Unveiling Artistry in Early Childhood Music

Praise for *Unveiling Artistry in Early Childhood Music*

"Engaging and comprehensive – Gleaned from decades of teaching young children, here is everything a teacher needs for confident teaching of infants through elementary grades, along with a generous sampling of Pinzino's captivating songs plus notes for their effective use. If I could own only one book on early childhood music, this would be it."
LINDA M. FIELDS, EARLY CHILDHOOD MUSIC SPECIALIST AND LIAISON TO PIANO TEACHERS

"Mary Ellen Pinzino's book *Unveiling Artistry in Early Childhood Music* offers a roadmap for nurturing musical artistry in young children. With numerous songs, tonal and rhythm activities, and reflections drawn from years of classroom music teaching, Mary Ellen Pinzino invites us to engage musically with young children in new and transformative ways."
ERIC BLUESTINE, AUTHOR OF *THE WAYS CHILDREN LEARN MUSIC*

"Perhaps the most salient aspect of this beautifully written book is the unwavering respect Mary Ellen Pinzino shows for the musical artistry of every child. The joy and wonder of music learning resonates on every page. The music educator who takes to heart the principles of learning embedded within this book will be joyfully rewarded."
ROSEANNE ROSENTHAL, PRESIDENT EMERITUS, VANDERCOOK COLLEGE OF MUSIC

"This book provides music educators with the foundation needed to go beyond just the joy of singing to the mastery of musicianship. It is a compass to aid early childhood music educators in navigating through the incredible possibilities young children can musically achieve."
JUDY MEYER HAYS, EARLY CHILDHOOD MUSIC SPECIALIST, ADJUNCT PROFESSOR, ILLINOIS WESLEYAN UNIVERSITY

"Are you searching for new insights and directions in the world of quality literature for young children? Do you wish you could find song repertoire that is age appropriate yet musically rich? The substantial scope of the songs and activities in this book will certainly aid any music teacher seeking to nurture musical skills and artistry within young children."
LEA LAMB, EARLY CHILDHOOD MUSIC EDUCATOR, CAROL STREAM, IL

"Pinzino's brilliance as a master teacher and teacher-of-teachers shines brightly throughout this practical and inspiring guide. A must-read for music teachers seeking to engage and nurture the musical minds and artistry of young children."
JOY MORIN, MUSIC LEARNING SPECIALIST AND PIANO PEDAGOGUE

"The logical sequencing of skill development is well thought out using numerous musical examples that reinforce skills and concepts for teacher and student. Lesson plans are thorough, well defined, clearly articulated, appropriately timed, and complete. Each lesson reflects a keen understanding of age-appropriate activities that build confidence in participation in a positive, nonthreatening atmosphere."
REBECCA NELSON, DEAN EMERITA, COLLEGE OF EDUCATION, NORTH PARK UNIVERSITY, CHICAGO, IL

"The young brain is remarkably adept and efficient at learning, but every child is also an artist, highly expressive and without self-consciousness. The author provides insightful concepts, content, and methods for maximizing the appropriateness and effectiveness of early childhood and elementary age music education."
BRUCE DALBY, EMERITUS PROFESSOR OF MUSIC EDUCATION, UNIVERSITY OF NEW MEXICO

"Pinzino's book is a treasure box for early childhood music educators and others who work with children, filled with songs, activities, insights, and guidance. Pinzino distills decades of experience with young children in music to provide this resource-packed volume. Her emphasis on artistry with young musicians helps practitioners deepen children's musical experiences."
LISA HUISMAN KOOPS, PROFESSOR OF MUSIC EDUCATION, CASE WESTERN RESERVE UNIVERSITY

"Mary Ellen's book provides a comprehensive window into her many years of teaching young children music. While influenced by Edwin Gordon, Mary Ellen puts her considerable experience to paper in an easily understandable sequence of events. If you are interested in stretching your knowledge of what is possible in the early childhood music classroom, this book is for you!"
ROBERT ROONEY, EARLY CHILDHOOD AND ELEMENTARY MUSIC TEACHER, HANOVER PARK, IL

"Mary Ellen Pinzino has crafted a beautiful book that will be helpful for music teachers of many levels of ability and experience in teaching Early Childhood Music. This book facilitates the development of artistry in both children *and* teachers. The resources and path forward are readily accessible here!"
PATRICIA WURST CICHY, ASSISTANT PROFESSOR OF MUSIC EDUCATION (RETIRED), PROVIDENCE COLLEGE

"In this book, Mary Ellen Pinzino invites us into the child's world of musical discovery, offering rich, descriptive examples for each stage of musical learning and challenging us to rethink familiar assumptions about young children's musical abilities and artistry."
JENNIFER S. MCDONEL, DIRECTOR OF MUSIC EDUCATION, RADFORD UNIVERSITY

"The author understands the need for readiness in musical development and coaches the reader with knowledge, field-tested material, encouragement, creativity and permission to explore one's own artistic voice as the content of this book takes root."
RENEE VANDE WEGE, MUSIC TEACHER AND CHORAL DIRECTOR, ROCKFORD, MI

"Inspiring, insightful, and lavishly—indeed almost poetically—written, Pinzino's guide empowers educators with practical tools to unlock young musical minds. A must-read for fostering a generation of expressive, confident, and joyfully artistic musicians."
RON MALANGA, MUSIC EDUCATOR/PEDAGOGY SPECIALIST

Unveiling Artistry in Early Childhood Music

A Guide For
Music Teachers

Mary Ellen Pinzino

Copyright © 2025 Mary Ellen Pinzino
First Edition 2025

All rights reserved. No part of this book may be reproduced or transmitted in any form or by any means, electronic or mechanical, including photocopying, recording, or by any information storage and retrieval system, without prior written permission of the author.

Published by Come Children Sing Institute
Homewood, Illinois
www.comechildrensing.com

ISBN 978-0-9718717-1-7 (pbk.)
ISBN 978-0-9718717-3-1 (hbk.)
ISBN 978-0-9718717-4-8 (ebook)

Book design by Adam Hay Studio, UK

*Special thanks to my husband, Gerald J. Pinzino,
for his ongoing support, wisdom, and humor
throughout my entire career.*

Contents

Introduction — xi

Part 1

1. Communicating Musically — 2
2. Making Sense — 23
3. Advancing Musically — 49
4. Propelling Progress — 78

Part 2

5. Taking It To a Higher Level — 107
6. Reveling in Music Reading and Writing — 130
7. Soaring in Song — 175

Part 3

Etudes — 206

1. For Getting Started — 207
2. For Planning Lessons — 219
3. For Choosing Songs — 229

Appendices — 253
Notes — 265
Bibliography — 269
Song Index — 270
Index — 271
Permissions — 274
About the Author — 276

Introduction

Little children are pure joy. They make us smile. They give us hugs. They inspire us as musicians and teachers with the depth of their artistry beneath such innocence. I invite you to join me in unveiling the wonder of young children's artistry.

This book addresses the development of little children's artistry from infancy through the primary grades. It presents the characteristic behaviors of young children's artistry, its progression of development, and its musical needs, with both practical and pedagogical considerations. The role of the musical mind, movement, playing music, and song in the development of young children's artistry unfolds throughout. The book also addresses the development of artistry in teaching early childhood music, offering perspectives and practices that facilitate the development of artistry both in young children and in teaching. You'll find an abundance of songs and activities to use in the classroom and playful ideas that will trigger your own creativity. You'll find guidance for teaching various ages and materials that serve for both professional development and classroom use.

I have had the privilege in this field of teaching all ages from birth through graduate students. It was always the youngest children who taught me the most about music learning and the development of artistry. I had spent a number of years teaching high school choral music and elementary general music before becoming directly involved in early childhood with two young sons. I began teaching early childhood music in the mid 70's, before music classes for young children became a popular offering. I led classes for little children through the local community college and university, and developed quite a following in the south suburbs of Chicago. I opened the Come Children Sing Institute in 1984 as a center for research and development in music learning, and developed an extensive early childhood music program and children's choral program. Many families attended for a full decade, so I was able to foster and witness the development of children's artistry from infancy through advanced choral performance.

Doing a presentation on early childhood music at a national music educator's conference in Chicago (MENC/NAfME), a year or so before opening the Come Children Sing Institute, changed the trajectory of my career. I took a bus load of over twenty moms and twenty tots from my classes at Governors State University for demonstration. I met Edwin Gordon in the elevator upon my arrival at the conference. I didn't know his work, but had heard that he was doing some research with young children and music. I introduced myself and invited him to my session that morning. I went to his sessions that afternoon and was surprised to learn that he had attended my morning session. He invited me to join him and his wife for dinner that evening, saying that he thought we had a lot of common ground. That began an association as colleague, student, and friend that lasted until the year he died (2015).

I spent many long weekends at Gordon's home throughout those years, discussing with him the process of music learning and teaching, particularly in relation to very young children. Gordon's primary strength was as researcher and mine as practitioner.

We challenged and influenced each other and always came away with more questions. We both looked to young children to find answers.

The many years of association with Edwin Gordon stimulated for me greater study, writing, composing, and researching. I wrote Edwin Gordon profusely for a lot of years, reflecting on what I was seeing in the classroom with little children and with older children in relation to his research, often coming to different conclusions. I was also reading extensively about speech and language development during that time. New insights led me in new and different directions as Gordon began to formalize his ideas about early childhood music. The long weekends at his home during that time generated lively discussions. The more he formulated his views, the more I challenged them, as they did not align with what I was seeing in the classroom. He welcomed my challenges, commenting once that if we always agreed with each other, we'd have no reason to grow. He encouraged me throughout those many years to keep writing, questioning, and following through on my inquiries in the classroom to see what I might learn. This book presents my findings.

The successful early childhood music classes that I had developed pre-Gordon transformed from a program using delightful children's songs and music activities into an even more joyous program rich in music learning and rich in the development of children's artistry. Each year three- and-four-year-olds became more developed than the year before, requiring ongoing experimentation with advanced dimensions, yet the children were still not old enough for kindergarten. I grew along with the children throughout those years, developing many new materials, songs, and activities, as there was nothing available to feed the unprecedented growth that such young children were exhibiting. I composed hundreds of songs for children of all ages, only to realize much later that I was studying not only music learning and the development of children's artistry, but also song and its role in that process. The many songs became part of the Come Children Sing Institute SONG LIBRARY.

The Come Children Sing Institute grew into five different levels of weekly classes for little children before they reached kindergarten, a chorus for kindergarten and first graders who had been through the younger classes, and choruses for long-term students from second grade to high school, in addition to graduate courses for music teachers. Outreach to Head Start programs and other settings brought materials and practices developed at the Come Children Sing Institute to additional pre-K, kindergarten, and older children who did not have the long-term background. Each setting confirmed and further clarified my findings about music learning and the progression of children's artistry. Later developments generated a virtual campus that includes online classes for young children and parents, the Come Children Sing Institute Online Teacher Education Center, and the SONG LIBRARY.

Many years in the choral field also greatly influenced my work with young children. I had developed children's choruses at the local community college and university prior to developing the children's choral program at the Come Children Sing Institute. I became involved in the children's choral movement, which grew immensely during the years on the floor with little children. I was later able to serve for a couple of years as college choral conductor, serving one of the Chicago City Colleges and the University of Illinois at Chicago, where I found still greater validation for my findings about music learning and the development of artistry. Long-term engagement in the choral art provided experience with artistry that impacted my work with little children as well as with older singers, while my experience with little children impacted my work with older singers.

This book presents the perspective that evolved through many years of teaching and classroom research on the process of music learning in young children and the development of little children's artistry, impacted by the work of Edwin Gordon, the choral field, parenthood and grandparenthood, and hundreds of little children that I have had the privilege to teach. My hope is that this book will stimulate greater research on the process of music learning in early childhood and the development of young children's artistry; that it will give voice to little children's artistry in your classroom; and that it will give voice to young children's artistry in the field of music education.

Part 1

1
Communicating Musically

Children's artistry is awe-inspiring. It is highly musical and sensitive to every musical nuance. It is full of joy and full of reverence for the art. It is most accessible in very young children, yet it is not often discussed in relation to early childhood music. Little children's utter charm and delight in song and music activities blind us to the depth of their artistry. We as a field of music education have only begun to uncover the wonder of young children's artistry.

Little children are born artists with a natural capacity to learn music just as they do language. Early childhood music teachers have the privilege and obligation to engage little children in song and music activities that promote music learning, to draw the artistry out of every child, and to provide for the development of children's artistry.

Generations of parents and teachers have used music with little children to calm or excite, to enhance learning, and to entertain. Preschool teachers have employed music to facilitate the development of language, body awareness, and social skills. Research on music learning in the last fifty years has taken early childhood music to a new level. Findings have spawned greater understanding of how little children learn music, awareness of the importance of music instruction at very young ages, and all kinds of music classes for little children.

Some of us on the floor with little children have been on the ground floor throughout this fifty- year evolution, researching the process of music learning in young children, developing materials and techniques to meet young children's musical needs as they grow, and teaching teachers and parents about young children's music development. Many successful years of teaching little children as well as older children led to the opening of the Come Children Sing Institute, a center for research and development in music learning which offered classes for children from birth through thirteen. An extensive early childhood music program and children's choral program presented the unique opportunity to nurture and witness music learning in children from the time they were in diapers through their participation in advanced choral performance, as many children attended for ten or eleven years. Meeting children's ongoing musical needs from infancy through advanced children's chorus led to a perspective on music learning informed by the choral art, leading to greater understanding of artistry in young children and its progression of development throughout childhood.

The Come Children Sign Institute had the benefit of its director's many years as colleague, student, and friend of Edwin Gordon, during much of his research on music learning in early childhood.[1] The renowned researcher and this experienced practitioner regularly compared notes from their different perspectives on their findings with little children, influencing and challenging each other, and often leading to differing views.

This book presents the findings of this teacher's research through many years of teaching, highly influenced by Gordon's work, but also informed by many years in the choral field, study of the process of speech and language development, and hundreds of little children, leading to extensive inquiry into the process of music learning, song, and the development of children's artistry.

The unveiling of artistry in early childhood music necessarily includes both children's artistry and artistry in teaching early childhood music. This book addresses both. Part 1 provides for the development of children's artistry with all ages from birth through eight, guiding implementation throughout. Each of the four chapters of Part 1 presents various aspects of music learning in young children and then shifts gears into a section on "Artistry in Teaching," offering perspectives and practices that facilitate the development of young children's artistry. Part 2 addresses more advanced dimensions of music learning to add through multiple, successive years of instruction, including music reading and vocal/ensemble development. Part 3 offers Etudes with materials to use in the classroom, guidance in using those materials, and professional development that transfers directly to the classroom.

Principles presented in this book apply to musical age rather than chronological age, as children grow through a continuum of development musically, whether they come to us as infants or as primary grade youngsters. Guidance, materials, and practices are offered for all ages from babes in arms to young choral artists, including children growing under our tutelage throughout early childhood.

This book is designed for both those embarking on teaching early childhood music and those quite accomplished as early childhood music teachers. Topics introduced in Chapter 1 are revisited regularly. The musical mind, movement, playing music, song, and the role each plays in the development of young children's artistry unfold gradually throughout as children and teachers develop. Musical examples throughout the book include a multitude of songs for all ages across the continuum of development.

You as a music teacher may or may not be experienced teaching little children. You may find that this book aligns with some of your current practices, or you may discover a whole new paradigm for early childhood music. The experience or lack of experience that you bring, accompanied by your own special gifts, offer a rich perspective from which to witness the budding and blooming of little children's artistry. Your unique journey up to this point will yield insights that you may not have otherwise been able to glean, and that colleagues you might think more competent cannot envision from their perspective.

Giving voice to young children's artistry takes time. Children need time to grow as artists, and teachers need time to grow in developing children's artistry. We cannot develop artistry in children or teaching by trying an occasional idea from this book. It takes ongoing commitment to mine the treasure of little children's artistry, continuing effort to maximize musicality, and willingness to be an artist ourselves in the early childhood music classroom.

Speaking to the Musical Mind

Little children are our finest teachers. We can learn more about the workings of the musical mind from young children than we can from any other age. We just have to learn to communicate with it. The more we learn to speak directly to the musical mind, the more transparent it becomes.

The musical mind learns music in much the same way that the thinking mind learns language. It needs a "sound environment" for immersion in its native tongue and interactivity with loved ones who respond to its efforts to express itself. The greatest difference between how the musical mind learns music and how the thinking mind learns language is in the native tongue of the musical mind.

Rhythm and melody speak to the musical mind. Words speak to the thinking mind. The musical mind does not process words, yet we as music teachers have traditionally assumed that our well-meaning words reach and teach the musical mind. Words actually get in the way of the musical mind's processing of rhythm and melody. We have to let go of our wordiness and speak to the musical mind if we want to give voice to children's artistry.

We know that we can compel the imagination of the thinking mind with a good story and take it on quite an adventure, yet we find it hard to believe that we can compel the imagination of the musical mind and take it on a musical adventure without words, stories, or explanations. Little children are masters of non-verbal communication. Our well-meaning words throughout music activities interrupt the musical mind aurally, just as intermittent walking in front of a TV screen interrupts what is going on visually. It is pure rhythm and pure melody that capture the musical mind, accompanied only by movement.

Getting a group of little children happily engaged in delightful songs and music activities can easily lead us to believe that we have reached the musical mind. Learning to speak the language of the musical mind, however, leads us to discover far more, taking our classes to a higher level. Little children are artists. They perceive the nuances of music with the sensitivity of poets and musicians. We have to communicate artistry through artistry. Intimate communication with the young musical mind inspires the exciting journey of unveiling the brilliance of young children's artistry.

Changing the Narrative

> "Once upon a time there was a little dog who loved to run. He ran day after day. He ran after the ball. He ran after the truck. He ran after the butterfly. One day, he ran up to the top of the hill, and then do you know what happened?"

A group of little children would now be in the palm of your hand. The musical mind responds the same way to a compelling musical narrative without any words. An appropriate rhythm narrative or melodic narrative can similarly draw the musical mind in to follow every twist and turn of the musical "story," without words, without explanation, and without talk between musical segments, when presented through multiple repetitions.

Figure 1.1 Rhythm Narrative—Duple Meter

Figure 1.1 presents an example of a rhythm narrative. We offer multiple repetitions of the rhythm narrative vocally on the neutral syllable "bah," chanting expressively, as if delivering a favorite nursery rhyme, compelling the young musical mind and immersing it in its native tongue of rhythm.

Figure 1.2 Tonal Narrative—Dorian Tonality, Duple Meter

The melody in Figure 1.2 offers an example of an appropriate tonal narrative. We sing multiple repetitions of the tonal narrative on the neutral syllable "too," compelling the musical mind and immersing it in its melodic native tongue.

The more successive repetitions of Figure 1.1 or Figure 1.2, the more children attend to the musical narrative, and the more the narrative spins its magic on the musical mind. An appropriate musical narrative for little children holds the musical mind captive when presented through many successive repetitions, accompanied only by musical movement.

Music acquisition in young children is so similar to language acquisition that we can always look to the process of learning language when in doubt about the process of learning music. Little children learning language or music need immersion in the native tongue in order to develop. They need to interact with loved ones who speak the language, whether learning language or music, and in the process they attempt to communicate, to make meaning.[2]

The thinking mind gets immersed in language day in and day out, with built-in loved ones who speak the language and respond to the young child's expression throughout the early years. It is up to us as music teachers to create the "sound environment" within which the musical mind can thrive. It is up to us to provide for immersion and to be the loved ones who respond to the musical mind's expression. It is up to us to provide the context in which the musical mind can "make sense" of rhythm and melody—a sense of beat and a sense of pitch.

The musical mind "makes sense" out of beats in relation to each other and it "makes sense" out of pitches in relation to each other. The organization of beats gives rise to meter. The organization of pitches gives rise to tonality. The great variety of meters and tonalities offers a wellspring of raw material for rhythm and tonal narratives that excite the musical mind, and each takes the musical mind on a new adventure. (Etude 1 is designed for teachers to develop greater competence and confidence with the various meters and tonalities.) It is meter and tonality that provide the gateway to children's artistry.

The power of meter and tonality over the musical mind is hard to imagine by our thinking minds, and meter and tonality each generates a different kind of power. Meter incites energy and compels the musical mind, holding little children's attention. Tonality casts a spell over the musical mind as if transporting it to some kind of dream world or higher level of consciousness.

Children's focused attention to meter and to tonality can evoke a "deer-in-the-headlights" stare that is so intense that parents in attendance wonder what their child finds that is so fascinating. Babies, preschoolers, and older children all exhibit such focused attention to meter and to tonality. The longer the musical narrative goes on, the more children attend and the longer we witness such intense focus. Ending a tonal narrative can jarringly break the "magic spell," as does ending a good story.

Children's intense focus on rhythm and tonal narratives looks as if meter and tonality are satisfying a deep thirst within little children, and that the little ones just cannot get enough. Their riveted attention to meter and to tonality appears as reverence for the art itself. We have traditionally relied on words to songs, actions, or playful sounds to get little children's attention, when the most powerful force over the musical mind is naked meter and naked tonality.[3]

The ongoing, intense, and focused response of little children to meter and to tonality can be in complete contrast to the joyful, enthusiastic response we generally elicit. Let us not be fooled into thinking that little children struck by the wonder of the art are not happily engaged in music. The pensive "deer-in-the-headlights" stare is a very musical response. We have to broaden our practice to nurture the deeper wisdom of the young child's musical mind.

Art Song Speaks

Little children under the spell of tonality are enthralled by "art song" that arises out of that tonality. They receive the art songs like true artists, exhibiting a kind of spiritual awe. They absorb the words as sounds intertwined with meter and tonality in one artistic whole when they are under the spell of tonality, rather than as words that interrupt the musical mind. Appropriate art songs for tender ages transport the musical imagination to new horizons.

The Frog and the Cherry Petal

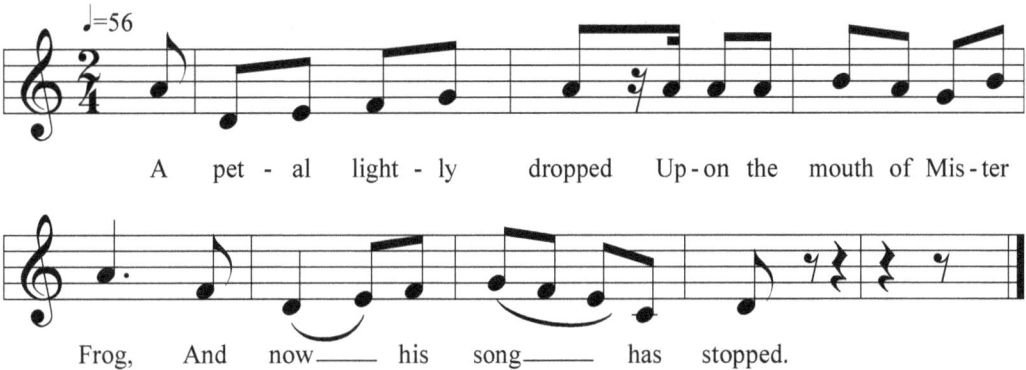

Figure 1.3   Art Song—Dorian tonality, Duple meter

The Frog and the Cherry Petal (Figure 1.3), with its text a translation of a Japanese haiku, offers an example of an art song for young children. Little artists of all ages have demonstrated that the most compelling and most musical experience of a little art song arising out of tonal narrative is through multiple successive repetitions, accompanied only by musical movement. Children from birth throughout early childhood stay focused throughout those many successive repetitions.

The young musical mind's communication through its intense focus is just as strong as the little tot's classic "again, again." Imagine holding such young children's attention through the length of four-to-eight successive repetitions of the tonal narrative presented in Figure 1.2 and then without verbalization, moving directly into eight-to-twelve repetitions of *The Frog and the Cherry Petal*, all presented with your voice, accompanied only by musical movement. Witnessing the power of tonality over the young musical mind throughout the entire length of the experience is stunning, making us rethink our assumptions about the young child's attention span. Appropriate art songs arising out of tonality provide intimate experience with the art. They feed the young child's very being, while broadening our notions about songs for young children.

Some of us have run very effective music classes for little children without musical narratives or art songs for young children, engaging tots and parents in delightful songs and music activities with joyous participation from all. Learning to communicate with the musical mind takes our teaching to new horizons, as we continue to lead utterly charming music classes that engage parents and children together in delightful songs and music activities, while also compelling the musical mind, propelling music learning, and giving voice to children's artistry.

Movement beyond Words

Little children know that music and musicians have to move. They understand that movement is the life blood of music; that without movement, music is lifeless. Children's unbridled movement to music reflects the very essence of music—the vibrance of life itself. The young child is literally on the same wave length with music and resonates with his whole body—the prime musical instrument. Children are "moved" by the music.

Little children are highly musical. They may not yet be able to sing tunefully, move rhythmically, or even stand up, but even infants "dance" with music. Movement is the most immediate expression of the musical mind. It is the "embodiment" of musicality. Movement makes music tangible. It is a means for the young child to interact with—to touch, to hold, and to chew on—music.[4]

Movement is our most powerful means of communication of all that is musical. *Movement is the sign language of music.*

We can express every musical nuance through movement, without words, images, or labels, and without props or stories. We as teachers of early childhood music have to move beyond using movement to reflect words or images with little ones.

Children love being bunnies and butterflies, but the words and images actually get in the way of the musical imagination. They put the thinking mind at the forefront rather than the musical mind. We are all familiar with the vase/face figure-ground illusion in which we look at the figure one way and see a face, and look at it another and see a vase. Both the vase and the face are present, but our perception of the figure depends upon what we see as the foreground. Similarly, the thinking mind and the musical mind may both be present, but the one in the foreground dominates.

Language, which speaks to the thinking mind, is paramount in the life of young children and necessarily puts the thinking mind in charge. Words and images may effectively stimulate movement like bunnies and butterflies to serve other kinds of learning, or to contrast weighted movement with flowing movement, but they do not serve music learning.

The irony is that both weighted movement and flowing movement are essential to music learning. That movement, however, has to be triggered by the music itself, or by our non-verbal model of movement with music, not by labels. It might even look like butterflies or bunnies, but with the musical mind in charge.[5]

Our musical movement in the context of music speaks to the young child's musical mind. Words that describe musical movement speak to the thinking mind. The more we engage in movement that reflects musicality rather than words, the more movement serves the development of children's artistry.

We know so much more now about music learning in early childhood, about children's musical needs and capabilities, and about the development of children's artistry. It is imperative that we as music teachers and as a field of music education grow to meet the musical needs of little children. We will see as this book unfolds that movement then becomes the embodiment of the developing musical mind as well as joyful activity. Props take on new meaning as musical instruments for "playing music" as well as for participation. Songs become the vehicle for children's artistry in addition to joyful interaction with music and community. The more we understand about the young child's musical mind, the more we can meet little children's musical needs.

Playing Music

Professional musicians and little children both heartily engage in "playing music." That is how they practice music. Playing music can be sheer joy and utterly musical for both the professional musician and the young child.

Little children learn through play. They manipulate, build, tear down, compare, and sort. They hypothesize and then try again and again, revising hypotheses as they make discoveries about their world. The musical mind does the aural equivalent of manipulating, building, tearing down, comparing, and sorting the properties of rhythm and of tonal (pitch-related aspects), revising hypotheses through greater experience as it makes discoveries about rhythm and about tonal.[6]

Our growing understanding of the young child's musical mind can lead us to create an enchanting musical playhouse within which children learn by playing music. We provide a "sound environment" for the development of the musical mind, plus delightful musical opportunities for little children to interact with rhythm and tonal. We can create a playful, yet highly musical setting where little children become absorbed in playing music, just like the professional musician.

We have often used toys and other props in music activities to entice participation, but attractive objects can also distract or derail the musical mind that is not fully attuned to meter or tonality. They draw attention to themselves, unless the musical mind is at the forefront. A little child whose musical mind is captivated by meter follows our lead and will use a toddler hammer as an instrument for engaging in meter. The child whose musical mind is not yet compelled by meter uses the hammer as just a pounding toy. Meter or tonality has to dominate every activity we do with props, so that each prop becomes a vehicle for the expression of the musical mind rather than something to attract children's attention or keep them busy.

The young musical mind compelled by meter or tonality brings so much greater depth to children's musical interaction with toys and other attractive items. The musical mind is fully engrossed with the magic of meter or tonality, with the props serving as catalyst to give voice to the musical mind vocally, in movement, or both. Props become musical instruments for little children, engaging the children in playing music—practicing music with the joy and heartfelt expression of a musician.

Props provide a tangible way for the musical mind to playfully explore the properties of meter in the context of meter and the properties of tonality in the context of tonality. They offer a hands-on way for children to animate the wisdom of the musical mind and activate the voice and body to "make sense" of meter and tonality. The focused attention of the musical mind, coupled with the delight of the props, make practicing music a joy.

A child in play doesn't distinguish between what is real and what is imaginative. Little children just play, making up what they need as they go, whether the thinking mind or the musical mind is at the forefront. We capture the musical mind of four-year-olds with a rhythm narrative, don fire hats with all hands on a rope as if a hose, and with the ongoing rhythm narrative we're all firefighters chanting in the meter to put out an imaginary fire. The musical mind is at the forefront, with meter leading the way, while the little firefighters enthusiastically chant the meter to douse the fire. No words are spoken. No explanation or instructions given, no invitation to pretend. We simply create the "sound environment" and become as enchanted as the children in playing music.

Any number of attractive objects can become musical instruments when we capture the musical mind and engage musically with the props. Household items not usually associated with music, or that generate activity not typically in the day-to-day lives of little children, can become delightful musical instruments for young children. Start a rhythm narrative, bring out a dry, four-inch paint brush, and nonchalantly start "painting" the wall while continuing the rhythm narrative. Keep the meter going and give each child a dry two-inch paint brush. The children immediately "paint" the wall with us, chanting the meter. The ongoing musical narrative dominates the activity, with all happily practicing music.

The musical mind at a later point in time unexpectedly replays bits and pieces of music heard in classes, as if contemplating what it has heard. That tendency of the musical mind and the activities we design for playing music lead little children to spontaneously practice music at home, with either the musical mind or the props triggering the practice session. The hammer in the toy box may stimulate a child's chanting while pounding. The little painter may paint the wall at home with a paint brush or kitchen spatula while chanting, practicing music with great joy.

The clever parent of an uncooperative tot turns a spoon into an airplane circling the child's mouth, charming the little one into enthusiastic participation. We can similarly charm little children of all ages to enthusiastically engage in playing music with the heart and soul of a musician.

The young musical mind is so compelled by meter and tonality that even shyness cannot hold it back. Parents are sometimes surprised when their clingy little one who won't go to Grandma approaches the music teacher to interact musically one-on-one. Little children lose themselves in meter and tonality. Couple that with children losing themselves in play and we can have every little child with us at every step of the way, throughout highly musical classes.

Little children love being musical. They love practicing music. Playing music is the process and the product for little children, just as it is for professional musicians. We have the opportunity to entice children into playing music in a highly musical setting throughout early childhood, meeting their growing musical needs and giving voice to children's artistry.

A Word about Song

Song is a powerful force of early childhood. It charms and entertains, calms and excites, and it invites participation. There's a song for everything in life, whether handed down through the ages or spontaneously made up by a little child. Song is also a major component of the musical art, offering a continuum of musical complexity and artistry from the simplest song through high art.

Music teachers have traditionally chosen songs for little children based on song words. We might choose songs for their seasonal, social, or cultural merit, but how often do we choose songs for their musical merit? We want songs that appeal to little children, but we as a field of music education have hardly begun to appeal to the musical mind of little children. Our prime criteria for a song for little children have usually been that the children love it. Children also love songs that feed the musical mind, draw them into the art of song, and serve as a vehicle for the expression of young artistry.

Children learning language encounter nursery rhymes, fairy tales, sensitive little poems, and lovely little stories throughout early childhood. Some literature for little children is simply for fun. At the other end of the spectrum is fine poetry, with its sound, imagery, and artistry that captivate even the youngest children. Somewhere in between is quality prose, which is more sophisticated than children's speech, yet not such high art as poetry. Progressive difficulty in children's literature provides for ongoing growth in language.

The young child's musical mind urges us to broaden our horizons in song literature for little children to provide for the kind of growth afforded in language. "Play songs" can be chosen for their words that delight and invite participation. At the other end of the spectrum are "art songs"—the poetry of song literature—songs that invite sheer musicality. Somewhere in between are "gem songs," the quality prose of song literature that feeds developing musicianship and provides for ongoing growth. Little children revel in far more musically sophisticated song literature than we have ever thought appropriate for young children. Song graciously accommodates, as it encompasses the full range of the art.

Play Songs

Songs that have traditionally dominated music activities for young children are most often play songs. They serve a multitude of purposes, generally delighting all and eliciting participation. We choose play songs for their words, and the words are often the driving force for movement, props, or games. Play songs can include finger-plays, seasonal songs, and play-parties. The words rather than the music lead the way, putting the thinking mind at the forefront and serving many kinds of learning, though not necessarily music learning.

Who Can Walk Like a Duck?

Figure 1.4   Play Song—Major tonality, Duple meter

David Has a Dirty Face

Figure 1.5   Play Song—Major tonality, Duple meter

Who Can Walk Like a Duck? (Figure 1.4) and *David Has a Dirty Face* (Figure 1.5) offer examples of play songs for little children. The songs charm children and parents alike, inviting movement, participation, and parent-child interaction.

Art Songs

Art songs that give voice to little children's artistry speak for themselves, as they draw the artistry out of every child and draw every child into the art of song. Quality art songs for tender ages are the poetry of song literature for young children. They feed and challenge the musical mind at every level, just as poetry does with language. Art songs that give voice to children's artistry, like fine children's poems, know no age, but touch all as fine art.

Words are a critical component of an art song, but for far more than their literal meaning. Words come with their own sound and imagery. They have their own rhythm, which drives the rhythm of the song. They have their own expression, which influences melodic line.

A well-written art song for children is a vocal stage play, with the intertwining of text, rhythm and melody serving as the staging, scenery, and costumes for the dramatic delivery of text. A quality song for young children brings the various dimensions of text, rhythm and melody into one artistic whole, transporting little children into their own artistry and that of the song.

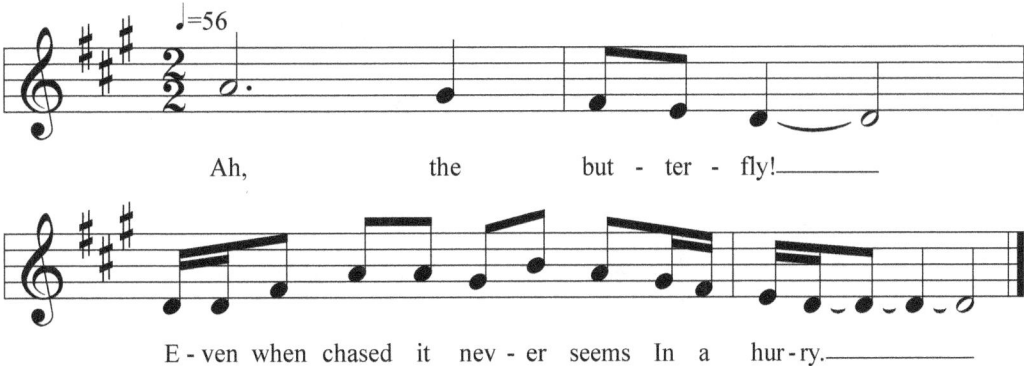

Figure 1.6   Art Song—Lydian tonality, Duple meter

The Frog and the Cherry Petal, presented in Figure 1.3, and *Never in a Hurry* (Figure 1.6) offer examples of art songs for young children. Each of the texts is a translation of a Japanese haiku. Each song is in a different tonality and each song is set in the vocal range that most serves the young musical mind. Art songs that most compel the musical mind are in tonalities other than Major tonality. Experience with rhythm and tonal narratives in the various meters and tonalities develop the musical readiness for the art song. An art song growing out of a tonal narrative in the same tonality provides for little children to receive the song as poets and artists, without explanation about the words, without props, and without musical instruments.

Art songs speak to the musical mind. Movement is the only appropriate accompaniment with an art song for young children—movement propelled by the music rather than the literal translation of the words. Multiple, successive repetitions of an art song with movement mesmerize little children, immersing and engaging them in the art. Emerging artistry thrives on such intimacy with the art.

Gem Songs

Gem songs are the prose of song literature for young children. These little gems feed developing musicianship. They are more musically sophisticated than play songs, yet not as high art as art songs. Gem songs offer well-set playful texts in a variety of tonalities and meters, capturing the musical mind, while the texts charm the thinking mind. Gem songs become more complex musically as children grow, just as stories for young children become more complex as children grow in language.

Figure 1.7   Gem Song—Minor tonality, Duple/Triple meter

Figure 1.8 Gem Song—Dorian tonality, Unusual Paired meter

Otto Would a Riding-Go (Figure 1.7) and *Under the Chair* (Figure 1.8) offer examples of gem songs for young children. The two songs are set in different tonalities and meters and in a vocal range that best serves the young child's musical mind. *Otto Would a Riding-Go* is a setting of a Swedish folk rhyme, with the complexity of shifting meters that accommodate the rhyme. The playful words of *Under the Chair* are set in a more difficult meter. The challenging rhythm in each of these songs reflects the rhythm of the words. Both songs invite playful activity while exciting the musical mind.

Gem songs, as children grow, become a musically higher level of play songs, as demonstrated by *Otto Would a Riding-Go* and *Under the Chair*. The play in gem songs, however, is the musical play between rhythm, melody, and text, as much or more than the playful words. Little children delight in the musical sophistication of gem songs as well as in the play suggested by the words.

Experience with rhythm and tonal narratives in the various meters and tonalities develop the musical readiness for gem songs just as they do for art songs. Little children without experience with meters and tonalities could surely engage in the playful gem songs in figures 1.7 and 1.8, however, they would relate just to the words and the activity, as their musical minds wouldn't have the readiness to comprehend the music content. Similarly, little children could happily engage in a game in a foreign language, but they still wouldn't understand the language. Teaching to the musical mind prepares children for more and more difficult musical material, whatever the song words might be.

Gem songs, like art songs, are best experienced through multiple successive repetitions, accompanied only by movement. Preceding the song with a tonal narrative to set up the tonality of the gem song helps the musical mind to receive the gem song as a musician. Multiple successive repetitions of a gem song hold the musical mind captive throughout. Gem songs, like art songs, invite intimacy with the art itself. They serve children's developing artistry accompanied only by movement, without explanations of the words, without props, and without instruments. (Additional songs for young children, including art songs and gem songs in the various tonalities and meters can be found in the Come Children Sing Institute SONG LIBRARY. [7]

Our greatest challenge in expanding our concept of song literature for little children is in our own dependence upon song words. Our choice of songs, activities, movement, and props most often reflect the literal translation of the words. A quality art song or gem song, however, is a *musical* translation of the words. Our role is to engage children in the musicality of that musical translation through our own artistry in singing and movement.

We have to trust the artistry of little children to rise above our own dependence upon song words. We also have to trust and unleash our own artistry. We can, indeed, non-verbally communicate to little children the wonder of the art that drew us into this field, and engage them in song repertoire that propels music learning and the development of children's artistry.

Song is a vibrant force of early childhood and of the early childhood music class. Little children's artistry implores us to embrace the broader expanse of the continuum of musical complexity and artistry inherent in the fine art of song. Quality art songs and gem songs for young children are little kernels of the art of song waiting to bloom in the musical minds and bodies of little children—little artists, waiting to bloom in songs that merit their artistry.

Artistry in Teaching

We as teachers of early childhood music love little children. We thrill at the joy of their very being, their enthusiasm for life, and their zest for music. The marvel of young children's artistry is equally thrilling. Its progression of development, its characteristic behaviors, and its musical needs present a dimension of little children that just adds to their wonder.

The brilliance of the young child's musical mind deserves our greatest gifts as teachers of early childhood music. We are trained musicians. We are trained as teachers. We might even be experienced teachers, attuned to child development, or good with young children. Our love of little children, our musicality, and our awareness of the process of music learning are essential in teaching early childhood music. There is, however, another element that drives success in the early childhood music class, though it is not regularly addressed in methods classes, music studies, or research in early childhood music. The progression of developing young children's artistry depends not only on our understanding the young musical mind and meeting its musical needs, but also on our developing artistry in teaching music to young children.

Little children simply grace us with their presence. They have no preconceived notion of classroom decorum, participation, or orderly group activity. They might join in; they might make a fuss; they might walk away. It is up to us to draw in every child and inspire willing participation and cooperation.

Any parent can attest to how strong-willed an infant, toddler, or preschooler can be, or how difficult it might be to get a little one to go along with anything. Yet we as early childhood music teachers can make our classes irresistible to a whole group of strong-willed little ones by the music content we choose and how we implement that content. We can magically get little children in the palm of the hand in every class we teach, with each child happily participating by their own free will and delivering on cue.

Little children are natural learners. They are enthralled when something is right for learning. It is we teachers who have to do things differently when our very young learners don't do as we might have hoped. Little children's compliance or lack thereof with everything we do guides us to become better teachers. We can be highly informed by books or mentors, but little children are the master teachers.

Long-term research at the Come Children Sing Institute, fed by many earlier years of teaching little ones, necessarily included investigation into the process of music teaching as well as music learning in early childhood. The Institute grew with the children to provide music instruction for little children who attended four or five consecutive years before entering kindergarten, as well as multiple years after. The little children developed so quickly by the process presented in this book that every year became a new challenge as to where to take them next. Their musicality was so far beyond what might have been previously thought possible, yet they were still in diapers or not yet old enough for kindergarten. This led to a lot of experimentation with music content, song, activities, and techniques, comparing musical responses across ages and levels of development, and comparing the process of music learning in little children to that of older children. Many insights were gleaned during these years of inquiry about drawing little children of all ages into every activity throughout every class through multiple years. *Artistry in Teaching* sections in Part 1 of this book offer perspectives and practices of teaching early childhood music that facilitate the development of children's artistry and promote artistry in teaching.

Sculpting Energy

A master teacher of early childhood music is an artist with children's energy and its dynamic interaction with musical energy. Appropriate music content is not sufficient. We have to become aware of everything we do with children and how it affects their energy as well as how it affects the musical mind.

> Children's energy abounds. It is the raw material that every child brings to class. Direct it wisely and you can create a very satisfying experience for everybody. Ignore its power and it can defeat whatever you try to do.
>
> Children's energy is like putty in your hands. You can shape it, stretch it, play with it, create with it, enjoy it, transport it, and engage with it. Children's energy is your greatest ally, though it requires your awareness and developing skill to fully enchant, leverage, manipulate, maneuver, and engineer children's energy.[8]

The musical materials we choose, the way we put them together, and the way we execute them impact children's energy. The level of movement, the props we use, and the transitions between activities affect children's energy. Every technique we employ and every element of our class routine influences children's energy. Music teaching and learning can soar when we effectively sculpt energy. Every class session then becomes an artistic composition from start to finish that shapes, builds, and resolves the enactment of energy, as well as a rich musical experience. The effective sculpting of energy charms both children and accompanying adults to get on board at the start of class and enjoy the ride throughout an exciting forty-five- to fifty-five-minute musical journey, disembarking only after the final song.

> Parents, out of necessity, generally learn to leverage children's energy. They plan to stop at the grocery store with their little one after a feeding and before a nap, assuring that the child will be in a cooperative state at the grocery store. They bring a favorite toy in case they get stuck in a long line at the check-out. They pull out a snack in the car to keep the child going a little longer. Parents know how to distract a child with a favorite little squeaking toy when the child is attracted by something unsafe. Parents know how to gently relax a child who

is overexcited. Parents regularly charm children through the mundane chores of changing a diaper or putting on a snow suit.[9]

We can similarly charm little children into happily engaging throughout an entire music class. We can creatively leverage children's unbounded energy and use it to serve musical needs. We can skillfully feed the momentum that carries little children from start to finish, taking the musical imagination of all in attendance on a joyous and satisfying musical journey.

Sculpting children's energy and musical energy into one artistic whole is a wonderful creative challenge. It can assure the full engagement of children and accompanying adults throughout the entirety of the class. We all know how quickly a little one can dissolve into tears and how easily a group of excited youngsters can get out of hand. We know the palpable energy that a favorite song can stir, the physical energy that can be charged through movement, and the excitement with props. We're discovering the power of meter and tonality to focus the musical mind and how verbal communication can break the magic—the musical energy that compels the musical mind. We can make the most of energy generators and more calming influences by building and discharging energy strategically throughout the class session, keeping children's energy on an even keel, while feeding the musical mind and giving voice to children's artistry.

Viewing the process of sculpting the energy dynamic of an early childhood music class as if we are directing a children's play helps us to take a step back from music learning to create an artistic whole. A well-executed children's play carries the audience from start to finish without interruption, inviting participation, but with careful planning to sustain the momentum throughout. It runs seamlessly, without mundane talking, awkward pauses, or time to decide or prepare what comes next. Transitions are purposefully staged. Props magically appear and disappear. Surprises come out of nowhere, and every moment is fresh, gracefully moving to the next. The totality of the experience creates a kind of magic, an aura that transports children and accompanying adults from the world of everyday life into the world created by the play.

Our classes can flow just as seamlessly, without mundane talking, awkward pauses, or time to decide or prepare what comes next. We can make props musically appear and disappear. We can artfully plan transitions that lead to the next activity or that provide for the musical mind to savor the meter or tonality it has just experienced. We can create classes with momentum that carries little children from start to finish, with every moment fresh, gracefully moving to the next. The overarching artistic whole creates the aura, the magic that transports children and accompanying adults from the world of everyday life into the musical world that we create.

We have to examine everything we do in the early childhood music classroom in relation to both how it affects children's energy and how it affects the musical mind. We can too easily fall into old habits or techniques we have picked up from others, without even questioning their musicality. Artistry in teaching sizzles when little children are in the palm of the hand and engaged in sheer musicality.

Sculpting energy is effective with little children of all ages in any size group, with any number of parents, teachers, or aides. It sustains momentum, keeping both children and adults with us. Dead space is an invitation to a group of little children to become unruly. It's also an invitation to attending adults to talk. Our seamless children's play, with its high level of musicality and pacing of little children's energy, entices children and parents together to go along with the flow, without any hesitation from children and without parents trying to coach their child. The artistic whole propels children and attending adults from start to finish, stimulating cooperation and enthusiastic participation from all.

Deliberately sculpting children's energy and its dynamic interaction with musical energy is an ongoing process, as we will see throughout this book. Every class we teach can become an artistic whole that provides for music learning, the moderation of children's energy, and the development of children's artistry. We can transport little children and accompanying adults on a magic carpet from the beginning of class until the final note has sounded.

Mining for Gold

We as teachers of early childhood music are fortunate to have a ready-made laboratory for the study of the musical mind, with the potential to unveil the purest, most authentic musicality. The more we learn to nurture the young musical mind and develop artistry in teaching, the more the musical mind reveals itself.

We have to become keen observers of little children, taking in everything just the way they do. We have to tune in to children's non-verbal communication, body language, and energy, as well as their musical output or lack thereof. Little children's response is as dependent upon our practices as it is on the music content. The toddler who hides in Mommy's arms or doesn't want to take a turn serves as a mirror of our teaching. We have to take a step back, reconsider both music content and implementation we thought appropriate, and then create and test alternate hypotheses in our laboratory. Music activities that align with young children's musical needs, delivered with practices that align with their emotional needs, are irresistible to young children.

Our little artists are perfect learners. Anything that doesn't work in the classroom is either because the music content is not right for our children or our implementation of the content is not right for them. Whatever a child or group does or doesn't do can be a clue pointing to what we need to examine in our laboratory, including rhythm and tonal content, our techniques, and the differences in the way the musical mind processes rhythm and tonal. It is fruitless to develop multiple techniques to try to get music content to work, when the issue is with the music content itself, or to conclude that the musical material is not right for the musical mind, when the issue is with implementation.

We have to be willing to challenge our own practices and beliefs about early childhood music. We might, for example, find better ways to interact musically with individual children while also compelling the musical mind of others. We might find that some tonal narratives focus the young musical mind on tonality more than others. We might find greater similarities or differences between the way the musical mind processes rhythm and the way it processes tonal.

We can always count on the authentic musical response of our little children to validate, challenge, or expand our understanding of the process of music learning, but can we always count on our own willingness to alter music content or practices in order to further unveil children's artistry? It is easier to trust an authority than it is to trust ourselves as researchers in the classroom, and it is easier to follow a formula than it is to engage in inquiry with young children. Little children have a way of humbling the most accomplished teachers and researchers, yet they can teach us more about the workings of the musical mind than any other age.

The wonder of young children's artistry begs for greater examination of the process of music learning, appropriate music materials, and implementation practices. A little insecurity in the classroom reminds us that we have much to learn about teaching early childhood music. Our little laboratories offer ongoing opportunity to create hypotheses and alter music content, activities, and practices over time until we find answers to our questions or new insights that move us forward and can move our field forward.

Every class we teach provides a fully-equipped laboratory for the exploration of the music teaching and learning process, the questioning of principles, practices, and music content that have defined our teaching, and the fine-honing of practices and techniques that facilitate successful teaching and learning. Each day of teaching is an opportunity to search and re-search in our classrooms for greater insights into music learning in young children and for practices that yield the greatest growth in children and in us as teachers. Our little laboratories invite us to mine the riches of children's artistry.

> Teaching music requires ongoing dialogue between your increasing awareness of the process of music learning and your students' demonstration of that process. Each informs the other and leads to adjusting content, ordering of activities, energy management, and techniques.[10]

Our day-to-day hypotheses in the laboratory illuminate our path as we learn to reach the musical mind more intimately, continue to uncover the process of music learning, and further unveil the development of children's artistry. We can explore in our classes while sustaining momentum by sculpting energy, whether or not those explorations are enlightening. Some of our investigations may lead to securing current thinking or practices, while others lead to more questions, greater challenge about what we are doing, and ongoing research.

We may teach music to little children in community classes, daycare, preschool, elementary school, or online. We may have anywhere from fifteen to sixty minutes with a class. We may or may not have accompanying parents, teachers, or aides. We might have babies, toddlers, preschoolers, or children in kindergarten and older. We might have pre-K classes of mixed ages, mixed experience levels, or groupings by age and experience. We might have a tuition-based program, a private school setting, or a daycare setting with whomever happens to show up any given day. Every context offers a rich laboratory for our study of the development of children's artistry in early childhood.

The more classes we teach, the more ages we teach, and the more consecutive years we teach second, third, fourth and fifth year students before they reach kindergarten, the richer our laboratory becomes and the more we can uncover the process of music learning in early childhood. We can compare children's responses in one group to that of another of the same age, or different age but same level of experience with us. We can compare the effectiveness of one prop, technique, or activity with that of another, and test our findings with different ages or different experience levels. We witness the musical growth in little children through successive years, charging us to meet the ongoing musical needs through multiple years. Three-year-olds, for example, who have been with us since infancy, are musically ready for far more than beginning three-year-olds, and will challenge us even more as four-year-olds. Where do we take these children? They are still just three and four years old, with inarticulate speech and imprecise tunefulness and rhythmicity, yet their musicality, like their ability to communicate, demonstrates great depth of understanding. Our laboratory provides for ongoing inquiry into the process of music learning and teaching at every level and in relation to every other level.

Active inquiry in our classroom laboratory makes us far better teachers, as it guides us to become more astute in observing little children's subtle cues, while exercising greater flexibility, playfulness, and creativity. New insights take us to greater understanding of the process of music learning, more appropriate music content, and more effective practices in teaching. Searching and re-searching in our classroom leads us to greater confidence, greater insights, and a greater variety of creative activities and techniques that can serve all ages. Mining for gold in our classroom stimulates greater artistry in teaching.

2
Making Sense

Unveiling the young musical mind opens horizons in music teaching and learning that we never thought possible with young children. Those little musical minds are brilliant, with the capacity to absorb, make sense, and use music content just as little children do with language. The challenge for us is in understanding how the musical mind works so we can effectively teach to meet the musical needs of the young musical mind.

We all have some sense of how to speak to little children so that they can understand what we are saying, and we know how to respond to little children's attempts to make meaning with words, however fragmented they might be. We have to learn to do the same with the young musical mind—to address it in a way that it can understand our music content, and to musically respond to its attempts to make musical meaning, however fragmented they might be.

We can easily assume that we have reached the musical mind or that young children are learning music when they are happily engaged in music activities, but the young musical mind needs so much more in order to develop. A lot of music activities facilitate different kinds of learning, but those activities do not necessarily promote music learning.

> Water, too, can be a delightful vehicle for learning, and children engage regularly with water. They bathe in it, wash their hands in it. They play in wading pools, sprinklers and water tables. They explore the properties of water with pitchers and sieves, developing foundations for math and science, the readiness for understanding measurement and volume. Yet these delightful experiences do not begin to teach a child to swim. It takes ongoing experience of immersion and thoughtful coaching over a long period of time to develop the young child's natural capacity to sustain himself in water and propel himself by his own steam.
>
> Similarly, it takes ongoing experience of immersion in music and thoughtful coaching over a long period of time to develop the young child's natural capacity to sustain himself in the wonder of the art and propel himself musically by his own steam. The many delightful music activities that serve so many areas of learning do not begin to tap the musical genius of the young child.[1]

The young musical mind can process rhythm and melody with the same depth of understanding that little children demonstrate with language. We are the ones who have to stretch musically and pedagogically to meet the musical needs of the young musical mind. We are the ones who have to go beyond common music materials and practices with little children to be able to give the young musical mind what it is so ready to receive, to process, and to use. The young musical mind offers a clean slate, unencumbered by expectations. Our effort to reach and teach the young musical mind—even when it stretches us beyond our comfort zone musically and pedagogically—can lay the foundation for a lifetime of music making.

Sense-Ability

Little children with a set of stacking cups explore, sort, and compare the cups. They create hypotheses about how the cups go together, revising those hypotheses as needed as they try different ways to put them together and make discoveries about relative size, nesting, and stacking. They might even notice that color is not a factor in relative size. Their stubby little fingers manipulate the cups as they try to figure them out even before they are a year old. They go back to those cups day after day and try again, drawing concrete conclusions about relative size and how to stack those cups. We can't see their newfound insights, but we witness their growth in stacking the cups.

Give the young musical mind various meters or tonalities to absorb and it will do much the same aurally, as it tries to figure out how beats relate to each other or how pitches relate to each other. It will create and revise hypotheses, and given the opportunity, will go back regularly to try to make sense of meter and tonality. Little children do this before they can even sit up or stand, making discoveries that lead to an aural understanding of meter and of tonality.

It is hard for our thinking minds to comprehend the capability of the young child's musical mind and the aural processing that takes place. It is, however, just as dynamic as the more tangible process we observe with little children manipulating cups. We cannot see the musical mind's process or newfound aural insights, but we can witness its growth by its musical response when we meet its musical needs both rhythmically and tonally.

Rhythm underlies melody in music and in the musical mind, and provides the foundation for music learning. Ongoing exposure to a variety of meters provides for the musical mind to begin to make sense of rhythm. It stimulates the musical mind to explore beats in relation to each other, to aurally grasp the organization of beats, and to attend to beat groupings and the division of beats. The variety of meters helps the musical mind to discover macro beats (big beats), micro beats (smaller beats), and the relationship between the two—the factors that define meter.

Figure 2.1   Duple, Triple, Unusual Paired

Figure 2.1 offers an example of Duple meter, Triple meter, and Unusual Paired meter. Duple is the easiest meter to learn, but the musical mind will learn Duple meter most efficiently by regularly engaging with a variety of meters. It is the contrast between meters that prods the musical mind to learn, just as the contrast between stacking cups prods the thinking mind to learn. The young musical mind absorbs the more difficult meters just as it does Duple. Ongoing immersion and interactivity in a variety of meters stimulates the musical mind to "make sense" of meter—a sense of meter, which serves as an aural structure within which rhythm makes sense to the musical mind—a kind of an internal grid in which rhythm falls into place.

Ongoing exposure to a variety of tonalities similarly stimulates the musical mind to make sense of tonal—to explore pitches in relation to each other, to discover the pull of the resting tone, and to aurally grasp the organization of pitches in relation to that resting tone. The variety of tonalities helps the musical mind to aurally discover the factors that define tonality.

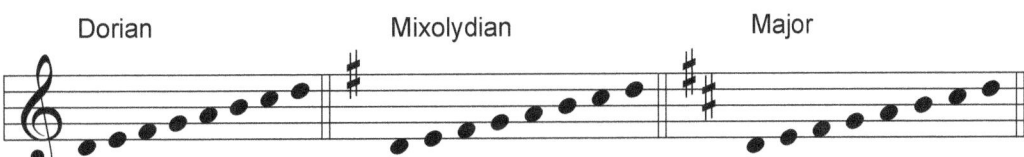

Figure 2.2   Dorian, Mixolydian, Major

Figure 2.2 offers a scale of Dorian tonality, Mixolydian tonality, and Major tonality, all with the same resting tone, but distinguished by the unique relationship of pitches to that resting tone. The young musical mind will make greater sense of the more common Major tonality when regularly engaged with a great variety of tonalities. The contrast between tonalities in sound stimulates the musical mind to "make sense" of tonality—a sense of tonality, an aural framework within which tonal makes sense to the musical mind—a kind of spatial soundscape, in contrast to the more contained rhythmic grid.

The young musical mind is most compelled by the less common meters and tonalities. Duple meter is most immediate, but so common that it does not compel the musical mind as much as the more difficult meters. Major tonality is so common that the young musical mind does not attend to it as it does the more unusual tonalities. Ongoing experience with a great variety of meters and tonalities leads the young musical mind to process Duple as a meter and Major as a tonality, rather than as the common background of day-to-day life. (See Appendix A for meters and tonalities used in this book.)

A developing sense of meter blooms into rhythmicity and a developing sense of tonality blooms into tunefulness. Little children need a lot of practice to get to that point, just as they need a lot of time to learn to speak fluently. A developed sense of meter will ultimately provide for precision in any meter, steady tempo, and momentum in performance. A developed sense of tonality will ultimately lead to singing in tune in any tonality, quality tone, and expression of line. Greater understanding of how the young musical mind processes both rhythm and tonal guides us in providing for its growth and development. (Etude 1 provides for teachers to develop greater competence and confidence with the various meters and tonalities.)

Moving Right Along

A sense of meter and a sense of tonality in the process of development are both propelled through movement. Sustained, flowing movement mobilizes the musical mind captured by meter or tonality, embodying rhythm and tonal knowing.

Flowing movement that stimulates the musical mind and body engages the whole body. We plant our feet on the floor, and with arms extended in space, we activate knees, hips, shoulders, and arms. We keep the whole body moving throughout the entire musical experience. Our flowing movement makes the flow of music more tangible for little children, as we become that flow of music, with its ongoing energy in flight.

The young musical mind captured by meter or tonality is "moved" by our accompanying flowing movement and that of attending adults, whether or not the children are yet ready or able to engage in flowing movement themselves. Babies experience flowing movement in the arms of a parent, while little toddlers might just watch or imitate our flowing movement, perhaps with only an arm. Preschoolers, kindergarteners, and primary grade youngsters might surprise you with how musical their flowing movement can be. Children's flowing movement gives us a glimpse of the depth of children's artistry.

Flowing movement reveals a most basic, yet most developed response of musicality. It speaks to and for the musical mind of little children and the professional musician who subtly moves in performance with the flow of the music. Little children's "deer-in-the-headlights" stares with meter or tonality might become even wider or more intense as we engage with flowing movement, as little children seem to show even greater reverence for the art with the addition of flowing movement.

We might think that we are facilitating music learning by using stylistic or Laban terminology, or exploring body parts in space, but words that prompt movement keep the thinking mind at the forefront of the activity. Full body flowing movement in response to meter and tonality keeps the musical mind at the forefront. The music does the prompting.

Music flows, whatever the style. Our flowing movement reflects that flow. Try to avoid giving into pulse when engaging in flowing movement, even if your movement feels much the same across various meters and tonalities, styles, and tempos. Flowing movement sustains momentum between and through the beats, unencumbered by time and weight.

Figure 2.3 Triple narrative

Figure 2.3 presents a rhythm narrative in Triple meter. Try chanting it on "bah" while engaging in flowing movement without regard to beat. Go through multiple successive verses engaging the whole body in movement, freely activating hips, knees, arms, shoulders, and hands simultaneously, moving with the music. We can tread the flow of music like we tread water.

Our full body flowing movement becomes a non-verbal invitation for children and attending adults to join us in flowing movement. It communicates that there is no right or wrong way to move, and entices children and adults to freely engage the whole body in flowing movement. A group of little children and attending adults engaged in flowing movement, with musical minds held captive by the music, becomes a community of artists engaging in sheer musicality.

Adding Weight

Flowing movement is foremost in developing musicality and it provides the groundwork for movement on the beat. Flowing movement is the backdrop upon which we place weight to create beat and meter. Macro beats carry greater weight than micro beats. The musical mind with a developed sense of meter is mindful of macro beats and micro beats simultaneously, with appropriate weight distribution. Macro and micro beats provide the foundation upon which melodic rhythm is placed.

We can facilitate the young musical mind's development of a sense of meter by directing its attention to macro beats and to micro beats through movement. Our movement to macro beats contrasted by our movement to micro beats makes each come alive for little children, and it makes the difference between macro beats and micro beats more tangible. It also invites children to engage with macro and with micro beats in movement. Little children need a great deal of experience moving to macro beats and moving to micro beats in a variety of meters in order to develop a sense of meter. (See Appendix A for macro and micro beats in the meters used in this book.)

A little tot who is able to stand alone often sways or bounces at the knees when hearing music, even if just a TV ad. The young musical mind wisely engages the weight of the body in response to music. We have traditionally encouraged beat activity through clapping, tapping, or playing a rhythm instrument, but none of these embody the musical mind as does engaging the whole body in weighted movement. Using lower body weight with macro beats and with micro beats is most productive in developing a sense of meter. Swaying macro beats and bouncing at the knees on micro beats put the musical mind in motion to develop a sense of meter.

A rhythm narrative such as the example in Figure 2.3, through multiple successive repetitions, provides the "sound environment" for engaging children in movement with macro and micro beats, just as it did for flowing movement. Chant the narrative on "bah" and keep it going, demonstrating movement on macro beats by swaying, shifting body weight with each macro beat. Switch to knee bouncing on micro beats on the next verse or phrase. Alternate swaying movement with macro beats and bouncing movement with micro beats on successive verses to keep the contrast between macro and micro beats alive in the young musical mind, complete with appropriate weight distribution.

Include an occasional verse of swaying macro beats while simultaneously bouncing micro beats, communicating the relationship between macro and micro beats through movement, with the bounce into macro beats adding energy to the greater weight of the macro beats. The musical mind has to become mindful of both macro and micro beats in order to precisely perform melodic rhythm, and has to become mindful of macro and micro beats simultaneously.

The embodiment of rhythm knowing can be propelled by engaging the tongue with full body weight movement. Try "tonguing" macro beats with the rhythm narrative in Figure 2.3—deliver eight bar phrases of macro beats on an aspirated "too" rather than "bah," while swaying macro beats throughout. Children and attending adults will follow your lead. Switch to bouncing and "tonguing" eight bar phrases of micro beats with the aspirated "too." The body tends to follow the tongue, so tonguing macro beats and tonguing micro beats while moving with them offers a way to facilitate little children's bodily connection to macro and to micro beats.[2]

Imagine engaging little children in movement through successive repetitions of the rhythm narrative in Figure 2.3 in a sequence such as this, all without losing a beat:

1. Flowing movement through several repetitions on "bah,"
2. Weighted movement through several repetitions on "bah," alternating macro beat and micro beat movement with each verse,
3. Tonguing macro and micro beats with weighted movement for several eight-bar phrases, alternating phrases of macro beats and phrases of micro beats on the aspirated "too,"
4. Weighted movement with both macro and micro beats, swaying and bouncing for several repetitions on "bah,"
5. Flowing movement for a couple more verses on "bah."

You might find it hard to believe that little children could be focused that long with such a seamless activity, but when we reach the musical mind and hold it captive, little children are more than willing to engage with us throughout. They love practicing music and are happy to engage with us on a regular basis in this kind of extended activity in each of the various meters.

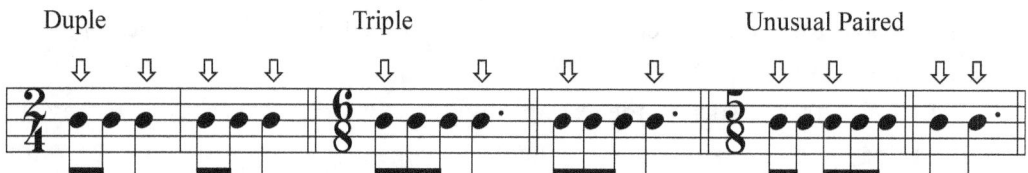

Figure 2.4 Macro beat weight, Duple, Triple, Unusual Paired

Figure 2.4 offers examples of macro and micro beats in Duple meter, Triple meter, and Unusual Paired meter, with arrows indicating weight on macro beats in each meter. (See Appendix B for weight distribution with additional beat groupings in unusual meters used in this book.) The difference between delivering macro and micro beats at the right time in any meter and delivering them at the right time with appropriate weight distribution is the difference between lifeless and exciting performance, even with professional musicians.

Flowing movement and weighted movement propel tonal development as well as rhythm development. Sustained flowing movement in tonal narratives and art songs reflects melodic line and supportive breath between and through the beats, energizes musculature for singing, and animates tonal knowing. Movement mobilizes the musical mind, whether it is processing rhythm, tonal, or the two together. It embodies rhythm and tonal knowing as the musical mind moves toward tunefulness and rhythmicity.

Making Meaning

The young child immersed in language vocally plays with sounds and begins to make meaning with those sounds. The playful "buh buh buh" can evolve into a request for a book or bottle. The young child's understanding of language is far greater than his ability to speak, so meager attempts to communicate can sound like babble. A little child's garbled speech may be unintelligible to us, but that doesn't mean that the child is not trying to communicate. A parent who senses that their little one is trying to create meaning responds to the child's speech as if the child is speaking fluently, filling out the child's utterance with what the parent thinks the child might be trying to say. A child's "buh" might be met with something like, "Book? Would you like to read a book?"

Similarly, the young child immersed in the various meters and tonalities attempts to use his voice to express the musical mind. His garbled attempts at rhythm and at tonal may be unintelligible to us, but what might sound like babble in the context of meter or tonality is most often a young child's attempt to make meaning musically. The young musical mind understands far more than the child's meager attempts to communicate. Little children often voice "bah" in response to our delivery of a rhythm narrative on the syllable "bah," or "too" in response to our delivery of a tonal narrative on the syllable "too," as if commenting musically in response to what they have just heard. They might even deliver "bah bah" in rhythm or "too" on the resting tone. Little children might also initiate "bah bah" or "too" at home in response to the musical mind's occasional replay of what they have heard in class. They are practicing music.

The parent of a child learning language sets up the model for dialogue with a little child in multiple ways. Playing "Peek-a-Boo," for example, elicits a child's show of delight—a kind of back and forth dialogue—even without inviting a verbal response. Another model for dialogue is created when the parent points to an object and asks, "What's this?" The parent may answer his own question with another question, "Is this a ball?" The game of identifying objects compels babes in arms. A nine-month-old might initiate the interaction by pointing to something and uttering "Dis?" The questioning vocal expression from parent or child sets up the expectation for a response. Little children love such interaction and will engage repeatedly, often communicating "again, again," even if just by enthusiastic wriggling movement rather than words.

The supportive parent of a little child learning language also simplifies sentences into single words or short phrases that carry meaning, often led by the child who sums up entire thoughts in a single word or utterance that only a parent understands. "Go sye" might be met with a parent's "Go outside? Do you want to go outside?" The child grows with each encounter as the parent engages with short language forms with the child, responds to the child's meaning, and fills out the child's response so the little one can hear in context what he might have been trying to say.

We can similarly offer short musical units of rhythm or tonal in the context of meter or tonality, making it easier for the young musical mind to deliver rhythm or tonal meaning. We can encourage little children's attempts to make meaning musically by offering opportunities for music dialogue. We, like parents scaffolding children's speech, can provide the musical context, support, and model that help the young musical mind to have its say.[3]

"Conversing" in rhythm or tonal, as in language, is dependent upon mutual understanding. We prime the pump for one-on-one musical interaction by offering short rhythm or tonal segments in the context of a meter or tonality in group activities. We present short units of rhythm or tonal and leave space after each for response, encouraging group echo, even if we do the echoing, perhaps accompanied by attending adults.

Figure 2.5 Short Units—Triple meter

Figure 2.5 offers an example of a couple of four-beat rhythm patterns in Triple meter, with each followed by space for echo. We could engage little children in multiple verses of the rhythm narrative presented in Figure 2.3, setting up the context of Triple meter, and then without losing a beat, present patterns like these on "bah," with the silent measures for echo. We then go right back into the rhythm narrative, re-establishing the context of Triple meter, which dominates the activity throughout.

A series of short rhythm or tonal segments in the context of meter or tonality, with silent space for group response, expands a rhythm or tonal narrative and compels the musical mind. Leaving space for response, with or without echo, provides for the musical mind to replay silently what it has just heard and sustains the focus of the musical mind. The short musical segments become familiar to the children through the group activity, as does the back and forth interplay of musical interaction, providing musical context, musical content, and a model for one-on-one musical interaction.

O-Solo-Me-O

Children learning language and children learning music grow by both listening and "speaking," which go hand-in-hand. The more the child listens, the greater his understanding and the more he knows to say. The more the child speaks, or attempts to express himself, the more focused his listening becomes. A child's output sparks greater attentiveness to the nuance of delivery, whether language or music, heightening both listening and self-expression. Input and output feed on each other, so it is essential that we provide both continuing experience with rich musical input and ongoing opportunities for little children to interact with us musically one-on-one. We can then develop independent musicians who are able to express the budding brilliance of the young musical mind.

We can draw little ones into musical one-on-one interaction that, like "Peek-a-Boo," playfully sets up the model for dialogue and delights little children every time, while immersing them in the various meters, tonalities and smaller segments within those meters and tonalities. We can cultivate each child's ability to make musical meaning independently—the musical equivalent of speaking. We can draw little children into ongoing solo response both rhythmically and tonally by the time they are two-years-old, and nurture development in each child throughout the early years.

Little children willingly engage in solo response when meter or tonality compels the musical mind, the musical interaction aligns with the musical mind's development, and the one-on-one interaction is inviting. These three factors require that we keep the meter or tonality as the dominant force of any activity, that we be aware of the way the musical mind develops both rhythmically and tonally, and that we are conscious of the emotional as well as the musical needs of our little artists.

Four types of activities are presented here that stimulate group and one-on-one response with little children of all ages, while serving the development of the musical mind. These core activities—Rhythm Dialogue Activity, Resting Tone Activity, Macro/Micro Beat Activity, and Tonal Dialogue Activity—provide for immersion and musical interaction with rhythm and tonal segments in the context of meter and tonality. They invite echo response in group activities, draw children into solo response, and provide for little children's ongoing music development with increasing musical difficulty throughout early childhood. Props take on new meaning in these activities, as they become not only musical instruments for practicing music, but also vehicles for practice in speaking one's mind—the musical mind.

Rhythm Dialogue Activity

The young musical mind compelled by meter engages in Rhythm Dialogue Activity as readily as a young child engages in playing "Peek-a-Boo." Little children who have been immersed in various meters and rhythm patterns within those meters immediately understand our invitation to dialogue in rhythm, with our offering no more than a four-beat rhythm pattern chanted as a "question." We leave four beats for a child's "answer," and then pose another four-beat "question." A smile, movement, or shy head-turn of a babe in arms demonstrates awareness of the playful rhythmic interaction well before a vocal response is offered. Rhythm Dialogue Activity, like "Peek-a-Boo," sets up an enticing model for one-on-one interaction with built-in time for response. Figure 2.6 offers a sample for Rhythm Dialogue Activity in Duple meter.

Figure 2.6 Rhythm Dialogue Activity, Duple

Set up the context for Rhythm Dialogue by chanting a rhythm narrative in the meter and then, without losing a beat, chant the initial four-beat rhythm pattern on "bah," using vocal inflection that makes the rhythm pattern sound like a question. Leave four beats for response, whether or not the child offers a response, and then present the next four-beat pattern on "bah" as a question in the meter, leaving another four beats for response. Keep the meter running throughout Rhythm Dialogue Activity, with or without a child's response, continuing to immerse children in the ongoing meter and in the individual rhythm patterns. A series of four rhythm patterns offered as questions, with each followed by four beats, creates a substantial rhythm narrative that sustains the meter as the dominant force of the activity, keeping the musical mind of all in attendance with us while we engage with individuals.

The four silent beats provide time for response and time for the musical mind to replay what it has just heard, serving the development of the musical mind. A child might offer a single "bah" in response to our rhythm pattern or "bah bah bah" that is not in the meter. A child might offer a two-beat or four-beat rhythm pattern that is clearly in the meter. Another child might echo the pattern we presented, offer a different one, or even deliver a pattern in a different meter. Our rhythm patterns serve to reaffirm the given meter and the invitation to dialogue in the meter, whatever response we might receive.

Rhythm Dialogue is an ongoing process that is appropriate with every age. It can be done in any meter and with increasing levels of difficulty as children grow, challenging each group and each child at their own level. We can engage a group with multiple rhythm patterns, eliciting echo, improvisation, or both after each pattern, and we can engage individuals, offering a couple of patterns or more to each child, all without losing a beat. Each experience provides opportunity for children to practice delivering rhythm patterns, all without comment.

We engage regularly in Rhythm Dialogue Activity in all the various meters throughout early childhood. We learn to interpret little children's musical output and tailor our input to meet each child's musical needs at every level. We might respond to an individual with a pattern that simply re-establishes the meter, one that clarifies or expands what we think the child may have been trying to deliver, or one with greater rhythmic challenge, depending on the child's response. You might find yourself engaged in more expressive musical conversation with more developed youngsters, playfully offering some rhythm patterns with the vocal expression of "comments" or "commands" as well as "questions."

We can create irresistible Rhythm Dialogue Activities that draw the youngest into one-on-one interaction. A toy microphone, puppet, or any number of different kinds of props can be effective in eliciting solo response in Rhythm Dialogue Activity. The more children engage with the various meters through rhythm narratives, and the more they engage in the short rhythm units in Rhythm Dialogue Activity in group activities, the more willing and better equipped they are to engage in rhythm dialogue in any meter. Note the simplicity of the rhythm in Figure 2.5. Familiar rhythm patterns with just macro and micro beats in the easiest meter are most inviting as the initial experience in drawing little children from immersion into one-on-one interaction, including children whose immersion has been only through online recordings.

Rhythm Dialogue Activity with solo response, as defined here, scaffolds each child in making music with a loved one who responds to the child's musical meaning, fills out and models what the child is trying to say, and leads each child to more advanced music making. It models for attending adults how to interact musically with their child at home and how to respond to a child's meaning. Rhythm Dialogue Activity develops the young child's readiness for one-on-one tonal interaction.

Resting Tone Activity

Little children generally engage one-on-one with rhythm more quickly than they do with tonal, as if tonal is more intimate for the musical mind. The seemingly less personal interaction of Rhythm Dialogue Activity teaches the musical mind to speak for itself, priming it to speak up tonally.

The most immediate tonal response for the young musical mind is the resting tone, the organizing force of tonal. Our singing the resting tone between short tonal segments in an established tonality strengthens a developing sense of tonality and gives voice, literally, to what is hovering in the young child's musical mind, making the resting tone more tangible. Our singing a series of tonal segments, each followed by the resting tone, compels the musical mind, with tonality dominating the activity. The young child then quite naturally fills in the resting tone between segments, whether vocally or just within the musical mind. Giving the young child the opportunity to anticipate the resting tone, which is then reinforced by our singing the resting tone, serves the developing sense of tonality, whether or not the child is yet able or willing to sing the resting tone. Figure 2.7 offers an example of a Resting Tone Activity in Dorian tonality.

Figure 2.7 Resting Tone Activity, Dorian

Establish the context for Resting Tone Activity with a tonal narrative in the tonality, key, and meter of the Resting Tone Activity. Sing the first tonal segment of the Resting Tone Activity on "too." Take an audible breath and then sing the resting tone on "too." Sing the next tonal segment similarly, followed by an audible breath and then the resting tone. Gesture so that children breathe with us and sing the resting tone with us. The more adept they become in singing the resting tone with us, the more we can offer just the tonal segments, gesture, and breath, with children singing the resting tone. Four tonal segments, each followed by a breath and the resting tone create a substantial tonal narrative that sustains the tonality in the musical mind, keeping all in attendance with us while we engage with individuals.

The audible breath after each tonal segment provides a bit of a pause, giving time for the young musical mind to anticipate the resting tone, which then magically appears in sound. The breath also summons tonal knowing. Our audible breath serves as a virtual breath for young children, mobilizing the young musical mind to sound the resting tone, whether internally or externally.[4]

Tonality dominates Resting Tone Activity, immersing all in the tonality, continually reinforcing the resting tone, and feeding the musical mind throughout. Notice that the tonal segments are presented with just macro and micro beats. The neutral syllable "too" is used for tonal activities, rather than the more common "bum," as the deliberate use of the tongue, particularly with the "oo" vowel, elicits more precise intonation from both teacher and children.[5]

We continue to immerse children in the various tonalities and tonal segments within each, strengthening the resting tone in the musical mind in every tonality, whether with group activities or one-on-one activities. Resting Tone Activity in any tonality enhances the awareness of resting tone in all tonalities, and children's vocal response of resting tone in the context of any tonality reinforces resting tone response in any tonality. Little children may or may not initially sing the resting tone with us. We respond to each child's offering or lack thereof by continuing to deliver tonal segments followed by a breath and the resting tone, reaffirming the tonality and the resting tone in the musical mind.

Children who have been immersed in the various tonalities and tonal segments in each are familiar with the tonal segments followed by the resting tone, and they have already experienced Rhythm Dialogue Activity. We can create irresistible Resting Tone Activities that draw little ones into singing the resting tone, whether group activity or one-on-one activity. We might, for example, engage a group with or without adults in flowing movement in a tonal narrative and then sing the tonal segments in Figure 2.7, cueing the breath and squatting to sing the resting tone. Little children will follow, happily squatting with us each time we sing the resting tone, often breathing and singing with us as well. The activity for the children is akin to repeatedly playing "Ring-Around-the-Rosie" with all falling down. The young musical mind captivated by tonality compels the child to breathe and squat with us as if it is a natural expression of the resting tone. The breath mobilizes the musical mind and using the weight of the body in the squat reinforces the implied weight of the resting tone in the musical mind, making the resting tone more tangible and the "resting tone squat" that much more compelling.[6]

We can also entice little ones to sing the resting tone with a puppet who only sings the resting tone in response to our tonal segments, complete with breath. The young musical mind is so compelled by the power of tonality and resting tone that singing the resting tone repeatedly with a charming puppet is hard to resist. We might offer two or four tonal segments to each child, completing a phrase before moving to the next child. A toy microphone or set of telephones are also effective with Resting Tone Activity—the most basic tonal dialogue that prepares children for the more difficult Tonal Dialogue Activity.

Macro/Micro Beat Activity

A developed sense of meter is mindful of both macro and micro beats simultaneously, whatever the meter. Macro/Micro Beat Activity makes macro and micro beats more tangible and fortifies macro and micro beats as the driving force of each meter. The musical mind/body connection is activated with Macro/Micro Beat Activity, offering practice in embodying macro and micro beats with appropriate weight distribution in the various meters. Figure 2.8 offers an example of a Macro/Micro Beat Activity in Duple meter.

Figure 2.8 Macro/Micro Beat Activity, Duple

Set up the context for Macro/Micro Beat Activity by chanting a rhythm narrative in the meter and then, without losing a beat, chant the first eight bars of the Macro/Micro Beat Activity on "bah," shifting body weight side to side with macro beats, while simultaneously bouncing at the knees with micro beats. Shift to "tonguing" four-bar phrases on an aspirated "too," bouncing at the knees and tonguing micro beats for two measures and then swaying and tonguing macro beats for two measures, alternating between the two both in sound and weighted movement so the young musical mind and body is immersed in the contrast between the two.

Go back to the beginning, chanting on "bah" with both macro and micro beat movement, as described, bringing the combination of macro and micro beat movement back into the chant after engaging in macro beats and micro beats separately. Tonguing macro and micro beats with little children shines an aural spotlight on macro and micro beats, clarifying what a child knows in sound. Engaging the tongue helps to bring the body in sync with the musical mind's awareness of macro and micro beats.

The tonguing section with movement is the heart of Macro/Micro Beat Activity. The opening chanting section invites children to engage in movement in the meter. The next section offers the opportunity to practice macro and micro beats in tonguing and movement, followed by bringing that practice back into context. We can carry the activity on through a number of repetitions, alternating tonguing sections with chanting sections throughout. Meter dominates the activity as we model macro and micro beat movement together in the chanting sections and separately in the tonguing sections. Little children readily engage in Macro/Micro Beat Activity. They enjoy the tonguing and the dramatic shift back and forth from macro beats to micro beats. The example in Figure 2.8 includes only macro and micro beats in Duple meter, making it effective as the initial experience in drawing little children into Macro/Micro Beat Activity. We engage children in Macro/Micro Beat Activity in the full variety of meters, with the difficulty of rhythm patterns in the first eight bars increasing in each meter as children grow.

We can employ props like pom-poms with Macro/Micro Beat Activity, and we can engage one-on-one with little children. The nature of Macro/Micro Beat Activity with a group, however, compels each child to generate his own macro and micro beats in sound and movement, so we can witness each child's developing competence within the group activity as well. Macro/Micro Beat Activity points toward ensemble as well as individual musicianship, with little children independently engaging together in the consistent meter and tempo.

The young musical mind/body connection needs Macro/Micro Beat Activity in a variety of meters. The contrast between meters strengthens the musical mind/body's connection to macro and micro beats in any meter, while the contrast in weight between macro and micro beats within each meter propels children toward both rhythmic precision and momentum, both individually and in ensemble.

Tonal Dialogue Activity

We have set the stage for Tonal Dialogue Activity with Rhythm Dialogue Activity, and with Resting Tone Activity, which is the most basic Tonal Dialogue. Gently moving children into Tonal Dialogue Activity serves tonal development, however skilled or unskilled children's tonal response might be within the activity. Figure 2.9 offers an example of Tonal Dialogue Activity in Mixolydian tonality.

Figure 2.9 Tonal Dialogue Activity, Mixolydian

Establish the tonality with a tonal narrative in the same tonality, key, and meter of the Tonal Dialogue Activity, providing a musical context for tonal dialogue. Sing the first eight bars of the Tonal Dialogue Activity on "too." The next section, with its short tonal segments, intentionally slows the tempo and adds beats to accommodate an audible breath before each tonal segment and response. Take a deliberate breath before delivering each tonal segment, and another deliberate breath in support of the child's response, whether or not the child responds. Note that the short tonal segments include very simple rhythm. End the activity by going back to the beginning, reinforcing the context of the tonality.[7]

The breath before each tonal segment summons tonal knowing. Our audible breath in each segment serves to scaffold and cue young children to mobilize the young musical mind, summoning tonal knowing, and generating energy for vocal production. A silent response from a child leaves space for the musical mind to replay what it has just heard, serving the musical mind of all in attendance. A child who might respond with just a breath does the same, but with the aid of the breath to summon tonal knowing even without a vocal response.[8]

Little children might respond in Tonal Dialogue Activity with just the resting tone, which is the first step to dialoguing tonally. Some might cling to the resting tone for response to each tonal segment, communicating that they are solidly in the tonality, though not yet ready to deliver tonal segments. Some children might echo our tonal segments or offer their own. Some might deliver something diatonically that is obviously in the tonality, but without discreet pitches, as if the musical mind is in the tonality, with the voice trying to express what the musical mind knows.

Immersion in the short tonal segments in group activities provides models for response and vocabulary with which to dialogue. We can engage little children in Tonal Dialogue Activity in multiple ways, including movement or props. A microphone, telephones, or puppets serve well with Tonal Dialogue Activity. A puppet or two can be helpful in modeling the response of a tonal segment rather than resting tone with children just moving into Tonal Dialogue Activity.

We respond to each child's offering as we did with Rhythm Dialogue Activity, singing what we think a child is trying to deliver, clarifying the short tonal segment, and resetting the tonality as needed. We regularly engage little children in Tonal Dialogue Activity in each of the various tonalities, making sure that tonality dominates the experience, sustaining the musical minds of all in attendance. Offering multiple tonal segments to each child for response creates an ongoing tonal narrative and gives each child substantial opportunity to respond in solo. Staying with an individual child through a musical phrase of tonal segments encourages musical response more than one segment per child.

Immersion in the variety of tonalities and tonal segments in Tonal Dialogue Activity in a group strengthens one-on-one Tonal Dialogue Activity in any tonality. Experience in Tonal Dialogue Activity with any tonality strengthens tonal dialogue in all tonalities. The ongoing experience of one-on-one Tonal Dialogue Activity with a more developed musician can serve a lifetime of music making, giving voice to ever-growing tonal skill.

Breaking down rhythm and tonal into bite-sized pieces in Rhythm Dialogue Activity, Resting Tone Activity, Macro/Micro Beat Activity, and Tonal Dialogue Activity provides basic vocabulary with which little children can make musical meaning. Each meter or tonality provides a musical context in which the short segments carry meaning. Immersing children in the various meters and tonalities and the smaller units within each develops the readiness for the musical mind to speak up.

Successive rhythm or tonal segments, with time for response or echo after each, extends the rhythm or tonal narrative, compelling the musical mind throughout. Adding full-body movement to the musical conversation mobilizes the musical mind while adding energy to response. Group engagement in the musical interaction offers opportunity for abundant repetition and expansion of the basic rhythm and tonal vocabulary that carry meaning, securing rhythm and tonal segments in the musical mind, while reinforcing meter and tonality. Engaging a group in the give and take of musical interaction through immersion in rhythm segments in the context of meter and tonal segments in the context of tonality, provides not only rhythm and tonal context, but also rhythm and tonal content, as well as modeling of rhythm and tonal interaction—all of which sets the stage for solo response.

Introducing one-on-one interaction to little children with Rhythm Dialogue Activity elicits the most immediate response and teaches little children how to interact musically one-on-one. Introducing Resting Tone Activity after successful Rhythm Dialogue Activity draws on the willing one-on-one interaction experienced with Rhythm Dialogue to elicit the more intimate solo tonal response. Introducing Macro/Micro Beat Activity for solo response after one-on-one experience with Rhythm Dialogue Activity and Resting Tone Activity builds on the previous activities with greater physical involvement, activating the musical mind/body connection. It also separates Resting Tone Activity from Tonal Dialogue Activity, which requires a more developed response than Resting Tone Activity.

Ongoing experience in rhythm and tonal narratives in the various meters and tonalities provides the necessary stimulation for the musical mind to compare and contrast meters and compare and contrast tonalities in the process of developing a sense of meter and a sense of tonality. Ongoing experience in Rhythm Dialogue Activity, Resting Tone Activity, Macro/Micro Beat Activity, and Tonal Dialogue Activity in the various meters and tonalities fortifies the developing sense of meter and sense of tonality while providing short rhythm and tonal vocabulary for little children to begin to make meaning. These activities each provide for developmental progression through music content of increasingly greater difficulty through multiple years, and together provide the groundwork for all higher levels of music learning. (Examples of the four types of activities in the various tonalities and meters can be found in the Come Children Sing Institute SONG LIBRARY. [9])

Artistry in Teaching

Little children read us like a book. They sense our warmth and sincerity, our respect for them, and our joy in teaching. Every move we make affects their participation and cooperation. Tuning in to little things that make a difference can enhance children's engagement, increase the musicality of our classes, and promote artistry in teaching.

Using and Not Using Props

Little children will explore anything we put in their hands and become absorbed in the item itself. The musical mind does the same aurally with meters, tonalities, rhythm patterns and tonal segments, which are all "aural toys" for the musical mind. They compel the musical mind just as any shiny object compels a little child, and they can pacify a crying child as effectively as a dazzling toy.

Appealing objects are often used to distract a young child, and they will distract the musical mind that is not fully engaged with meter or tonality. Giving the musical mind a chance to play with the "aural toys" over time, through multiple repetitions of rhythm and tonal narratives without props, assures that alluring objects won't get in the way of the musical mind's engagement with the aural toys. Minimizing props in the first few classes with beginners gives the musical mind a chance to wake up, experience, and explore the aural toys without the distraction of fascinating objects in hand. *Little children don't need something in their hands to keep them busy when the musical mind is busy.*

Sculpting energy and offering a seamless presentation does wonders to keep beginners of all ages with us without props, while we enchant them with meters, tonalities, movement, and song. Everything is new to beginning classes, so whatever we do is fresh and exciting, without expectations for objects in hand. There are many things we can do with beginning classes to add variety and interest with a minimum of props, including the use of play songs.

Movement can always shift energy and create variety. We might have children and accompanying adults engaged in full body flowing movement with a rhythm narrative and then move into group Rhythm Dialogue Activity or Macro/Micro Beat Activity. We might engage children with flowing movement with a tonal narrative and then move into group Resting Tone Activity, with each tonal segment followed by the "resting tone squat."

We can play a meter on a drum or a tonality on a recorder or other musical instrument to provide variety in the "sound environment." The intrigue of the musical instrument encourages just listening, generally heightening the musical mind's focus on meter or tonality.[10] We might add just one prop to a beginning class as a special treat—perhaps rhythm sticks for each child, or a single puppet that stays on our hand. The aural toys we have offered without props have the greatest power to capture the musical mind and develop little children's musical readiness to use props meaningfully.

Store-bought, homemade, or imaginary props can then become a grand addition to our longer-term classes, as they become musical instruments with which to practice music. The meter or tonality continues to dominate each experience. The way we introduce props, hand them out, and collect them are all part of sculpting energy to create the most musical and compelling experience.

> Start a rhythm narrative and then pick up a pair of rhythm sticks, pom-poms, or a toy hammer and play along with your chanting. The meter dominates the activity while our engagement with the prop wordlessly defines the prop as a musical instrument and demonstrates how it is to be used. Continue the chant while passing out the same prop to each child, increasing ensemble sound and activity gradually. Each child joins the ensemble using the prop in the same musical manner we've demonstrated, happily engaging in practicing music, whether chanting along or just engaging with the meter. Collect the musical instruments one child at a time while the rhythm narrative continues to dominate the activity. The crescendo and decrescendo created by distributing and collecting the instruments one-at-a-time add to the musicality of the overall experience and encourages cooperation from all.

A thoughtful approach to using props helps us to avoid challenges that can easily derail the musical mind, deflate children's energy, or over-stimulate them. We know, for example, not to expect toddlers to sit quietly with a prop in their hands, or come to attention amidst the collective din of a noisy prop. We know that little children want whatever they see that is attractive, so we keep props out of sight before and after we use them. We know that little children's manipulation skills are limited, so we avoid using props beyond their level of facility. Tennis balls roll away. Bean bags stay put. Passing a prop around the room can be difficult for little children, as can letting go of a prop, so we keep a single prop like a puppet or toy microphone in our own hands and use it to interact with each individual child. Games can also be difficult for little children. Something as simple as putting our hands on our heads or shoulders with a musical narrative can interrupt the musical mind, turning the activity into a follow-the-leader game directed by the visual rather than the aural.

Choosing props that match our musical intent also facilitates the effectiveness of props. Crisp movement with a toddler hammer, for example, works better for rhythm activity than for tonal, whereas scarves generally serve tonal better than rhythm. Pom-poms can suit rhythm or tonal, but they are particularly effective with rhythm. Using a prop for both rhythm and tonal activity within a single class period diminishes its effectiveness. Using the prop for rhythm activity in one class and for tonal in another is a better option, as each new use becomes a fresh experience.

Some props, like pom-poms, are most effective while standing, while others, like toddler hammers, are most effective while sitting, offering multiple options in sculpting children's energy, with the distribution and collection of props built into each activity. We might, for example, engage an entire group of youngsters, with or without attending adults, in jumping into hula hoops for group Rhythm Dialogue Activity, followed by sitting for a more calming Resting Tone Activity with a puppet. We might use scarves for the children to engage in full body movement for tonal activity and then go to a sitting position for a rhythm activity with toddler hammers. The shift between standing and sitting can help to regulate children's energy while offering many different types of experiences with both rhythm and tonal.

We can use props to stimulate both immersion and one-on-one interaction, effectively combining the two in one longer activity. We might, for example, engage children with pom-poms while immersing them in a rhythm narrative and then break into Macro/Micro Beat Activity with the pom-poms, swishing pom-poms on macro beats and flicking wrists on micro beats while tonguing.

A single puppet can be very effective for both group and one-on-one interaction if we have captured the musical mind. Puppets are very attractive to little children, so if we haven't yet captured the musical mind, children will just want to touch or hold the puppet. It is the sheer musicality of a puppet in relation to meter or tonality that draws a child into one-on-one musical interaction.

Children relate to each puppet as a little friend, and the puppet's musical response entices the children to interact with the music as the puppet does. The puppets do not talk. They just respond musically, leading or modeling appropriate musical response for the children. A puppet on our hand, with a mouth that our hand can open and close for musical response, is most useful. It is always a joy to observe a group of little ones spellbound by the puppet's musical response, when we are obviously manipulating the puppet right in front of the children and singing the music content and the puppet's response.

A puppet defined by a particular rhythm or tonal response is more effective with the youngest and least experienced children than a puppet who does both rhythm and tonal, or one who demonstrates skills in rhythm or tonal that are way beyond that of the children. Each puppet becomes endeared to the children for its defined musical response. "Resting Tone Rabbit," for example, only sings the resting tone in response to our tonal segments. The puppet's predicable response reinforces the resting tone in the musical mind while enticing little children to sing the resting tone with the puppet. You may surprise yourself by how creative you become with puppets to further explore the musical mind of more developed children.

Limited budgets prevent a storehouse of props, but there are many ways to acquire a variety of props through the years. We might be able to occasionally borrow a few items from a gym teacher or early childhood setting. We can make some props or use household items to cut cost. We might find promotional items like fire hats free.

A little imagination can turn anything into a prop. The classic see-through, restaurant sandwich baskets are delightful for playing "Peek-a-Boo" with the resting tone. A child-sized broom for each child invites full-body movement to sweep up macro beats and micro beats, alternating between the two with each verse of a rhythm narrative, with or without tonguing. Small promotional fly swatters can enable swatting the resting tone at the end of each tonal segment, singing along with it. A sell-out on small laundry baskets can offer the opportunity for each little tot to become a Jack-in-the-box, popping up on the resting tone. The baskets on a different day might become see-through hats for standing three-year-olds to lift off of their heads when singing the resting tone, and on another day they might serve as vehicles for rides with immersion activities.

We might repurpose instruments from an elementary school music program to meet the needs of younger children. Orff instruments, tone bells, and recorders, as examples, could be used to reinforce resting tone, with drums and other percussion instruments used for immersion or Macro/Micro Beat activity.

Props can be used differently to suit particular holidays or themes. A little imagination and a wagon full of pom-poms create a delightful hayride, with each child's ride carried by a different rhythm narrative in the meter which dominates the activity. Giving each child a couple of tickets for their rides adds a special touch, while encouraging waiting for their own ride. The ticket might also be used for each child to engage in Rhythm Dialogue before his ride, with perhaps the rhythm narrative tailored to increase difficulty in class immersion. Imaginary props can also be very effective as long as we engage in playing music rather than imaginative play. Meter or tonality has to dominate the experience.

Little children's imagination is so far beyond ours that we need only suggest something by our props and it becomes real. Don a visor, stand behind a level music stand, and you become a "crew kid" at a fast-food restaurant taking orders. Offer the opening "question" suggested for Rhythm Dialogue Activity in Duple meter and three-and-four-year-olds will enthusiastically get in line repeatedly to engage in Rhythm Dialogue as if placing orders.

We can engage little children in playing music in an endless number of creative ways, with and without props. We continue to fine-hone non-verbal communication throughout, with meters and tonalities dominating the experience as little children practice music. The more playful we become, the more little children engage, and the more musical and magical our classes can become.

Eliciting One-on-One Response

Meter and tonality capture the musical mind, while props serve as musical instruments for practicing music. This powerful combination draws children in, but how we draw children out can make or break any hope of getting little ones to interact with us musically on cue.

Parents of a two-year-old learn very quickly that whatever they want their child to do, the child will not, unless it is his own idea. The parents necessarily have to become very clever to charm the child into going along with anything. Coaxing musical response can turn any child into a two-year-old, with a will to defy any expectation or request, and determination to hold firm in his decision. On the other hand, alluring children into musical response can turn any child, including two-year-olds, into cooperative musicians, responding individually on cue.

> "Playing music" takes the little child into another realm where he happily loses himself in the wonder of his own musical imagination. Our role has to be that of an "ensemble musician", also caught up in "playing music," with the musical narrative prime and only non-verbal communication. The wonder of the young child's musical mind lost in "playing music" overrides shyness, fear, and stubbornness to engage independently in musical response.
>
> The trick is to get the children so caught up in that wonderful world of "playing music" that they lose themselves and all consciousness of self. Then they respond as musicians. It is only when we try to get them to respond with our words, logic, and reasoning that we jar them back into the "real world," where they once again become two-year-olds.[11]

We can charm little children into responding musically on cue. We can creatively propel little children from active group engagement to individual musical response. We have to handle every child with care, but it is the youngest children that need our most artful approach to eliciting willing one-on-one response. Babies and toddlers can be threatened by our attention. Three- and four-year olds, particularly those with preschool or pre-K experience, are usually more willing to function independently, but those who are not can be enticed in the same manner that we draw in younger children.

Our efforts to engage little children individually are often counterproductive. The youngest children, accompanied by an adult, are most content in our classes when we create the illusion of a little distance between teacher and child and respect their safe space with a loved one. We might greet each child with his name as the first measure of a four-bar chant in Duple or Triple meter while creating a nametag, essentially addressing the child indirectly while intriguing the musical mind. We might sing a song in class that uses each child's name, give each child a pair of rhythm sticks at some point in the class, or bid each good-bye. Trying to elicit individual musical response, however, can make little children more reluctant to respond than they would be if we create the illusion of distance from the start and let them soak in the experience on their own terms in the arms and laps of their loved ones. The musical mind needs its own time and space to process musical input in its own way.

Classes with twenty or more beginners, each with an attending adult, help to create the illusion of distance. We might even sit on a two-step folding stool or stepladder rather than on the floor with beginning classes, creating greater distance as well as presence, and assuring children's comfort by giving the musical mind the time and space it needs to absorb and process musical input. Classes that flow like a seamless children's play contribute to the illusion of distance, seemingly without direct attention to individual children.

We've all seen little children hide in a loved one's arms or legs when a stranger enters their space. The musical mind is equally shy and just as easily threatened. Little children are very protective of its soundness when we enter its space as an outsider. Children might, however, when given the necessary space, naturally dance along, spontaneously offer "bah bah" after a rhythm narrative, or sing the resting tone after a tonal narrative, all without our invasion of their musical space or direct attention to their response. Trying to interact with the individual child's impromptu offerings can diminish the spontaneity of the young child's musical expression. It can also interrupt the musical mind of the others in class, lessen the flow of the seamless class, and diminish musicality and artistry in teaching.

We can accomplish more with the youngest children in class by offering rich musical input than by trying to elicit output from individuals. Children have to absorb meters and tonalities just as they have to absorb their native language before they can make meaning. We can fully prime the little ones for one-on-one response by group exposure to meters and tonalities and rhythm and tonal segments. One-on-one interaction with the musical mind is highly intimate for young children, and the youngest will interact musically with us most willingly when we allow for the development of readiness both musically and emotionally.

Children under eighteen months of age may indeed engage in Rhythm Dialogue Activity or Resting Tone Activity, but not necessarily with us. Parents who regularly attend classes with their little one know that a child's initiated "bah bah" at home is an invitation for rhythm interaction. The parents may make up something that is no more rhythmic than the child's utterance, but they are trying to interact with their child musically as they do with language. Dialoguing with rhythm then becomes another option for parents to connect with their little one on the changing table, in the car, or while cooking a meal, just as spontaneous renditions of a play song may become part of their day-to-day activity together.

We stimulate parent-child musical interaction by our model in class, with or without online recordings for home use, and by gradually drawing little children into one-on-one response in our classes. We are priming the parents as well as the children to grow together in musical interaction. Parents, like the children, find rhythm more immediate than tonal, so interacting rhythmically with their little one develops greater adult and child readiness for tonal interaction.

Little children approaching eighteen-months-old, who have been with us for a couple of full terms, are ripe to allure into one-on-one musical response in class. These children are familiar with us, and they are familiar with the various meters and tonalities and rhythm and tonal segments. They have experienced group interaction in Rhythm Dialogue Activity, Resting Tone Activity, Macro/Micro Beat Activity, and Tonal Dialogue Activity.

We invite these children to stay for an additional ten minutes of "advanced activities" after their regular class. These little ones then continue with the immersion and delight of classes for beginners, while crossing the bridge to a more advanced class with one-on-one interaction. We sit on the floor with the children for the advanced activities, creating a more intimate setting. We use familiar musical narratives and rhythm and tonal segments, keeping the focus on the meter or tonality rather than on the child, and continuing to practice non-verbal communication. Attending adults stay with the children, but we offer irresistible activities that little children want to do by themselves.

Advanced activities can include a short series of rhythm activities and a short series of tonal activities, using props that invite children to engage directly with us. We might, for example, start chanting in Duple meter for a small group of sitting youngsters and engage in Macro/Micro Beat Activity with a puppet who dances to contrasting macro and micro beats in front of the children. We invite the children to dance with "Dancing Doggie," with the meter dominating the activity. We keep the puppet on our own hand and position it in front of each child, tonguing four bars of micro beats and four bars of macro beats. The puppet bounces up and down while tonguing micro beats and sways side to side while tonguing macro beats in front of each child, alternating phrases. Each child participates in his own way. Some might hold the arms of the puppet on our hand, and some might bounce and sway with the puppet. Some might just stare intensely.

This activity does not ask for one-on-one vocal response, but rather, gently nudges little ones toward one-on-one interaction with musical material that children already know and a delightful puppet. It also stimulates a little greater independence from their accompanying adult, paving the way for greater comfort with solo response the next week or even in the next activity. We might do exactly the same activity the following week in Triple meter, reinforcing independence as well as meter, while gently breaking in children who were not in attendance the previous week.

Another week of advanced activities might start with a narrative in Duple meter, and then we bring out a toy microphone. We hold it near our chin to deliver the opening two-bar "question" for Rhythm Dialogue Activity in Duple meter and then lean the microphone toward an individual child for response. The child may or may not deliver, but we leave space for a four-beat metric response and use the microphone ourselves for another rhythmic "question." We lean the microphone toward the child for the next four beats before similarly inviting Rhythm Dialogue from each individual child. We keep the microphone in our own hands and continue to offer familiar rhythm patterns and space for response, without losing a beat, without focusing on any individual child's response or lack thereof, and without applauding for individuals, which interrupts the musical mind of all. The meter just keeps on going, with the series of rhythm patterns creating its own rhythm narrative that dominates the experience and carries children beyond any hesitance to engage.

We can similarly entice the youngest or most reticent children to engage with tonal. We start a tonal narrative and within that aural context bring out "Resting Tone Rabbit," a puppet who only sings the resting tone. We sing familiar tonal segments in the tonality, and after each segment, Resting Tone Rabbit takes an audible breath and then sings the resting tone. The arm with the puppet cues the breath before the puppet sings, much as a conductor might. We invite children to sing the resting tone with Resting Tone Rabbit, and then continue the tonal segments, each followed by the puppet's breath and delivery of the resting tone.

We keep the puppet on our hand and position it in front of each child as we deliver a couple of tonal segments, with the puppet cueing the breath and delivering the resting tone after each. The puppet sings the resting tone, complete with breath, modeling in front of each child, whether or not the child sings the resting tone. The musical mind anticipates the resting tone, complete with breath. Little children, most often, sing the resting tone, just as a child jumps in to finish the final word of a favorite book or nursery rhyme that the parent left out.

We have allured children into one-on-one response in Resting Tone Activity, without focus on the individual child, his response, or lack thereof. The ongoing tonal segments with intermittent resting tone become the tonal narrative that compels the musical mind, while the puppet draws children into singing the resting tone.

Each successive week of "advanced activities" might include a rhythm or tonal activity for immersion and independent engagement in playing music, with another for one-on-one response. We might, for example, start pounding with a toddler hammer while chanting a rhythm narrative in Duple meter, passing out hammers while maintaining the meter. Children practice music with their little instruments while the rhythm narrative continues to engage the children actively in the meter. The children are participating independently, whether or not we invite solo response, and they independently return the hammer to us as we collect them within the meter.

We can do much the same tonally by singing a tonal narrative, putting a see-through, sandwich basket (restaurant-style) over our eyes, and starting Resting Tone Activity. We take the basket off of our eyes only when singing the recurring resting tone, as if playing "Peek-a-Boo" with the resting tone. We keep the tonal narrative going while handing out baskets to each little child. We continue to sing tonal segments, with each followed by the resting tone, unmasking the eyes and resting tone with the preliminary breath and singing of the resting tone. Children follow our lead, playing "Peek-a-Boo" with the resting tone and participating independently, whether or not they are singing the resting tone and whether or not we invite one-on-one response. Singing the resting tone in a game of "Peek-a-Boo" is hard for little children to resist.

The key to engaging very young children in one-on-one music response is to provide a sound environment that is so rich in music content that we keep the musical mind with us while gradually moving children forward, making sure that each new step is non-threatening. We can provide through careful planning and sheer musicality the training wheels for children to become independent musicians in our classes by age two, interacting musically on cue.

3
Advancing Musically

The young musical mind continues to become more transparent as we learn to engage with it, unveiling greater depth. It continues to challenge both common practice and research on music learning in early childhood. It continues to stretch us further to understand its brilliance.

Greater understanding of how the musical mind works in processing rhythm and tonal independently and together informs our teaching throughout early childhood. It guides us in selecting and improvising rhythm and tonal content that is appropriate for each group of children. It helps us to interpret and scaffold one-on-one interaction with every child. It guides us in choosing song repertoire appropriate for every age and level of development.

The musical mind works like a tower of blocks. Rhythm provides the foundation, with macro and micro beats the first two blocks. Melodic rhythm sits on top of macro and micro beats. The tower will fall if any one of the rhythm blocks—macro beats, micro beats, or melodic rhythm—are not secure in the musical mind. The tonal dimension is a block placed on top of melodic rhythm. A solid tower of macro and micro beats, melodic rhythm, and tonal can handle additional layers on top, including song words and instrumental accompaniments, but any single block in our tower that is not secure can topple the entire structure.

We are the prime source of nourishment for the young musical mind. It is up to us to build a solid tower of blocks in every child. It is up to us to detect which blocks are weakening the structure at any given time and to strengthen those blocks in individuals and in groups. It is up to us to secure towers that are strong enough to stay standing long after we are gone.

Young children cry when their needs are not met. The young musical mind, however, does not. It just tunes out. We can often sense a young child's needs, but our sense of what the young musical mind needs is not so intuitive—until we have a better grasp of the way the young musical mind works.

This chapter takes us deeper into the properties of rhythm and tonal and their effect on the young musical mind. It further addresses the combination of rhythm and tonal in melody and then adds song words, discussing how the intertwining of melody, rhythm, and text affects the young musical mind. Teachers new to the properties of rhythm and tonal that are discussed here may feel apprehensive about the importance of the greater complexity in relation to teaching little children. Rest assured that many of us have felt much the same as we've tried to understand in music theory what we were never taught in sound. Our own musical minds never had the opportunity to "make sense" out of the various meters or tonalities in sound, though our thinking minds were schooled in music theory. Etude 1 in Part 3 of this book is designed for teachers to develop greater competence in the various meters and tonalities through sound rather than through music theory. It is also designed to use directly in the classroom so that teachers develop with each classroom experience along with the children.

Rhythm

Rhythm provides the foundation of music and of the musical mind. Meter is determined by the relationship between macro and micro beats, which is unique to each meter. Little children validate Edwin Gordon's research on rhythm difficulty with both meters and rhythm patterns.[1]

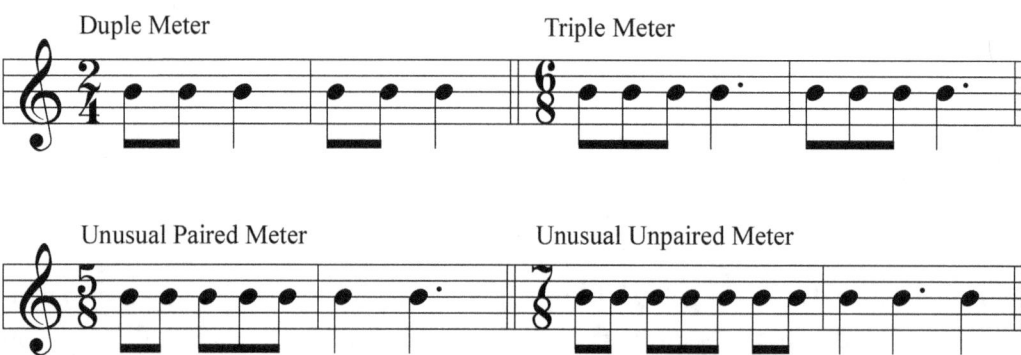

Figure 3.1   Duple, Triple, Unusual Paired, Unusual Unpaired (in order of difficulty)

Figure 3.1 presents four meters, showing the relationship between macro and micro beats in each meter. Duple is the easiest meter, with Triple more difficult. Unusual Paired meter is still more difficult, with Unusual Unpaired meter the most difficult of these four meters.[2]

Macro and micro beats serve as anchors in the musical mind in all meters. Melodic rhythm patterns placed on top of macro and micro beats can fall into place when macro and micro beats are secure in the musical mind.

Figure 3.2   Duple (melodic rhythm patterns, macro, and micro beats)

Figure 3.2, in Duple meter, shows melodic rhythm patterns in the top line in relation to macro and micro beats in the lower line. The musical mind that has developed the internal aural structure for macro and micro beats in this meter can process the melodic rhythm patterns of the top line without confusion. The process is the same in every meter, with macro and micro beats serving as anchors in the musical mind.

Figure 3.3 Triple (rhythm pattern difficulty)

Figure 3.3 shows rhythm patterns of various levels of difficulty in Triple meter. The first pattern with just macro and micro beats is the easiest. The next measure includes divisions, making it more difficult than the first measure. The third and fourth measures include elongations, rests, ties, and upbeats, with each function increasing rhythm difficulty more than the previous function. The greater the difficulty of rhythm patterns, the greater the demand on the musical mind to maintain macro and micro beats amidst the more challenging melodic rhythm. Every meter has macro and micro beats, divisions, elongations, rests, ties, and upbeats, each of which increases rhythm difficulty in the musical mind, in addition to the difficulty of the meter.[3]

Figure 3.4 Duple (difficult patterns), Triple (easier patterns)

The first line of Figure 3.4 presents a rather difficult line of Duple meter that includes rests, ties, and upbeats. The second line presents the more difficult Triple meter, but with easier rhythm patterns that include only macro beats, micro beats, and divisions. (See Appendix A for macro beats, micro beats and divisions in each of the meters used in the book.)

The young musical mind needs both macro and micro beats to become seated in any meter, and it needs to have the relationship between macro and micro beats reinforced throughout. The four bars of Figure 3.5 establish Triple meter, as the relationship between macro and micro beats is clearly defined and reinforced.

Advancing Musically   51

Figure 3.5 Triple (meter established)

The example in Figure 3.6 does not establish Triple meter, as it does not present both macro beats and micro beats in sound. It takes much greater skill for the musical mind to infer and sustain meter without the presence of both macro and micro beats.

Figure 3.6 Triple (meter not established)

The rhythm narratives that we choose for our young students have to both define and sustain the meter. The relationship between macro and micro beats has to be present in sound, establishing the meter, in order for the musical mind to process the meter. The relationship between macro and micro beats has to also be reinforced regularly, supporting and sustaining the meter in the musical mind.

Figure 3.7 Triple (established and sustained throughout)

Figure 3.8 Triple (not clearly established and sustained throughout)

Figure 3.7 presents a rhythm narrative in triple meter that establishes the meter immediately and reinforces the meter throughout. The rhythm narrative in Figure 3.8 is more ambiguous to the young musical mind, as it does not initially present the relationship between macro and micro beats in sound, nor does it reinforce that relationship throughout. The example in Figure 3.8 could be appropriate for far more developed children whose musical minds can infer and sustain the meter without the direct relationship between macro and micro beats in sound.

Awareness of rhythm difficulty guides us in meeting children's musical needs. It assures that we provide rhythm narratives and rhythm improvisations that speak to the young musical mind. It leads us in offering Rhythm Dialogue Activity (p. 32) and Macro/Micro Beat Activity (p. 36) to each group, and in responding to each child's solo offering. It also guides us in choosing appropriate tonal narratives and songs for our children.

Figure 3.9   Rhythm Dialogue Activity, Triple

Figure 3.9 presents an example of Rhythm Dialogue Activity in Triple meter. The first four-beat pattern establishes the meter. We can come back to that first pattern as often as needed to re-establish the meter. We might offer the second pattern in just macro and micro beats to reinforce the meter for children dialoguing with macro and micro beats or for children ready for more difficult patterns. The third line includes divisions, which we might use to add spice, to challenge children at the basic level, or to reinforce division patterns with children who are ready for more difficult patterns. The fourth line offers a still more difficult rhythm pattern which we might use for immersion or for dialogue, always tailoring our patterns to meet and challenge children's development.

We can further apply our awareness of meter difficulty and rhythm pattern difficulty to Macro/Micro Beat Activity, immersing children in rhythm narrative at the appropriate level of rhythm difficulty contrasted by a tonguing section with just macro and micro beats, all with movement. Figure 3.10 offers an example of Macro/Micro Beat Activity in Triple meter with division patterns.

Figure 3.10   Macro/Micro Beat Activity, Triple

The first section in Figure 3.10 immerses the young musical mind in divisions patterns, while the tonguing section brings the developing sense of meter back to just macro and micro beats. Going back then to the more difficult section brings the added benefit of greater definition of macro and micro beats in the musical mind while receiving the more difficult patterns.

Little children develop rhythmically in accordance with rhythm difficulty, demonstrating skill in Duple meter before Triple meter and in Triple meter before the Unusual meters. Duple and Triple meters serve very well to elicit response in one-on-one activities, as those are the meters children will be able to do first. It is, however, the contrast between meters through ongoing experience with Duple, Triple, Unusual Paired, and Unusual Unpaired that propels children's articulation in the easiest meters as well as the more difficult.

Children will be able to deliver macro and micro beats before divisions in any meter, and division patterns will precede more difficult patterns in each meter. Children that demonstrate some competence in Rhythm Dialogue Activity with both Duple and Triple meters with macro beats, micro beats, and divisions are well on their way, but they need a great deal of repetition to get to that point. We increase the difficulty of rhythm patterns throughout early childhood as children grow.

Tonal

The tonal dimension presents its own challenges independent of rhythm. The resting tone and fifth serve as tonal anchors in the musical mind, much as macro and micro beats serve rhythmically. The resting tone and the fifth are the same across tonalities. It is the "characteristic tones" in relation to the resting tone and fifth that distinguish one tonality from another. Figure 3.11 compares Dorian and Aeolian tonality to Major tonality and to each other, with all starting on the same pitch.

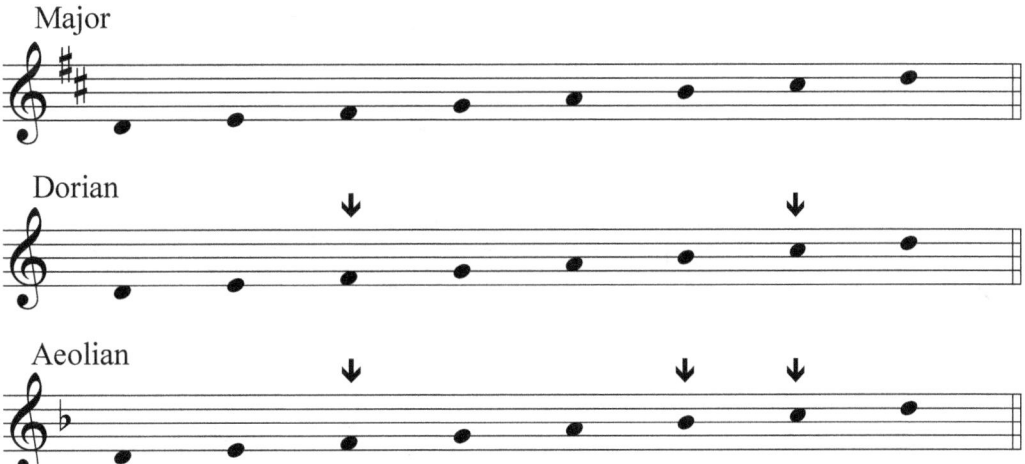

Figure 3.11 Major, Dorian, Aeolian (differences)

Dorian tonality differs from Major with its lowered third and lowered seventh. Aeolian tonality shares a minor third and lowered seventh with Dorian tonality, but Aeolian tonality also includes a lowered sixth. The lowered third and lowered seventh are characteristic tones of both Dorian and Aeolian tonality, but Dorian sports its characteristic major sixth, while Aeolian claims its characteristic minor sixth. Each combination of characteristic tones is unique to each tonality. (See Appendix C for characteristic tones of all tonalities used in this book.) Don't let the various key signatures throw you. We are accustomed to seeing a key signature in Minor tonality with the same key signature as its relative Major, but Dorian, Mixolydian, Phrygian, Lydian, and Aeolian also have the key signature of their relative Major.

The young musical mind, fortunately, does not process tonal through music theory. The more we engage with little children in the various tonalities with movement, the more our own musical mind bypasses our thinking mind, so that we, like the children, can become immersed in the unique sound of each tonality rather than trying to think our way through them.

The young musical mind processes tonality through sound, and it needs tonal narratives that clearly define and sustain tonality just as it needs rhythm narratives that define and sustain meter. The characteristic tones have to be presented in sound to establish tonality, and they have to be regularly reinforced in order for the young musical mind to sustain the tonality.

Figure 3.12 Dorian (establishes and sustains tonality)

Figure 3.13 Dorian (ambiguous tonality)

Figure 3.12 offers a tonal narrative in Dorian tonality that clearly establishes the tonality, with characteristic tones presented early and reinforced throughout. Figure 3.13 offers a tonal narrative in the same tonality, but the tonality is more ambiguous, as it does not include the characteristic major sixth of Dorian until the next to last measure. The musical mind could process the narrative in either Aeolian or Dorian before reaching the characteristic sixth. The young musical mind needs a fully defined tonality to be seated in that tonality.

We can establish tonality in a tonal narrative or tonal improvisation without all of the tonality's characteristic tones if the characteristic tones included clearly distinguish the tonality from all others. Phrygian, for example, is the only tonality with a lowered second, in addition to its lowered third and lowered sixth. Figure 3.14 presents Phrygian tonality with all of its characteristic tones.

Figure 3.14   Phrygian (with all characteristic tones)

Figure 3.15   Phrygian (without lowered sixth)

The Phrygian example in Figure 3.15 includes a lowered second, lowered seventh, and lowered third, without its characteristic lowered sixth, but Phrygian is the only tonality with a lowered second. The minor second, minor third, and minor seventh in Figure 3.15 make the example unmistakably Phrygian.

Figure 3.16   Mixolydian (with all characteristic tones)

Figure 3.17   Mixolydian (without major sixth)

Mixolydian tonality differs from Major tonality by its lowered seventh. Figure 3.16 offers an example in Mixolydian tonality. The example in Figure 3.17 also clearly establishes Mixolydian tonality rather than Major, because the repeated lowered seventh, presented early, along with the inclusion of a major third, clearly defines Mixolydian even though no sixth is present.

Figure 3.18   Lydian

Figure 3.19   Lydian (ambiguous tonality)

Figure 3.18 offers an example in Lydian tonality with its characteristic raised fourth presented early and reinforced. Figure 3.19 could be intended as Lydian tonality, but the characteristic raised fourth does not appear until the final measure, so even our own musical minds are likely to process this example in Major tonality, perhaps with an altered fourth. The young musical mind needs tonal narratives that clearly define tonality.

Figure 3.20   Pentatonic (ambiguous tonality)

The example in Figure 3.20 is Pentatonic, which has no fourth or seventh, so it does not define a tonality. The musical mind could therefore process this example as Major, Lydian, or Mixolydian tonality.

The musical mind developing a sense of tonality needs a presentation of tonality without ambiguity. The purity of the tonality, the characteristic tones that clearly define the tonality, and ongoing reinforcement of characteristic tones and resting tone are necessary for the young musical mind to develop a sense of tonality. Accidentals and shifting tonalities confuse the young musical mind. Shifting tonalities are a greater challenge for the developing musical mind than shifting meters.

Tonal properties are independent of rhythm; however, many years of research at the Come Children Sing Institute demonstrated throughout that children of all ages are far more able and willing to deliver tonal patterns when they are presented with the simplest rhythm.[4] The addition of simple rhythm to tonal patterns facilitates tonal output and yields far more musical one-on-one tonal interaction. Rhythm provides the vehicle for the musical mind's expression of tonal, compelling tonal knowing in the musical mind to speak up.

Basic tonal patterns in any tonality include 5-3-1, 1-7-1, 5-6-5, 5-4-3-2-1, 5-1, with the addition of 1-2-1 in Phrygian tonality and 5-4-5 in Lydian tonality to include all characteristic tones. The suggested set of patterns include all characteristic tones, and all but the pattern of tonal anchors, 5-1, include at least one characteristic tone of the tonality. Each of these patterns begins and ends on either the resting tone or fifth—the musical mind's reference points for processing tonality.

Figure 3.21 Tonal segments, Dorian

Figure 3.21 presents the basic tonal segments in Dorian tonality and Duple meter. Note that tonal patterns are presented with only macro and micro beats, with the weight of macro beats on the resting tone and fifth, adding weight to the tonal anchors in the musical mind and strengthening the developing sense of tonality.[5] Classes with some competence with tonal segments in Duple meter in the various tonalities may be ready for the same basic tonal patterns presented in Triple meter, with the weight of the macro beats in Triple meter falling on the resting tone and fifth.

These foundational tonal segments in the various tonalities provide tonal content for both group and one-on-one interaction in Tonal Dialogue Activity (p. 38). They can also be used in place of the more melodic segments in Resting Tone Activity (p. 34). These are generally the tonal segments that children who have been successful with Resting Tone Activity deliver initially in any tonality. The tonal segments can be done in any order once the tonality is established, but using the tonic 5-3-1 as the initial pattern with each individual helps to secure tonality. We can begin to expand tonal segments around the resting tone and fifth in any tonality (e.g. 7-2-1, 6-4-5), as these segments lead directly to the resting tone and fifth in the young musical mind caught up in tonality.

Little children just starting to dialogue tonally are usually more successful with the descending 5-3-1, 5-1, and 5-4-3-2-1 than they are with the ascending 1-3-5, 1-5, and 1-2-3-4-5. Tonal segments that lead down to the tonic seem to support the young musical mind more than those moving away from it. We can broaden tonal segments as children develop.

The difficulty of the various tonalities in relation to each other is inconclusive. The young musical mind is most drawn to the less common tonalities. Little children's responses can lead one to think that Major and Minor tonalities may be the most difficult for the young musical mind. Lydian always seems to be more difficult for little children than Dorian,

Mixolydian, Phrygian, and Aeolian. Phrygian is highly compelling for little children, but Dorian and Mixolydian seem to be the most immediate for one-on-one interaction, with Aeolian and Phrygian not far behind. The order of tonalities recommended here is Dorian, Mixolydian, Phrygian, Lydian, Aeolian, Major, and Minor, alternating tonalities with a minor third and those with a major third. The full variety of tonalities best serves the musical mind, leading to greater competence in any tonality. Children who deliver the resting tone or tonal segments in one tonality usually demonstrate the same level of skill in other tonalities.

The vocal range that is most accessible to the young musical mind and that makes the musical mind most accessible to us, is from middle C (C_4) to the B♭ above, with a tessitura between D and A. This initial singing range best serves the developing musical mind in tonal narratives, Resting Tone Activity, Tonal Dialogue Activity, art songs and gem songs.

> The initial singing range is where the musical mind makes the most sense of tonal—a sense of tonality. It is the range in which the musical mind learns to speak—to deliver tonal knowing through the voice. This beginning singing range serves for immersion and interaction with tonal narratives in the various tonalities with singers of all ages. This range offers the most immediate access to the musical mind—our portal for capturing the musical mind tonally, keeping it at the forefront, and taking it into the choral art, without the encumbrance of the thinking mind or vocal technique.[6]

We stay in this singing range to develop the musical mind throughout Part 1 of this book, with the exception of play songs, which are chosen for many reasons outside of music learning. Crossing the bridge to the higher singing range to develop the vocal instrument and ensemble singing with children in kindergarten and older is addressed in Chapter 7.

Melody

The combination of rhythm and tonal together directs the attention of the musical mind and can either support or challenge the musical mind's processing of either rhythm or tonal. The young musical mind in the context of melody needs for rhythm and tonal to support each other, strengthening each block in the musical mind's virtual tower of blocks. The intertwining of rhythm and tonal directs the musical mind's attention to either rhythm or tonal in the context of melody. Simple rhythm in a compelling tonality directs the attention of the musical mind to tonal. Complex rhythm in the same tonality upstages tonal, drawing attention to itself rather than to tonal. The power of rhythm to direct the young musical mind to or away from tonal is consistent in tonal narratives, tonal segments, and song. The simplest rhythm assures greater attention to tonal.

Figure 3.22 Phrygian, Triple (draws attention to tonal)

Figure 3.23 Phrygian, Triple (draws attention to rhythm)

Figure 3.22 presents a tonal narrative in Phrygian tonality and Triple meter. The simplicity of macro and micro beats in this example in Triple meter directs the musical mind to attend to tonal. The melody in Figure 3.23, which is also in Phrygian tonality and Triple meter, is couched in more complex rhythm, leading the musical mind to attend to rhythm rather than tonal. We choose melodies with simple rhythms when we want children to attend to tonal, and melodies with more complex rhythm when we want children to attend to rhythm.

The intertwining of rhythm and tonal can also serve to support both rhythm and tonal in the musical mind. Rhythm and tonal serve each other most in the context of melody when rhythm anchors (macro and micro beats) align with tonal anchors (resting tone and fifth), as each reinforces the other.

Figure 3.24 Mixolydian (rhythm and tonal anchors aligned)

The Mixolydian melody in Figure 3.24 presents macro and micro beats in Duple meter aligning regularly with the resting tone and fifth. The weight of macro and micro beats on tonal anchors adds strength to the resting tone and fifth, supporting tonal in the musical mind, while the implied weight of the resting tone and fifth aligned with rhythm anchors adds strength to macro and micro beats, supporting rhythm in the musical mind.

Figure 3.25 Mixolydian (rhythm and tonal anchors less aligned)

The Mixolydian melody in Figure 3.25 presents much less alignment between rhythm and tonal anchors than the example in Figure 3.24, making the melody far more difficult for the musical mind. The lack of regular alignment requires that the musical mind sustain both tonality and meter amidst the more puzzling melody, without the kind of built-in support provided in Figure 3.24.

Figure 3.26   Lydian (reinforcing characteristic tones)

The weight of macro and micro beats can also support tonal in the musical mind by aligning with characteristic tones of the tonality, reinforcing the tonality. Figure 3.26 offers a melody in Lydian tonality in which macro and micro beats regularly align with the characteristic raised fourth of Lydian as well as the resting tone and fifth, reinforcing the unique characteristic tone of Lydian in addition to reinforcing the resting tone and fifth.

Rhythm difficulty in melody that directs the musical mind to attend to rhythm rather than tonal increases tonal difficulty, as challenge in the lower blocks of the musical mind's tower of blocks affects the solidity of the tonal block on top.

Figure 3.27   Lydian (increasing tonal difficulty)

Figure 3.27 offers the same melodic line in Lydian tonality as that of Figure 3.26, but with more difficult rhythm, increasing both rhythm and tonal difficulty. Figure 3.27 could be appropriate for more developed students.

Figure 3.28   Mixolydian, Unusual Unpaired (increasing difficulty)

62   Unveiling Artistry in Early Childhood Music

A more difficult meter also increases tonal difficulty in the musical mind. Figure 3.28 offers a tonal narrative in Mixolydian tonality and Unusual Unpaired meter. Macro and micro beats align with resting tone and fifth throughout, or with the characteristic lowered seventh, supporting both rhythm and tonal in the musical mind. The difficulty of the meter, however, increases tonal difficulty, as the musical mind has to navigate tonality amidst the unusual meter. This tonal narrative would serve very well for long-term students with some rhythm and tonal competence in the various meters and tonalities.

Melodic contour, the shape of a melody, is another factor that impacts the musical mind. Abundant stepwise passages that spin around and between the resting tone and fifth support tonality in the musical mind, reinforcing tonal anchors and the direct relationship of characteristic tones to those anchors.

Figure 3.29   Aeolian (melodic contour supporting musical mind)

Figure 3.29 presents an example in Aeolian tonality that offers abundant stepwise passages that spin around and between the resting tone and fifth and include characteristic tones. The melodic contour, the presence of characteristic tones, and the alignment of rhythm and tonal anchors all reinforce tonality in the young musical mind.

Stepwise passages are easier for young children than skips. The young musical mind readily handles skips between the resting tone and fifth, with or without the third, and comfortably grows into skips within the harmonic functions that uniquely define each tonality. (See Appendix D for harmonic functions.) Musical lines that move down to the resting tone are generally easier for little children than those that move up to the resting tone, and melodies that begin and end on the resting tone are most accessible to the young musical mind. Melodies that start or end on the third or fifth require that the musical mind be mindful of the resting tone without its immediate or ending presence in sound, so they are more appropriate for more developed children.

The challenges of rhythm and tonal in melody, both individually and together, impact the musical mind. Adding words increases the challenge. The intertwining of rhythm, tonal, and text in song further impacts the development of children's artistry.

Song

Adding a layer of words on top of melody creates greater challenge for the musical mind, as its tower of blocks with macro beats, micro beats, melodic rhythm, and tonal have to be sturdy in order to secure the additional block of words. The difficulty of rhythm, melody, and text and how they work together all contribute to rhythm and tonal difficulty in the musical mind. The way rhythm, tonal and text come together can support the musical mind or increase the difficulty of rhythm, tonal, or text, individually or in combination. Songs that most support the musical mind are those in which the natural pronunciation of the words aligns with both rhythm and tonal anchors.

Lie A-Bed

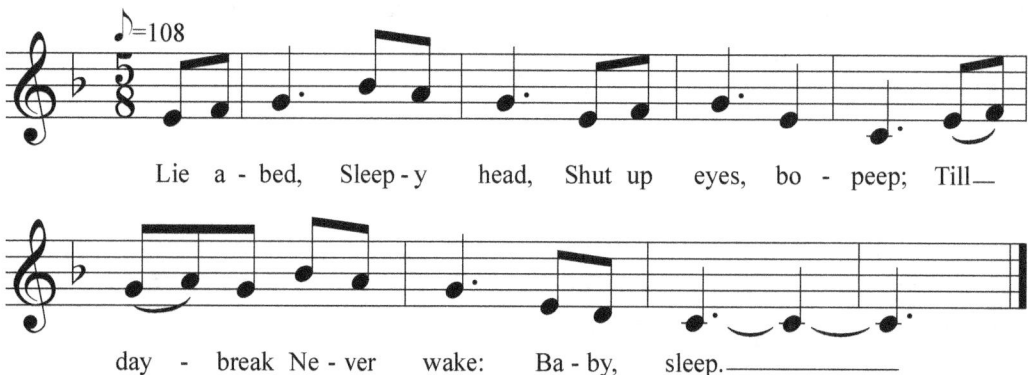

Figure 3.30   Mixolydian, Unusual Paired (rhythm anchors, tonal anchors, and text aligned)

Lie A-Bed (Figure 3.30) presents a lovely little text of Christina Rossetti set in Mixolydian tonality and Unusual Paired meter. Rhythm and tonal anchors align with each other and with the pronunciation of text, supporting the musical mind and the natural expression of text in the unusual meter.

Figure 3.31   Mixolydian, Duple (rhythm anchors, tonal anchors and text not aligned)

Figure 3.31 presents the same text with the same pitches and same durations in the easier Duple meter to demonstrate a lack of alignment between rhythm, tonal, and text. This example in the easier Duple meter is more difficult than the setting of the text in Figure 3.30 with the more challenging Unusual Paired meter, because of the lack of alignment between rhythm anchors, tonal anchors, and the natural pronunciation of the words. The setting in Figure 3.30 offers a lovely little song for young children, while that of Figure 3.31 is not worthy of children's artistry.

Understanding the way the musical mind processes rhythm and tonal, individually and together, and how they intertwine with each other and with words guides us in choosing appropriate musical narratives and songs for children at every level. Meter, rhythm, tonality, melodic contour, the way rhythm and melody work together, the way they present themselves in song, and the way they work with text affect rhythm and tonal difficulty in the musical mind. We can maximize our teaching by choosing musical material with "song architecture" that supports the musical mind, whatever the age or level of development of our children.

The Modest Violet

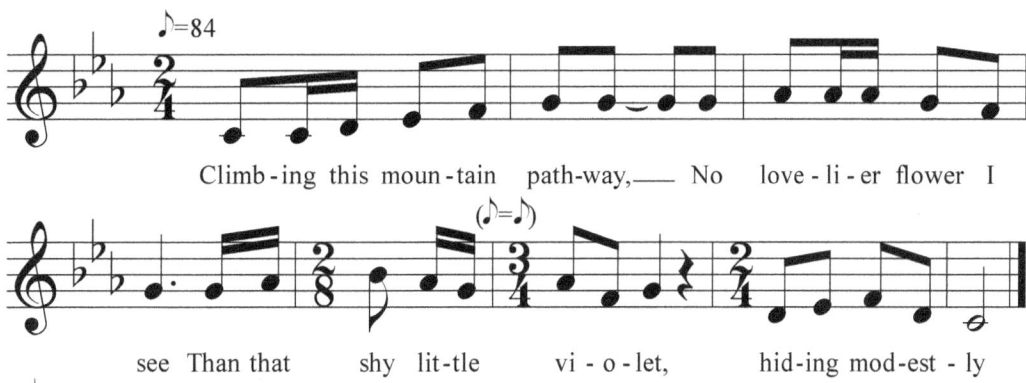

Figure 3.32   Aeolian, Duple/Triple meter

The Modest Violet (Figure 3.32) compels the musical mind with its setting in Aeolian tonality and shifting meter. Its song architecture both supports and challenges the young musical mind with the musical readiness for this song. Most of the melodic rhythm patterns are relatively easy, but the tie, elongation, and rest add difficulty, as do the shifting meters. Rhythm anchors and tonal anchors align and together they align with the pronunciation of the words, supporting each other in the musical mind. The meter is established very early in the song. The tonality is not fully established until the fifth measure when the lowered seventh confirms that the song is in Aeolian rather than Minor tonality. Aeolian's characteristic seventh, however, expands the melodic line upward and then comes down, rather than going directly to the resting tone, as children often hear in tonal segments, increasing the tonal challenge of the song. The melodic contour is primarily stepwise, spinning around and between the resting tone and fifth. The vocal range supports the young musical mind, while the song text, a translation of Japanese haiku, presents a bit of sophistication.

Notice how the song architecture of this little art song delivers not only the rhythm of the text, but also its expression. The melodic line and the energy of the line build to the peak of the song, framing that shy little violet musically, with the 2/8 and 3/4 measures inviting rubato as if to pause to cherish the beauty of the flower, with the quarter note rest supporting that pause before the line resolves. The song architecture of *The Modest Violet* supports the musical mind, and it prompts artistic expression.

We have explored in this chapter how the musical mind processes rhythm and tonal individually and together, and how the intertwining of rhythm, tonal, and text in song impacts the musical mind. Awareness of how the musical mind works guides us in choosing and improvising both rhythm and tonal content for our youngsters throughout early childhood. It guides us in choosing appropriate rhythm and tonal narratives, musical material for Rhythm Dialogue Activity, Resting Tone Activity, Macro/Micro Beat Activity, and Tonal Dialogue Activity. It guides us in choosing songs for every age and level of development.

The young musical mind is most ripe in early childhood. The more we learn to reach and teach the young musical mind, the more it teaches us about its musical needs. We grow with the children into a greater meeting of the minds—our musical mind and theirs.

Artistry in Teaching

Little children never cease to amaze and amuse the early childhood music teacher. They make us rethink everything we thought we knew about music learning in early childhood, challenge us to grow beyond where we've been, and prompt us to uncover gifts we never knew we had. They make us smile at their very being and inspire us to dust off our own playfulness. Little children facilitate the development of our artistry in teaching while we facilitate the development of little children's artistry.

Recognizing Progress

Little children grow musically in a fluid manner from birth throughout the early years. A child's demonstration of rhythm and tonal knowing progresses through a continuum rather than absolute stages. The measuring stick of music learning in young children is more related to what we put into the young musical mind than it is to the precision of what comes out.[7]

Little children learning to speak, whether in language or music, are in the process of making meaning. They understand far more than they are yet able to articulate. Their imprecise delivery, though it may sound like babble, is an attempt to communicate musically. Each child's musical articulation of their progress rhythmically and tonally is in process.

Little children focus on meaning rather than "pronunciation." They are generally unaware of the precision of their response in relation to the model as they grow. The two-year-old who communicates well, but whose speech is understood only by his parents, knows what he is trying to say, sing, or chant, whether we do or not.

The precision of a little child's rhythm or tonal response is generally inconsistent. A child's musical response at any given time can be as much a function of personality, mood, or whim as it is musical prowess. We might one day hear a precise resting tone from a child and another day not, or hear an imprecise resting tone in Resting Tone Activity and in-tune tonal segments in Tonal Dialogue, which is more difficult. A little child might engage in Rhythm Dialogue in Duple meter, competently delivering patterns that include divisions, yet two weeks later offer only the most basic patterns in the meter. He might also on either day deliver precise macro and micro beats in the same meter in Macro/Micro Beat Activity—or not.

Playing music through a variety of activities in the various meters and tonalities, with and without props, unveils signs of the musical mind's progress, giving us the broader picture of each child's rhythm and tonal development. Fleeting moments of rhythmicity and tunefulness over time exposes each child's development both rhythmically and tonally. The accumulation of moments of precision sheds light on the child's progress, as the occasional appearance of greater skill always demonstrates growth.

Witnessing and nurturing the rhythm and tonal response of each little child over time illuminates the path of young children's music development, even when solo responses are not articulate and not consistent. We just learn to better understand children's musical communication.

A three-year-old, for example, might in Rhythm Dialogue in Duple meter offer the same rhythm pattern to every pattern we offer, demonstrating security with the meter, as defined by that single pattern. The musical mind is communicating that it is solidly in Duple meter, whatever the difficulty of the patterns we present. Another child might in Rhythm Dialogue in Triple meter offer a pattern in Duple meter, communicating that he is not yet grounded in Triple meter, while demonstrating some security in Duple meter. Rhythm skill develops in little children in accordance with rhythm difficulty, so we will see progress in Duple meter before Triple, and progress in Duple and Triple before the unusual meters. Little children will demonstrate security with macro and micro beats before divisions in any meter. Developing facility with divisions in one meter helps a child move toward facility with divisions in the next more difficult meter, if macro and micro beats are secure in the more difficult meter.

Little children's demonstration of tonal development is generally consistent across tonalities. One who articulates the resting tone in one tonality can usually deliver the resting tone in any tonality. The recommended order of tonalities draws children into reaching new horizons, so we might get the first articulation of resting tone in Dorian tonality rather than Lydian.

Little children often deliver the descending pattern 5-4-3-2-1 in Tonal Dialogue fully in the tonality, yet without discreet pitches between the fifth and resting tone, demonstrating understanding of the tonality even with inarticulate delivery. Those children generally do much the same in any tonality, showing quite a sense of tonality, despite the imprecise articulation.

Little children engaged in Rhythm or Tonal Dialogue Activity may sometimes echo the rhythm pattern or tonal segment that we offer, but more often they deliver their own—usually rhythm patterns or tonal segments that they have heard in class. Dialogue in language involves responding to each other's meaning rather than repeating what was said. The child's speech regularly echoes words or phrases that he has heard his parents use, but in a context in which he creates his own meaning with the familiar words or phrases. The young musical mind engaging in one-on-one musical interaction responds to the teacher's musical meaning. Visual cues for a response of same or different speak to the thinking mind. Children's offerings that are different from ours, but within the established meter or tonality, demonstrate greater security in the meter or tonality than an echo response. Little children are the ultimate improvisers. They know how to take an idea and respond to it in like fashion, creating their own meaning.

Every solo response offered by a child is a gift, however meager it might be. Each deserves our sincere musical response and non-verbal encouragement. Each has something to teach us about early childhood music development by its precision or lack of precision. We learn by comparing a child's solo response to his response in a similar group activity.

We learn by comparing a child's rhythm development to his tonal development. We learn by comparing a child's response from one activity to another, from one day to the next, and from one age to another.

The effectiveness of a particular prop or activity we design can influence children's response, but we can usually determine its impact by the response of the entire class. The child who seems to lag behind the class in precise rhythm or tonal delivery is not necessarily any less gifted than those who seem to be more precocious. A two-year-old that is fully tuneful and rhythmic may, indeed, be musically endowed, but a long-term five-year-old student who is not yet fully tuneful and rhythmic is not necessarily delayed in development. A seven-year-old that is slower to develop than the rest of the class may demonstrate unshakable precision both rhythmically and tonally as an eight-year-old.

> Little children march to the beat of their own drummers developmentally. Some walk at nine months, others not until eighteen months. Some start talking before one year, others not until closer to two. Some become potty-trained in their first year and a half, others not until three or four years old. We cannot claim giftedness or developmental delay, but rather, marvel at the process of normal growth and development and the uniqueness of the beat of each child's own drummer.[8]

Every group of youngsters will demonstrate varying levels of rhythm and tonal development, even if the children are the same age and have had the same instruction, and each child's rhythm and tonal development will demonstrate different levels of articulation of rhythm and tonal knowing. We accommodate all by designing our classes to serve immersion as well as interactivity, using children's responses to guide us in gradually increasing the difficulty level of musical material, whatever the precision of rhythm and tonal articulation within the group. Each child's rhythm and tonal precision will indeed bloom as we scaffold each solo response, provide many opportunities for practicing music, and offer music content that supports and challenges their level of rhythm and tonal output.

Parents and children around a dinner table with one child in a high chair, one on a booster seat, and one on the kitchen chair engage in dinner conversation, with parents accommodating each child's development as needed, perhaps simplifying for the youngest or cleverly challenging the oldest. We in our classes, like those parents, can engage in musical discourse that reaches all, accommodating each child as needed, simplifying for some and cleverly challenging others.

There is always more difficult music content to challenge the more developed children, which serves as immersion for those whose output doesn't keep pace. The long-term class continues to move forward, guiding our choices of appropriate activities and musical difficulty for the class. Every child absorbs what he needs from the rich music content and uses it as he grows, whatever his output at any given time. We cannot hasten the process. We can only improve our teaching to more efficiently and effectively give voice to children's artistry.

Getting in Sync

Parents regularly scaffold little children in speech and in physical activity. They help a child say what he is trying to say and they help him do what he is trying to do. A tot on a small ladder may need just a bit of support to lift that little body to the next rung. We have served to scaffold children's musical response as they learn to speak the language of the musical mind, and we have stimulated the musical mind/body connection through singing, movement, and playing music. We now turn our attention to the physical part of that musical mind/body connection, and how we might help our little musicians physically to do what they are trying to do when the musical mind is ready and willing but the little body is not.

Giving a child a hand can help the child bring the well-bred musical mind and body together, as hand-to-hand contact offers a kind of physical scaffolding. A teacher's hand has even helped the occasional music teacher finally pull the musical mind and body in sync in an unusual meter when they were traversing the room in the meter hand-in-hand. Scaffolding children physically can serve to not only support them in bringing the musical mind and body into alignment, but also to support children through the quantum leap of aligning as a musical ensemble.

Lending a hand to long-term students who have engaged extensively in meters, tonalities, rhythm patterns, and tonal segments can help each child experience momentarily what it feels like when their own body is in sync with their musical mind. A hand-to-hand link with a child can help to align the child's musical mind and body, as if our own musical mind/body connection communicates to the child's through our hands.

Long-term students from the age of two are comfortable interacting with us one-on-one in Rhythm Dialogue Activity, Resting Tone Activity, Macro/Micro Beat Activity, and Tonal Dialogue Activity. We can take children further in each of these activities by occasionally offering hands-on support, as our little budding musicians attempt to align the musical mind and body.

We engage children in Rhythm Dialogue Activity, jumping on the initial macro beat of each rhythm pattern, perhaps over a rope secured to the floor, or into hoops laid out on the floor, with or without accompanying adults. We lead the group with our jump and patterns on "bah." The group follows, echoing our rhythm patterns as they jump over the rope or hoop and we echo the patterns with them. Taking a child's hand and jumping into rhythm patterns with the child communicates physically to the child's musical mind/body connection. Our jump into each rhythm pattern naturally models the activation of weight and breath with the jump. Our model serves a bit like a conductor's breath cue and downbeat and invites accompanying adults to take their own child's hand and jump into rhythm patterns in Rhythm Dialogue. An adult's hand communicates meaningfully to a child whether it is musicality, physical activity, or safety crossing a street.

We can similarly lend a hand in Resting Tone Activity. We might, for example, establish a tonality and engage with tonal segments on "too," each followed by a breath and a jump into the resting tone. We hold the hand of an individual child and jump with the child on the breath into the resting tone. Each child may or may not sing the resting tone, but holding the child's hand throughout with our jumping and singing the resting tone communicates physically to the child's musical mind/body connection. We can apply this to any tonality and our model invites accompanying adults to do the same with their little ones.

We can also give a hand to individual children as they leap from a small perch or mini-trampoline into a large bean bag chair on the resting tone, guiding their jump with our hand rather than our jumping. Our own physicality, energy, breath, and singing of the resting tone in relation to each of the tonal segments help the little body to experience greater musical mind and body alignment, even if momentarily. Our assistance serves like the boost to the next rung on the tot ladder. The deliberate breath summons the musical mind while the jump summons the body to be in sync with the musical mind, with the weight of the body aligning with the implied weight of the anticipated resting tone. The guidance of our physicality and musicality that transmits hand-to-hand assures a safe and musical landing.

Physically scaffolding the young child's musical mind/body connection can become even more pronounced with Macro/Micro Beat Activities. We start a rhythm narrative on "bah" and take an individual child's hands while facing the child, extending one arm forward and the other back with bent elbow, switching arm positions on micro beats through four bars of tonguing micro beats, followed by switching arm positions on macro beats through four bars of tonguing macro beats. We alternate four bars of micro beats with four bars of macro beats, both in tonguing and movement, in whatever meter we have chosen. We might follow up with the original rhythm narrative while continuing movement. This physical interchange with macro and micro beats delights all while giving each child a greater "sense" or "feel" for bodily movement that is in sync with the meter—his own body in sync with his own musical mind. The hands-on support can also be done by accompanying adults with their own children or with older children in pairs.

Scaffolding the musical mind/body connection in Tonal Dialogue Activity can support sustained singing. We establish a tonality and engage with tonal segments while facing and holding both hands of a child, with our feet on the floor and the child on a mini-trampoline. We sing a tonal segment and then lead the child with our hands and arms into a breath and jump on the trampoline, echoing our tonal segment on "too" while jumping on each pitch. We sing the echo as needed. We can do the same activity with the child standing on the floor and our jumping and singing with them hand-in-hand, or just singing with them and guiding their jumps with our arms. The lifting bounce of the mini-trampoline, however, does more dramatically simulate or stimulate sustained breath while singing.

The lift of our arms with the breath into the jump on the first pitch of each tonal segment communicates hand-in-hand a supportive breath which serves both the musical mind and the body. Our hand-in-hand connection throughout tonal segments with continued jumping on each pitch facilitates sustained breath with sustained singing. We can employ the mini-trampoline in any tonality with a series of tonal segments for each child. We can do the same with a short tonal narrative, scaffolding a child's sustained breath and sustained singing through the narrative. We might add to each turn a jump off of the trampoline into the resting tone. Children are always quick to get in line for another turn to leap into new growth.

Our hands, arms, and energy, as well as the child's act of jumping, are communicating non-verbally to the child the kind of energy needed to power the voice. You may be surprised when you hear a child sing tunefully for the first time while jumping. The physicality of jumping is a powerful activator of the musculature needed to propel the voice. The support of our hands holding the hands of each child while jumping and singing communicates physically to young children much of what children's choral conductors try to communicate verbally to older singers.

Hands-on scaffolding can be used with multiple ages and can be used for different purposes. Long-term students who are still not old enough for kindergarten are generally ready to engage in aligning as an ensemble, whether or not their little bodies and musical minds have yet to align rhythmically or tonally. The rich musical input over time and their extensive experience in practicing music provide the readiness for the new challenge that will not only scaffold the individual musical mind/body connection, but also bring the children together as an ensemble. We move toward nurturing an ensemble by stepping back from one-on-one physicality and stepping into more of a conductor's role, scaffolding the group rather than the individual.

We may have previously used pom-poms for a number of activities, perhaps both rhythm and tonal, but engaging longer-term children in Macro/Micro Beat Activity with pom-poms can propel ensemble growth. We start a rhythm narrative and hand out a pair of pom-poms to each child. We lead the group with a pom-pom in each of our hands, moving one arm up and the other one down on macro beats, switching arm positions with each macro beat, with pom-poms swishing with each change of motion. We move to a verse of micro beats, flicking the wrists of both hands together, and then move back on the next verse to the large sweep with macro beats. The children experience not only the difference in weight between the feel of macro beats and micro beats, but also the difference in spatial length and wind resistance between macro and micro beats, which becomes palpable with the swish of pom-poms. Adding tonguing amplifies the swish while bringing the musical mind and body into greater sync, as the body follows the tongue. We are providing for each child to feel the sync of their own body with macro and micro beats, along with the sync of everybody doing precisely the same thing at the same time, offering a dramatic experience of ensemble.

A number of props can serve for ensemble with Macro/Micro Beat Activity, including rhythm sticks (tapped on the floor rather than together) and hand drums. We start a rhythm narrative vocally with all sitting, put a hand drum on the floor in front of us, demonstrate without verbalization, and then provide a hand drum for each of the children. (Placing the hand drums on the floor deadens the sound, promoting ensemble unity.) We lead children in playing macro beats on the drums with both hands together, lifting arms after each macro beat, animating the greater length of macro beats in time and space, contrasted by short strokes for micro beats. Alternating verses of macro beats with verses of micro beats promotes the musical mind's awareness of macro beats and micro beats simultaneously, which is necessary for the delivery of precise rhythm. We might lead part of a group of four- and five-year-olds not yet old enough for kindergarten to play macro beats while the rest of the group plays micro beats, having them switch parts on cue as we improvise rhythmically in the meter on "bah".

Note that engaging in Macro/Micro Beat Activities with pom-poms or drums does not teach the musical mind macro and micro beats. The visual model with inexperienced youngsters engages the thinking mind, bypassing the musical mind. Ensemble activities described here are for the musical mind that already knows macro and micro beats, whether three-years-old or eight. The visual cue with long-term students serves to scaffold the musical mind/body connection, helping the body to align with the musical mind's developing sense of meter. Inexperienced children need micro beats before macro beats in the tonguing sections, as micro beats establish the meter and the length of macro beats. The Macro/Micro Beat Activities presented here for more developed youngsters suggest macro beats first in the tonguing sections, scaffolding the ensemble with the dramatic difference in space between macro and micro beats.

We are at this point leading the group by chanting a rhythm narrative or improvising rhythmically on "bah," accompanied by macro and micro beats on the drums, rather than leading the ensemble with rhythmic improvisation on another percussion instrument. Our vocal chanting and the macro/micro beat movement that we lead with the drums provides the scaffolding to better align individual children's musical minds and bodies, as well as to bring them into sync as an ensemble. Children who function well in ensemble with hand drums may be ready to maintain macro beats and micro beats on their drums while we improvise on another percussion instrument.

We have not had to use the terminology of macro beats and micro beats throughout these activities, as the children know macro and micro beats in sound and movement and our modeling one or the other with pom-poms or drums makes it clear which to play in ensemble. We can use the terms informally as the ensemble follows our lead from a few bars of one to a few bars of the other, having the children switch back and forth with the verbal label, supported by our model. (Labels are addressed in Chapter 5.)

We can engage in Macro/Micro Beat Activity in ensemble with pom-poms or drums in any meter. Four- and five-year-olds not old enough for kindergarten can generally handle this ensemble experience competently in both Duple and Triple meters. Ensemble activity in the unusual meters helps to secure greater competence in Duple and Triple meters, while challenging the ensemble.

Pairs of ten-foot PVC pipes can provide a very exciting full-body experience in ensemble with children four years and older. A pair of parallel pipes on the floor several feet apart makes an inviting "boat" for a number of little bodies to get into. Children sit on the floor between the pipes, facing forward, with one child in front of another and little legs stretched out alongside the person in front. We control the pipes from the front of the boat as we face the team of rowers with all little hands on the pipes. We start a rhythm narrative on "bah," lift the pipes off the floor, and the children follow as we power the boat with one arm forward and the other back, alternating arms on macro beats as we tongue four- or eight-macro beat phrases. We then move to tonguing and ensemble movement on micro beats with the same length phrase, with children working in sync with our support. We continue the rhythm narrative on "bah," alternating verses of macro beats and micro beats in movement, and then go into another round of tonguing and movement. We can also raise and lower our arms on successive macro beats, raising the pipes up and down in unison, contrasted by lowered arms pumping back and forth on micro beats, alternating in successive verses. The "boat" gives all of the children the experience of their own little musical mind/body connection being in sync with the meter and with the ensemble, as unlike the previous activities, the group is physically connected as an ensemble. They are "playing music" in ensemble. Four- and-five-year-old children that have the readiness find particular joy in this activity with unusual meters.

We can use recorders to create a most surprising and musically satisfying tonal ensemble before the children are old enough for vocal ensemble. We all know how variable the open pitch on a recorder can be, demonstrated by a child who picks up a recorder and blows it like a whistle. It is stunning to see a group of four- and five-year-olds not yet old enough for kindergarten playing the open pitch on a recorder in ensemble, perfectly in tune.

We establish a tonality vocally, using the open pitch on our recorder as the resting tone, and engage children in group Resting Tone Activity on "too." We switch to playing a tonal narrative and tonal segments in the same key on the recorder, stopping regularly to sing the resting tone with the children. We continue the tonal segments on the recorder, gesturing to the children to sing the intermittent resting tone while we play the resting tone on our recorder. We sustain the tonality vocally while handing out a recorder to each child and helping each one hold the recorder with two hands at the bottom, so as not to cover any holes. We keep the tonal narrative going vocally so the tonality dominates the experience rather than the physical challenge, while we non-verbally assist each child in playing the resting tone on his recorder. Adding one recorder at a time to the ensemble, while maintaining the tonality, keeps the experience highly musical. We might deliver melodic segments on our recorder with all of the children playing the resting tone after each, or have the children play the resting tone on macro beats or micro beats while we play a tonal narrative in the same tonality.

This ensemble experience evolves into our improvising in any tonality on the recorder, always with the open pitch as the resting tone, while the whole group of youngsters plays the resting tone with us throughout, perfectly in tune. We can add a rhythmic challenge with children who have the musical readiness by having part of the group play macro beats while the other part of the group plays micro beats, all on the resting tone, switching on cue while we improvise in the tonality over the accompaniment. Four- and five-year-old children who are at this level can generally handle any tonality in either Duple or Triple meter, tonguing macro or micro beats on the instrument.

The sensitivity of the young musical mind to tonality and intonation with the recorder in ensemble is breathtaking. Improvising on our recorders over such fine accompaniment is satisfying as a musician as well as teacher. An entire group of children still not old enough for kindergarten can engage in ensemble perfectly in tune and in rhythm on recorders. Even an eighteen-month-old sibling who attended his own weekly music class as well as tagging along to his sister's class has been known to grab the recorder out of his sister's hand and play the open pitch perfectly in tune without overblowing. The young musical mind is a powerful force, amplified by the musical mind/body connection. It is up to us to find ways to scaffold it so that it can fully express itself.

Priming Parents

Classes with infants, babies, and toddlers necessarily include parents or caretakers. We might effectively charm children and entice participation, but we also have to draw in parents and caretakers, nurture their role with the children, and entice their participation. Practices and procedures recommended in this book are as effective with accompanying adults as they are with little children.

Sculpting energy effectively assures that adults as well as children go along with the flow, minimizing opportunity for adult chatter or child coaching. Immersion activities saturate parents with meters and tonalities just as they do children, so parents grow along with their little ones, developing the musical readiness for parenting more advanced activities. Play songs engage parent and child in songs that can spontaneously be sung or made up at home, while art songs take parents as well as children to a higher level of musicality. Rhythm Dialogue Activity teaches parents a way to "play music" with their little one at home, and how to respond when their child initiates rhythm activity. Our transforming common toys and household objects into musical instruments charms parents as well as little children and guides them in playing music with their little ones at home.

The experience of our highly musical classes and children's willing engagement teach parents more than we could ever explain about music learning. Parents may or may not be enthralled by the rhythm and tonal material we present, but they are enthralled by their little one's absolute focus on that material and their child's initiation of "bah bah" at home. They are enamored by their babe-in-arms' enthusiastic response upon entering our classroom in successive weeks, and their obstinate two-year-old's willing cooperation. Parents witness that our classes compel a whole group of antsy little ones week after week and offer quality time between parent and child. Our classes become an oasis of joy for parent and child as well as a highly musical experience.

Parents naturally sing, dance, and play with their little one when nobody is watching. We can elicit the same by focusing on the children and effectively sculpting energy, so that children and parents board our train together as playmates when the class begins and don't step off until the journey has ended. Over-instructing parents can intimidate them, make them self-conscious, and diminish their spontaneity with their child. The more we sculpt energy to seamlessly carry children and parents from start to finish, the less we need to instruct attending adults. Parents in a beginning class need only an invitation to be themselves with their child, and the awareness that extraneous noise is disruptive.

"Just sing along, move along, play along, or go along with your child and with the music. If you have a noisy or crying child at any point, please walk out of the room with them until they are ready to come back in. (And thank you for turning off your cellphone!)"[9]

We might in successive weeks casually offer a similarly brief bit of information before we begin class.

"You might pay particular attention today to the occasional "deer-in-the-headlights" stare you might see in your child. That intense focus tells us that we are reaching your child's musical mind. We often think that a child has to be happily bouncing or dancing to be musical, but that focused stare is a highly musical response."[10]

Many parents of very young children are inexperienced and vulnerable. They need our support and appreciation. Parents make quite an investment in our classes, often paying tuition, driving a distance, juggling a toddler and infant with a stroller and diaper bag in inclement weather, and continuing through multiple years. They deserve our utmost respect.

We may be the only adult in the day that reinforces a parent's sense of their child. We become a colleague of the parent, celebrating the wonder of their child, as we uncover the child's artistry, how naturally musical the child is, and the potential the child has for music learning. We are one of the few who believe in the child as much as the parents do, as we know the power of the young child's musical mind and the capacity for musicality. We offer parents a glimpse of a dimension of their child that they are not equipped to release themselves, and rejoice with them in each new step the child takes in the direction of musical independence.[11]

Parents, as well as their children, grow each week through our well-designed classes. They sense the greater beauty and difficulty of art songs and the delight and challenge of gem songs. They know their children are learning and that they are learning something the parents don't know how to teach and that the local recreational music class does not teach. Parents are often amazed when their little one willingly engages one-on-one with the teacher with such earnest musical response.

Parents in more advanced classes become more the emotional support than musical, as they witness the children's growing musical independence. Parents sit back and watch the delightful playfulness that enthralls their little one as the children enthusiastically engage in Rhythm Dialogue Activity, Resting Tone Activity, Macro/Micro Beat Activity, and Tonal Dialogue Activity, practicing music with great joy and musicality.

More developed classes that move into rhythm and tonal syllables, music reading, and music writing speak volumes to parents, as they witness their little ones who are not yet old enough for kindergarten doing things the parents never learned to do. Parents who are not musicians, who have attended classes with their child through multiple years, find themselves reading music to their children at home.

Parents of young children are fully engaged in their child's language development and witness first-hand the similarity between their child learning language and learning music. They know the time and amount of repetition it takes for their little one to develop, and often relate to the process of their child's music development more easily than our colleagues. Our job is to model and provide the context for parent and child to engage joyfully in a highly musical, seamless class that draws both children and parents, and that inspires both children and parents to be their beautiful, natural selves with each other.

4
Propelling Progress

Little children are full of life, full of energy, and full of love. They are highly sensitive, naturally playful, and very expressive. Those same qualities are embodied in our chosen art. We have to preserve those qualities in children and in music. We have to channel the vibrance of children into the vibrance of music, while teaching to the musical mind, so that music can come alive, children can come alive, and children's artistry can come alive.

Little children so graciously lead us to discover that we cannot separate music from life, that we cannot separate music from movement, and that we cannot separate musicality from music content. We have to reclaim our own energy, joy, and enthusiasm for life, and we have to reclaim our own musicality. We have to allow ourselves to become wrapped up in the nuance of music—to embody the artistry that we want to elicit.

We are musicians. We have experienced the beauty of line, the compelling energy of rhythm, and the drama of their union. Little children with a background in the various meters and tonalities, flowing movement, and macro/micro beat movement are ready to explore musical nuance in the energy of the line through movement.

> The energy of the line is the impassioned life-force of musical nuance. It is the musical energy created by the coming together of every musical detail. It is the musical drama of the song that results from the intertwining of rhythm, melody, and text. It is the musical impact of a rest, an upbeat pattern, a consonant, ascending or descending pitches, repeated pitches or rhythms. It is the intensity, the capriciousness, the building, the resolution, the twisting and turning of line created by the unique musical detail of each song.[1]

Communicating the energy of the line through movement provides a tangible way for little children to experience and embody musical nuance, to "feel" the unique musical expression of each piece of music. Our engagement in the energy of the line in movement, like our engagement in flowing movement and macro/micro beat movement, activates the young musical mind and body, whether or not the children are yet ready or able to engage in the energy of the line in movement themselves. Little children of all ages are mesmerized by such musicality.

The youngest might display a "deer-in-the-headlights" stare or imitate a particular gesture, while three- and four-year-olds engage in full body movement, capturing musical nuance in their own way. Children five and older with a background in the various meters, tonalities, and rhythm and tonal segments, as well as flowing movement and macro/micro beat movement, have the readiness to fully engage in movement with musical nuance.

Exploring the musical energy of a song in movement by ourselves in front of a mirror or video platform is always helpful, as our movement with the energy of the line becomes the sign language for the young musical mind/body connection to explore the expressive import of a song in movement. Our own movement with the energy of the line can embody flowing movement and macro/micro beat movement, while also embodying articulation, style, and expression.

Figure 4.1 Mixolydian, Duple

Wake Up, Jacob (Figure 4.1) presents a setting of an American rhyme in Mixolydian tonality and Duple meter. This little gem song offers a delightful and highly musical experience in movement and song. The energy of the line expressed in movement draws children right into the art of song.

Sing the song through repeatedly, starting with flowing movement using hips, knees, shoulders, and outstretched arms. Move into macro/micro beat movement with weight in the lower body, and then explore the energy of the line in movement through several more verses. Use arms and hands to capture the musical nuance of the line. Start hands in close proximity and draw them apart on the tied half note. Feel the resistance with growing tension and volume on the long note. The energy of the line, mirrored in our movement, then snaps like a rubber band into the rhythmic "Jacob," followed by the smooth, long notes that again build tension and anticipation of the burst on the word "break-in'." The energy of the line then changes entirely into the playful, final statement. Use hands to articulate words expressed in line. Explore the drama of the song in movement with each successive verse, as you and the children discover the powerful energy of the line inherent in this little song.

Repeating the song multiple times gives children the extended opportunity to explore and express the energy of the line in movement, discovering the power of musical nuance as they learn to sing the song. Vocal placement in the beginning singing range enables kindergarteners to become the song in movement and voice in ensemble, without the encumbrance of vocal technique. Multiple repetitions make the experience more and more exciting, as little children revel in such musicality.

Our exploration of the energy of the line in movement through many repetitions of song communicates expression, articulation, and style, all without verbalization, and invites children to embody the energy of the line in movement. It demonstrates that there is not just one way to move and invites children to explore the energy of the line with their own bodies and their own artistry. Teacher and children together become a community of artists engaged in sheer musicality.

The energy of the line in movement serves for children like a sandbox of energy in which to build line, explore its twists and turns, and bring it to repose. Multiple repetitions of a song provide for children and teacher to build again and again, each time uncovering greater musical detail and expressing greater musical nuance in movement. Each different art song or gem song that promotes children's artistry offers a new experience with the energy of the line in movement—building a line, articulating words, capturing style, and interacting with musical detail—all without verbalization, offering little children tangible experience with a broad range of musical nuance.

Quaint Fancy

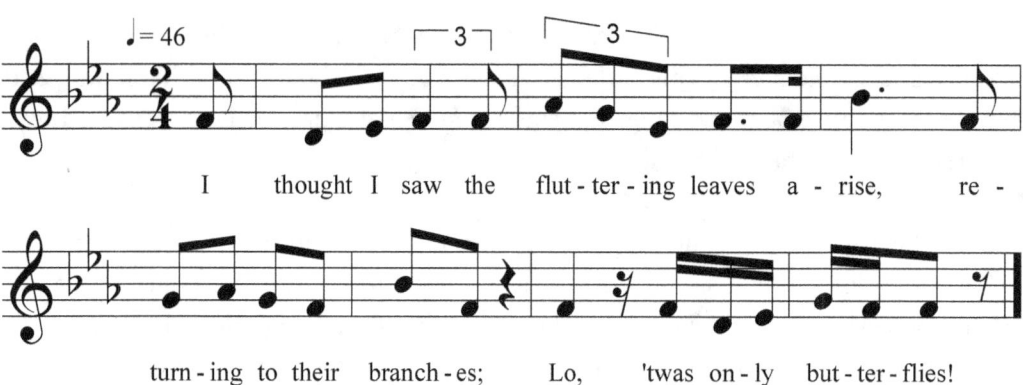

Figure 4.2   Mixolydian, Combined/Duple

Quaint Fancy (Figure 4.2) offers quite a contrast from *Wake Up, Jacob* in Figure 4.1, both in movement and musical nuance, with each musical detail contributing to a very different energy of the line. This little art song is also set in Mixolydian tonality, but with two different meters—Combined and Duple. Combined meter, like a combination of Duple and Triple, is made up of paired macro beats of equal duration, but with one macro beat divided into two and the other into three micro beats. Children well-versed in the four meters presented earlier in this book are ready for rhythm narratives, rhythm patterns, and then songs in Combined meter.[2]

Explore the song in movement using flowing movement in the upper body and weighted movement with macro and micro beats in the lower body. Keep the song going and explore the melodic rhythm of the song with arms and hands amidst the flow and weight of the body through several verses. Feel the turbulence of the shifting meter in movement through multiple repetitions. Build the opening line to the trumpeted "arise," and then bring the line to repose in expression and movement. Discover ways to place the quarter note after the rest in measure five, and to use the sixteenth note rest in measure six to better deliver the final figure. Articulate the words with your hands and feel the difference in the articulation of the sixteenth notes in the final figure compared to the rest of the song.

Figure 4.3 Major, Triple

Willie Boy, Willie Boy (Figure 4.3) offers yet another different kind of musical experience in movement with the energy of the line. The setting of the simple English rhyme in Major tonality and Triple meter could easily be trite, but the shifting tempos in Triple meter raise the song to a higher level of musicality. Explore the energy of the line of this little gem song in movement.

Activate full body, flowing movement with outstretched arms as you sing the song. Shift from side to side with the weight of macro beats in the first measure while bouncing micro beats, only to move differently in the second measure. Use arms and shoulders to capture the three quarter note micro beats in the second measure before moving again into the eighth note micro beats with bouncing knees. Move similarly throughout, reflecting with your whole body these shifting tempos of Triple meter and their impact on the energy of the line. Feel how the challenging rhythm directs the movement of the body to rhythm rather than to tonal, just as it does the musical mind. Contrast your movement in this song to your movement in *Quaint Fancy* in Figure 4.2, where the energy of the line is dictated more by the expression of the text.

The energy of the line includes and is influenced by the words of the song—the sound of the words and their meaning—as expressed through the musical line. The energy of the line reflects the musical setting of the words. The melody and rhythm of songs that are worthy of children's artistry are a musical translation of the words. Moving the energy of the line that is shaped by its words is very different from moving to the words of a song. Engaging children in movement of the energy of the line is engaging children in sheer musicality.

We as students of music practiced for hours to capture musical nuance in performance. Now movement is our instrument with which to engage in musical nuance through rhythm, melody, line, expression, articulation, and style. We incorporate flowing movement, macro/micro beat movement, and conducting movement as we explore the energy of the line. We are not dancers, but rather musicians, communicating musically to our little students the wonder of the art that drew us into this field.

Flowing movement and macro/micro beat movement are foundational. We continue to engage little children regularly in flowing movement and macro/micro beat movement. We take them a step further with movement with the energy of the line, applying flowing movement and macro/micro beat movement while also engaging with the musical drama of the song.

Children from kindergarten on demonstrate the direct transfer of experience with the energy of the line in movement to ensemble singing. The voice follows the body. The building of a line in movement generates the building of the line in singing. The articulation of the line in movement becomes the articulation of the line in singing. Movement of the energy of the line in any choral group leads to greater awareness and delivery of musical nuance in rehearsal and in performance.

We have addressed flowing movement, macro/micro beat movement, and movement with the energy of the line, offering multiple avenues for engaging children musically in song. Movement through multiple repetitions of art songs and gem songs in the various tonalities and meters gives children the opportunity to step inside each song and explore its rhythm, melody, text, and their combination in creating the energy of the line. The musical mind internalizes the song in all its musical detail, expressing itself through movement.

Toward Tunefulness

Each child in movement, whether flowing movement, macro/micro beat movement, or movement with the energy of the line, moves in his own way and in accordance with his own physical and musical development. Children have to be able to sing just as freely, in accordance with their own physical and musical development. We provide the opportunity for children to practice expressing the musical mind's knowing through ongoing engagement in movement and singing, inviting the musical mind to embody its rhythm and tonal knowing. The young child most often embodies rhythm first, demonstrated initially by moving to music; then demonstrated through Rhythm Dialogue Activity; and then through some precision in macro/micro beat movement. Tonal embodiment may appear with just a sing-song voice, but precision starts showing with Resting Tone Activity and then Tonal Dialogue Activity. Tuneful singing in the context of song generally takes longer.

Tuneful singing in young children varies as much as clarity in speech. A two-year-old may be tuneful without any instruction, while a seven-year-old with extensive instruction may not yet always sing tunefully. We provide the rich aural environment for the development of the musical mind through the early years, and we provide the ongoing opportunity for movement and singing. We engage with children one-on-one in Resting Tone Activity and Tonal Dialogue, encouraging and scaffolding the musical mind's tonal expression at every level. We stimulate singing at home and prime parents to sing with their children. Tuneful singing, however, will emerge in each child's own time frame.

A child who can sing a resting tone and a few tonal segments tunefully in the various tonalities may not yet be able to string several tonal segments together in song, just as a young child who can communicate in words may not yet be able to speak in sentences. Add a song text to a string of tonal segments and the difficulty level increases, often toppling the musical mind's tower of blocks. Add group singing as yet another block on top and even the sturdiest towers can fall apart.

A child not yet in kindergarten might, for example, engage in movement in the energy of the line with the song *Wake Up, Jacob* in Figure 4.1, exploring and expressing musical detail beautifully through movement, but without yet being secure in singing the song. The body, however, is one with the energy of the line and the musical mind is fully into the tonality and meter. The same child delivers nicely in Resting Tone Activity and Tonal Dialogue Activity. The rest will follow if we continue to feed the musical mind. Everything we do to develop the musical mind develops the voice. It is the musical mind that directs the voice into tuneful singing, quality sound, and the expression of line. It just takes a while for the young child to fully align the musical mind and the voice, with each child on his own unique timeline.

We might be tempted to try to shortcut the process. Teaching young children the words to a song to sing in unison is counter-productive, as children can sing the words without singing the music. Trying to get children to take their voice higher with the likes of siren sounds puts the thinking mind rather than the musical mind in charge. Putting little children on stage adds an unnecessary block to our still unstable tower of blocks, making everything else less steady. There is an emotional readiness involved in ensemble singing that doesn't fully bloom until about five years old, regardless of music development. Allowing the voice to develop in its own time before kindergarten will pay off in the long run; because when the voice finally catches up to the musical mind of a child with a rich background in meters, tonalities, and movement, that child's delivery of a song worthy of children's artistry will be utterly musical.

We might want to rush the move into the higher singing range, but it is the musical mind that directs in-tune singing. The beginning singing range speaks directly to the musical mind and stimulates singing in response. The higher range adds the block of vocal technique on top of an unsteady tower of blocks. The transition to the higher singing range and the development of vocal technique is appropriate for children in kindergarten and older who have a background in the various meters, tonalities, and rhythm and tonal segments; and a background in flowing movement, macro/micro beat movement, and movement with the energy of the line. The development of the vocal instrument in the higher singing range and ensemble singing is addressed in Chapter 7.

We might encounter a new group of seven-year-olds or even three-year-olds who are seemingly tuneful. The musical needs of older beginners or seemingly developed younger children, however, are the same as those of beginning toddlers, whether or not they are tuneful. Beginners of all ages need immersion in the various meters and tonalities and substantial experience with one-on-one activities in order to develop the musical mind, whatever their demonstrated level of tunefulness and rhythmicity. Everything we do with older beginners is necessarily remedial. Songs and activities in the various tonalities and meters that serve the musical mind also serve the voice and develop the readiness for the higher singing range and meaningful ensemble experience with children five and older.

Beyond Play Songs

A song that serves the development of young children's artistry compels the musical mind. It holds its own without accompanying instruments, body percussion, or props. The song's melody and rhythm are the musical translation of its text, reflecting its sound, meaning, and expression. Children's artistry knows the difference between a song with a sensitively set text and one with words that are packaged in music.

Songs that serve the development of young children's artistry are most often in a tonality other than Major, as the less common tonalities most compel the musical mind. They are set in a variety of meters, with the meter of each song reflecting the rhythm of its words, shifting meters as needed to accommodate the text. The songs are set in the initial singing range, and they are short, inviting multiple repetitions for prolonged engagement in their musicality, accompanied only by movement.

A song that serves young children's artistry clearly defines and reinforces meter and tonality in the musical mind. Rhythm anchors, tonal anchors, and the pronunciation of text align in support of the musical mind. Even a trite text can morph into a highly musical song when well-set with challenging rhythm that is aligned with the natural pronunciation of words. *Willie Boy, Willie Boy* in Figure 4.3 offers such an example, as well as demonstrating that a song in Major tonality with a well-set text can be worthy of children's artistry. A song that serves young children's artistry is age-appropriate and it meets the musical needs of the children, both supporting and challenging the musical mind at every level.

Songs that fit these criteria can be used in multiple ways with different ages and stages of development. We might, for example, use a little art song like *Quaint Fancy* in Figure 4.2 with babies and toddlers, with the song arising out of a tonal narrative in Mixolydian tonality, expanding immersion in the tonality while engaging children and attending adults in flowing movement. The musical sophistication of the song and the text difficulty would not be an issue in this context, as we are using the art song to extend immersion in the tonality. The shift from the tonal narrative to the song in the same tonality with shifting meters propels the tonality with a different energy, with Mixolydian still dominating the experience. We choose a song like this for very young children for the experience of the song in sound and movement rather than for singing, knowing the words of an art song serve the sound rather than interrupting the musical mind.

We might use the same song with developed four- and five-year-old children for experience in movement with the energy of the line. We might also use this song with developed seven- and eight-year-olds for movement with the energy of the line, leading deliberate articulation of text in movement to elicit singing with such musical articulation. We might transpose the song up a third to use as a choral warm-up with musically developed children seven and older, providing an experience in choral artistry. Each different use of this song immerses children in the tonality, compels the musical mind, and engages children in the song's artistry.

Song architecture guides us further in choosing songs that meet the musical needs of each group of children. Musically developed four- and five-year-olds not yet in kindergarten may, for example, capture the energy of the line in movement in *Quaint Fancy,* but the shifting meters, challenging rhythm, and challenging text make the song more difficult to sing; as do starting and ending on the fifth rather than the resting tone, and the song moving up rather than down to the resting tone. We might use that song for movement with the energy of the line with this age and choose a different song to promote singing.

Songs worthy of children's artistry that are the easiest for young children to sing compel the musical mind. Their song architecture supports the musical mind at its level of development. They have simple rhythm that directs the musical mind to tonal, which directs the voice. They have texts that are age-appropriate. Songs that meet these criteria, but that have slightly more difficult rhythm, both support and challenge the musical mind.

Three short songs below serve children at different ages and levels of development. All are in the vocal range that serves the musical mind. The songs differ in their musical complexity and sophistication of text. Choosing age-appropriate songs that meet children's musical needs and range of expression provides for young singers of all ages to grow as artists with effortless ease.

Little Bubble

Figure 4.4 Dorian, Duple

Little Bubble (Figure 4.4) offers a simple little gem song that compels the musical mind with its setting in Dorian tonality and Duple meter. The simple meter and simplicity of rhythm directs the musical mind to attend to tonal. Rhythm anchors and tonal anchors align and together they align with the pronunciation of the simple text. Rhythm, tonal, and text support each other. The meter is established very early in the song. Dorian tonality is established with its characteristic tones, though it doesn't include the lowered seventh until the end of the song. The melodic contour spins around and between the resting tone and fifth and consists primarily of steps, further supporting the musical mind. All of these factors, together with the simple text and beginning singing range, make the song easy for three- to five-year-olds to sing. The song architecture of *Little Bubble* enables the young musical mind steeped in meters and tonalities to fully process the song and easily engage with it in singing.

Hear How the Birds

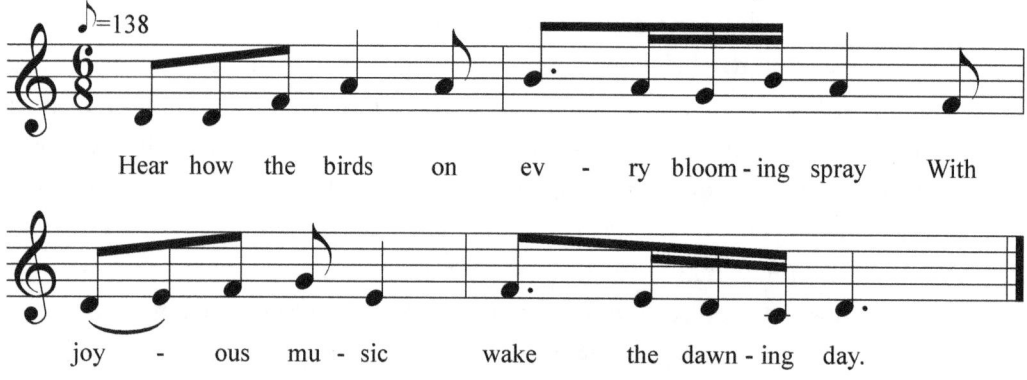

Figure 4.5 Dorian, Triple

Hear How the Birds (Figure 4.5) offers a more difficult song with a more sophisticated text by Alexander Pope that would be more fitting to elicit singing from a group of six- and seven-year-olds with a background in meters and tonalities. The little song compels the musical mind with its setting in Dorian tonality and Triple meter. The text dictates the rhythm and melody, which in turn, express the text. The melodic contour, establishment of meter and tonality, and alignment between rhythm anchors, tonal anchors, and text support the musical mind. Triple meter adds greater difficulty than *Little Bubble*, and melodic rhythm patterns are more difficult as well. The somewhat melismatic treatment of the word "joyous" adds a bit of vocal difficulty as well as an opportunity for greater artistry. This song both supports and challenges the musical mind at this level.

Engaging six- and seven-year-olds with a background in meters and tonalities in *Hear How the Birds* through movement—flowing movement, macro/micro beat movement, and movement with the energy of the line—offers an immersive experience in Dorian tonality, Triple meter, and sheer musicality, while inviting singing. Multiple, successive repetitions provide for children to step into the song and explore rhythm, melody, and text from the inside, absorbing the poetic text in the process. Their singing becomes increasingly musical through multiple verses, as does their movement, while the musical mind becomes increasingly moved by the song and children become increasingly moved by their own artistry. This song, transposed up a third, could also serve well as a choral warm-up with more developed children.

O Sailor, Come Ashore

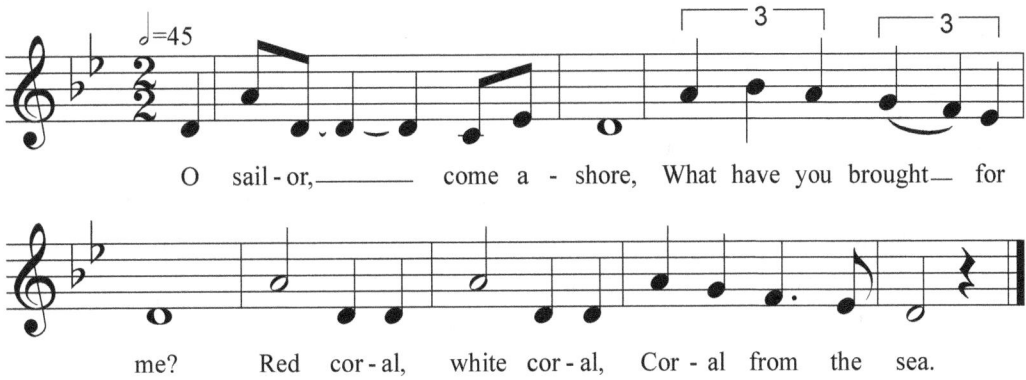

Figure 4.6   Phrygian, Duple/Triple

O Sailor, Come Ashore (Figure 4.6) offers still greater challenge, captivating the musical mind of more developed children seven and older. The sophisticated text by Christina Rossetti adds a dimension of maturity, while switching from Duple to Triple meter in Phrygian tonality offers greater rhythmic challenge, as do the ties and opening upbeat. The slow tempo adds difficulty, though children who are competent in a meter can generally handle the meter at any tempo. The song establishes Phrygian tonality immediately, but meter is less obvious, increasing the difficulty still more. Melodic contour, vocal range, and alignment of rhythm anchors, tonal anchors, and text support the musical mind. Rhythm and melody are dictated by the text, and the shifting meters and melodic twists and turns reflect and deliver the expression of text. The song both supports and challenges the musical mind at this level. This song, with movement of the energy of the line, nicely serves older children who need experience in the singing range that serves the musical mind. It also makes a lovely choral warm-up for more developed singers when transposed up a third.

Hear How the Birds (Figure 4.5) and *O Sailor, Come Ashore* (Figure 4.6) could be considered art songs or gem songs, as sometimes that distinction is in the ears of the beholder, especially when the text and the musical setting are somewhat sophisticated. Seven-year-olds with sufficient background in tonalities and meters receive both the poetry and the musical nuance of these songs as choral artists, happily engaging in movement and song and reveling in their own artistry. Those without a background in meters and tonalities receive such songs with the judgmental thinking mind rather than the musical mind, preferring upbeat songs with immediate texts. Meters and tonalities offer the gateway to children's artistry. Our understanding of the way the musical mind works, and how song architecture impacts the musical mind, guides us in choosing songs for children that meet their musical needs at every level.

The songs we choose serve as the vehicle for the expression of young children's artistry. They engage little children in the wonder of the art and in the wonder of their own artistry.

Cueing the Musical Mind

We know that it is easier for a little tot to leave a favorite activity if we prepare the child that we are going to leave in five minutes, rather than suddenly announcing that it is time to go. The musical mind also benefits when we prepare it for what is to come—in sound. Preceding an art song with a tonal narrative in the same tonality is one way to prepare the musical mind for the tonality of the art song to follow. The tonal narrative establishes the tonality prior to the song, making it easier for the musical mind to receive and process the art song in the intended tonality, rather than having to try to make sense of its tonality. The narrative in the tonality serves to prime the pump, so to speak, so that the musical mind aligns with the song to come. The tonal narrative enables the musical mind to become mindful of the tonality and "soundly" prepared to receive the art song within that tonality. Another example of preparing the musical mind for what is to come is to precede Rhythm Dialogue Activity with immersion in the same meter so the children are seated in that meter and can respond from within the meter.

We can use a shortcut to prepare the musical mind for the meter or tonality to come, a kind of code language—in sound rather than words. The shortcut for meter, or rhythm prep, unmistakably defines a meter in sound by setting up the unique relationship between macro and micro beats in the given meter. It also establishes the tempo of what is to come. The shortcut for tonal, or tonal prep, unmistakably defines a tonality by setting up the unique relationship between pitches as they relate to the resting tone and fifth. It also establishes the key of what is to come. Tonal and rhythm preps speak directly to the musical mind, cueing and eliciting the desired response of the musical mind as efficiently as a parent's question to a child, "What do you say?" elicits "thank you." The meter and tonal preps become aural billboards for the child, with each meter or tonality easily recognized by the musical mind. They become a meta-language for the musical mind until it is sufficiently developed to associate a formal label with each meter and each tonality.

Rhythm and tonal preps established by Edwin Gordon are very effective. The rhythm prep for each meter establishes the relationship between macro and micro beats within a couple of measures, followed by a couple of silent beats that give the musical mind time to reflect on and process the meter.

Figure 4.7   Rhythm Preps

Figure 4.7 presents Gordon's rhythm preps for the five meters used in this book,[3] with just one beat grouping within each meter. (See Appendix B for additional beat groupings.) Playing the rhythm prep on a drum can help to establish the meter in the teacher's musical mind before presenting the prep vocally on "bah" for the children. We present the prep, complete with silent measure, and then move directly into the meter with the children.[4]

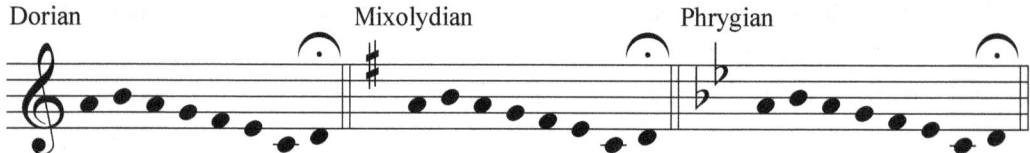

Figure 4.8   Tonal Preps

Figure 4.8 presents Gordon's tonal preps for three different tonalities,[5] all with the same resting tone. The sequence of tones, 5-6-5-4-3-2-7-1 is used with each tonality, with characteristic tones making each tonality unique in sound. The tonal prep, like the melodic contour that strengthens tonality in the musical mind, spins around and between the fifth and the resting tone, leading securely to the resting tone and including all characteristic tones. Holding the resting tone a bit longer than the other pitches gives the musical mind time to reflect on and process the tonality. The tonal prep establishes both the tonality and the key.

We can create a tonal prep for any song or tonal narrative by first locating the resting tone, which is often the final pitch of a song or tonal narrative for young children. We play the suggested sequence of tones, with the resting tone as the first degree of the scale, and use the key signature to guide us. Playing the prep on a keyboard or other instrument can help to establish the tonality in the teacher's musical mind before presenting the prep vocally on "bah" for the children. Using "bah" for the prep and "too" for the tonal narrative or song to follow keeps the prep purely functional. We present the prep, holding on to the resting tone a bit, and then move directly into the tonality with the children.

We have to think ahead to start each meter and tonality with a prep, but the benefit to the musical mind far outweighs any added effort. Each rhythm or tonal prep prepares and enables the musical mind to receive the meter, tonality, or song that follows with greater competence. Rhythm and tonal preps used with each activity and song provide a way for us to communicate directly with the developing sense of meter and sense of tonality. They provide code language in sound that not only sets up the meter, tonality, tempo, and key, but also helps the musical mind to distinguish between meters and between tonalities in sound, all without any use of words. They also help the teacher to distinguish between meters and between tonalities in sound, without the encumbrance of the thinking mind.

Rhythm and tonal preps serve rhythm and tonal activities with all ages and levels of development, as the preps speak directly to the musical mind, communicating far more than we can imagine with our thinking minds, and "formatting" the musical mind for each of the various meters and tonalities that follow. We begin each rhythm narrative, Rhythm Dialogue Activity, and Macro/Micro Beat Activity with a rhythm prep. We begin each tonal narrative, Resting Tone Activity, and Tonal Dialogue Activity with a tonal prep, directing the musical mind to tonal rather than rhythm. We can begin art songs and gem songs with both a tonal and rhythm prep, offering the tonal prep first, and then delivering the rhythm prep on the resting tone. We can additionally speak on the resting tone anything that we might want to say to the children, sustaining the tonality rather than breaking it with talking.[6]

Rhythm and tonal preps offer added benefits as children move into more difficult musical material. The young musical mind seated in the tonality and meter with a prep can better process musical narratives and songs that may not so clearly define or sustain tonality and meter. We can also use preps to cue the musical mind that we are changing the tempo, meter, key, or tonality.

We set up a meter and tempo with a rhythm prep, engage in a rhythm activity, and bring it to a close. We move on without any verbalization to the rhythm prep in the new tempo and then move directly into the new tempo. The musical mind that is familiar with the various meters and rhythm preps will sustain the meter and shift tempos. We can also use the preps to inform the more developed musical mind that we are switching meters. We bring the first meter to a close, deliver the prep of the new meter, and proceed in the new meter.

We can prepare the musical mind for a change of key within a tonality by bringing the first key to a close and then singing on the resting tone, "Now we're going to move the resting tone here," singing the new resting tone on the word "here," then delivering the tonal prep with the new resting tone and moving right into the new key. The musical mind that is familiar with the various tonalities and tonal preps will sustain the tonality in the new key. The words sung on the resting tone could even be in a foreign language, as they only signal change. The musical mind understands the rest. We can also inform the musical mind that we are switching tonalities by bringing the first tonality to a close, presenting the prep for the new one, and moving directly into the new tonality.

We can further meet the musical mind's needs by the way we order activities, hastening development by thoughtful placement of activities. The fledgling musical mind is not yet ready to process different meters successively or different tonalities successively. Separating activities in different meters with a tonal activity and separating activities in different tonalities with a rhythm activity supports the musical mind, which moves more easily from rhythm to tonal and back than it does from one meter to another or from one tonality to another. Separating meters and separating tonalities gives the young musical mind a chance to let each meter and each tonality sink in rather than confusing it with a different one. A tonal activity or song in a different meter does not confuse the young musical mind after a rhythm activity as much as another rhythm activity in a different meter.

We can effectively string several activities together in the same meter or in the same tonality, leveraging the musical mind's tendency to sustain a meter or tonality, which it does even after the music has ended. We can, for example, go from an activity for immersion in a meter to Rhythm Dialogue Activity in that meter, to Macro/Micro Beat Activity in that meter. We might offer the prep for a tonality, move into flowing movement with a tonal narrative, then to a Resting Tone Activity, concluding the series of activities in one tonality with an art song in that tonality.

We can learn to direct the young musical mind ever so smoothly by understanding its idiosyncrasies and accommodating its needs. Every class we teach gives us the opportunity to practice. We can learn to communicate so clearly with the young musical mind that we can even present various meters successively and developed four-year-olds stay right with us, as long as we precede each meter with a prep. We can switch from one tonality to another successively and again, staying with the same resting tone throughout, and developed four-year-olds know precisely what we are doing, as long as we precede each tonality with a prep. Using rhythm and tonal preps to set up each meter or tonality may feel awkward at first, but it will become as natural as using a keyboard to get a pitch for a song.

Whispers of Growth

Giving voice to children's artistry regularly prods us to move beyond our comfort zone to grow as musicians and as educators. Greater success each term accelerates children's development, making it an even greater challenge to take the same children still further in successive terms. We may regularly have to summon the power of determination when treading new ground, particularly when something doesn't initially work as we might have hoped. We, like the little tyke learning to walk, may be wobbly as we move forward, having to get back on our feet repeatedly as we continue to grow. The thrill of inspiring and witnessing the wonder of children's artistry as it continues to unfold term after successive term generates its own motivation, stunning insights, and unmatched satisfaction as teacher of early childhood music.

The more we learn to communicate with the wordless musical mind, the more intimate and the more magical the communication. We have the joy and privilege of becoming the musical mind whisperer.

Artistry in Teaching

Giving voice to children's artistry invites us to explore the depths of the young musical mind. It also invites us to explore the depths of our own creativity. Planning lessons that meet the musical needs of little children throughout early childhood stimulates our creativity, enlivening the imagination, triggering brainstorming, and igniting our teaching.

We can make every class, every week, highly musical, fully enchanting, and utterly joyous through multiple years of instruction. A thoughtful approach to planning lessons can assure that we meet children's ongoing musical needs and that we enable a seamless class with children in the palm of the hand. Developing skill in planning lessons leads to skill in teaching. Generating creative ideas in planning lessons leads to creativity in teaching. Cultivating artistry in planning lessons leads to artistry in teaching.

Putting It All Together

Thoughtful lesson planning, like a good GPS system, takes us where we need to go at every turn. We start with a basic framework to guide music content. We can streamline the process by approaching it through sets of three activities—rhythm activity, tonal activity, and song (RTS). Multiple sets of RTS can secure the ongoing presence of rhythm activities, tonal activities, and song at every level and assure a variety of meters and tonalities in every class.

Planning lessons through sets of RTS facilitates sculpting energy, as the components in each set can be arranged in any order, depending on what comes before, within, and after each set. We might, for example, arrange one set as RTS, another as TSR, and yet another as SRT. Sets of RTS make it easy to rotate meters and rotate tonalities, separate meters and separate tonalities, and provide contrasting meters and contrasting tonalities within each class.

Planning sets of RTS also promotes time management. Each RTS set can be allotted about ten minutes, though most will take less, so a twenty-minute class period could include at least two sets, while a fifty-minute class period could include at least five sets. The more RTS sets we fit into our classes, the more we can reach and teach the musical mind. Designing lesson plans by starting with sets of rhythm activity, tonal activity and song (RTS) is effective with all ages and levels of development, with or without attending adults.

Multiple sets of RTS provide the basic framework of our lesson plans. Unleashing creativity comes later in the process and later in this chapter. Figure 4.9 offers an example of how we might place meters—Duple, Triple, Unusual Paired, Unusual Unpaired—through four successive weeks with three sets of RTS in thirty-minute classes.

WEEK	1	2	3	4
Rhythm Activity	Duple	Triple	Un Pr	Un Unpr
Tonal Activity				
Song				
Rhythm Activity	Un Pr	Un Unpr	Triple	Duple
Tonal Activity				
Song				
Rhythm Activity	Triple	Duple	Duple	Un Pr
Tonal Activity				
Song				

Figure 4.9 Meters, four weeks (rotating and contrasting)

We can arrange the meters in many different ways, whether for two or five sets of RTS, as long as we rotate through the various meters and include contrasting meters in each class. The first rhythm activity in successive weeks in Figure 4.9 rotates through the four meters in the recommended order of difficulty, while the other two rhythm slots assure contrasting meters in each class and bring back a meter offered in previous weeks (after the first week). Note that there is at least one unusual meter in each class to provide the greatest contrast with the more usual Duple and Triple meters, and the fourth week includes one of the more usual meters to contrast with the unusual meters.

WEEK	1	2	3	4
Rhythm Activity				
Tonal Activity	Dorian	Mixolydian	Phrygian	Lydian
Song				
Rhythm Activity				
Tonal Activity	Mixolydian	Phrygian	Lydian	Aeolian
Song				
Rhythm Activity				
Tonal Activity	Phrygian	Lydian	Dorian	Major
Song				

Figure 4.10 Tonalities, four weeks (rotating and contrasting)

Figure 4.10 offers an example of how we might similarly rotate tonalities through the same four weeks of thirty-minute classes. We can arrange the tonalities in many different ways, whether for two or five sets of RTS, as long as we rotate through the various tonalities, alternating those with a minor third with those with a major third to provide the greatest contrast in each class. The first tonal activity in this example of successive weeks rotates through the first four tonalities in the order recommended in this book, while the other two tonal slots assure contrasting tonalities in each class and reinforce a tonality presented in previous weeks (after the first week).

WEEK	1	2	3	4
Rhythm Activity	Duple	Triple	Un Pr	Un Unpr
Tonal Activity	Dorian	Mixolydian	Phrygian	Lydian
Song				
Rhythm Activity	Un Pr	Un Unpr	Triple	Duple
Tonal Activity	Mixolydian	Phrygian	Lydian	Aeolian
Song				
Rhythm Activity	Triple	Duple	Duple	Un Unpr
Tonal Activity	Phrygian	Lydian	Dorian	Major
Song				

Figure 4.11 Meters and Tonalities (rotating and contrasting)

Figure 4.11 presents both rhythm and tonal as laid out in Figures 4.9 and 4.10. Our chosen layout can serve any level of development throughout early childhood, whether we design activities to include rhythm or tonal immersion, Rhythm Dialogue Activity, Resting Tone Activity, Macro/Micro Beat Activity, or Tonal Dialogue Activity, and whether for group or one-on-one activity. We can shift the ordering of RTS within any set to accommodate the activities we design and the sculpting of energy.

Laying out meters and tonalities for each class through successive classes assures that we keep all of the meters and tonalities alive in the musical mind throughout our tenure with the children. We can then design each class session to accommodate the experience level and maturity of each group. Each set of RTS within a single class is in relation to the first set we create, whether we teach twenty-minute classes with just two sets of RTS or fifty-minute classes with five.

Every class we teach is somewhere on the continuum from beginning to very long-term classes. Beginners need rhythm and tonal input. Long-term students, whether their second, third, fourth, or fifth year with us, need one-on-one activities that grow with the children, along with more difficult rhythm and tonal input. We can best accommodate beginning and long-term students with two different types of classes, whatever the age of the children and with or without attending adults.

- **Classes for Beginners**—Immersion in the various meters and various tonalities through rhythm and tonal narratives is prime with beginning classes. Also including group activities for Rhythm Dialogue Activity, Resting Tone Activity, Macro/Micro Beat Activity, and Tonal Dialogue Activity provides immersion in the smaller units of rhythm and tonal in the context of meter and tonality. Capturing the musical mind of beginners both rhythmically and tonally is done most efficiently through multiple repetitions of appropriate rhythm and tonal narratives with movement, without props, and with play songs for sculpting energy and overt engagement. An occasional art song might be included. Classes for beginners can serve a group of children for a term, a year, or longer, depending upon the length of each term, the time allotment for each class, and the particular combination of these with age and scheduling.

- **Classes for Long-term Students**—One-on-one interaction in the various meters and tonalities through Rhythm Dialogue Activity, Resting Tone Activity, Macro/Micro Beat Activity, and Tonal Dialogue Activity is prime with long-term students, with immersion continued. Rhythm and tonal narratives are expanded to include one-on-one interaction, building immersion into each one-on-one activity. Success with Rhythm Dialogue Activity one-on-one paves the way for success with one-on-one Resting Tone Activity; success with both serves one-on-one response with Macro/Micro Beat Activity; and success with the more difficult Tonal Dialogue Activity one-on-one is most easily achieved when children are comfortable with the other three activities one-on-one. Engaging children in one-on-one interaction is most effectively done through playing music with various props as musical instruments. Difficulty increases in immersion activities and in one-on-one activities as children develop. Art songs and gem songs are most appropriate for long-term students, with an occasional play song included, and far fewer songs are needed as rhythm and tonal activities expand. This type of class can serve second-year students, and it can serve third-, fourth-, and fifth-year students with the inclusion of new dimensions introduced in Chapters 5, 6, and 7.

Most of our rhythm content, whether for rhythm narratives, Rhythm Dialogue Activity, or Macro/Micro Beat Activity, is necessarily with macro and micro beat patterns in all four meters, moving into divisions. Including an occasional pattern with elongations, rests, ties, or upbeats can add a little spice, expand immersion, and challenge more advanced children who are secure with macro and micro beats and divisions, as can the addition of Combined meter.

Tonal content for tonal narratives, Resting Tone Activity, and Tonal Dialogue Activity is presented with the simplest of rhythm—primarily macro and micro beats in Duple or Triple meter. Appropriate tonal narratives in all tonalities support the musical mind as they spin around and between the resting tone and fifth and include all characteristic tones, with rhythm anchors aligned with tonal anchors and characteristic tones. Melodic segments for Resting Tone Activity and tonal segments for Tonal Dialogue Activity support the musical mind in the same way.

Tonal segments for Tonal Dialogue Activity in all tonalities include the basic 5-3-1, 1-7-1, 5-6-5, 5-4-3-2-1, 5-1, with the addition of 1-2-1 in Phrygian tonality and 5-4-5 in Lydian. All are presented with just macro and micro beats in Duple meter, with rhythm and tonal anchors aligned, and with each segment starting and ending on either the resting tone or fifth, All but 5-1 include at least one characteristic tone of the tonality. We can begin to expand tonal segments around the resting tone and fifth in any tonality (e.g. 7-2-1, 6-4-5) as children demonstrate the readiness for more.

Melodic segments for Resting Tone Activity include the parameters for the tonal segments of Tonal Dialogue Activity, but are longer than tonal segments to create greater melodic context for resting tone response, which is the beginning of tonal dialogue. Shifting the prompts from the slightly longer melodic segments for Resting Tone Activity (p. 34) to the shorter tonal segments for Tonal Dialogue Activity (p. 38) helps to elicit tonal segments from children in Tonal Dialogue Activity, rather than just the resting tone.

Groups demonstrating some competence in Resting Tone Activity in the various tonalities with Duple meter may be ready for the occasional Resting Tone Activity in Triple meter. Those somewhat successful with Tonal Dialogue in the various tonalities with Duple meter may be ready to encounter the occasional Tonal Dialogue Activity in Triple meter, all with the same tonal and rhythm parameters.

Our goal in early childhood music is to develop a sense of meter and a sense of tonality in the musical mind, body, and voice rather than to develop an extensive vocabulary of rhythm and tonal patterns. We scaffold, reinforce, strengthen, and monitor that developing sense of meter and developing sense of tonality in each child throughout the early years, creating activities and tailoring our one-on-one interaction with each child toward that goal. We offer the occasional rhythm pattern or tonal segment just beyond wherever the children are on their journey, while continuing to reinforce the most basic rhythm and tonal units. Children developing a strong sense of meter and tonality encounter and understand a broader vocabulary of patterns in the process, just as they encounter and understand language beyond what they are yet able to use.

Long-term classes are ready for us to stretch RTS sets to RRRTS, or TTTSRR, or other combinations, expanding the experience in any given meter or tonality. A series of activities within a meter or tonality can be highly musical, developmental, and delightful. Etude 2 takes you through the process of developing lesson plans for beginning classes and for longer-term classes, guiding you in the process. Chapters 5, 6, and 7 address more advanced dimensions for long-term classes.

We round out our lesson plans for all levels of development with songs. We might choose to use certain songs every week as signature songs, or we might use particular songs or a type of song at a predictable point in every class as an anchor in the class session. We can choose play songs, art songs, and gem songs as needed, and we can choose each song for a different reason. Play songs serve beautifully for sculpting energy in relation to rhythm and tonal activities, and for overt engagement with beginning classes and minimal props. Regular use of art songs and gem songs serve best with longer-term students, though art songs can mesmerize even a newborn babe. We might present an occasional art song following a tonal narrative with beginners after several weeks of immersion, or we might use one earlier to sustain the musical mind's focus with a rambunctious group of three-year-olds. Gem songs are musically most appropriate for more experienced youngsters. Play songs, art songs and gem songs can be chosen to fit each group of children. Art songs and gem songs, as we have seen in this chapter, increase in musical difficulty as children develop. This becomes particularly apparent as we move children in kindergarten and beyond into the higher singing range with the development of the vocal instrument and ensemble singing (Chapter 7).

We may have to build into our lesson planning a reminder to start every rhythm and tonal activity, art song, and gem song with a prep—rhythm, tonal, or both. We can make accessible a hand drum and a small, electronic piano keyboard for rhythm and tonal preps to secure our own musical mind before delivering each prep. The practice not only helps the young musical mind to grow, but also fortifies our own musical mind in flight, while our thinking mind attends to running a class.

We may be facing a group of babes in arms, a class of pre-K or second graders, or a class with both beginners and more experienced youngsters. We can create an effective lesson plan for every group using the same layout of meters and tonalities, similar rhythm and tonal content, and similar or different songs. Planning the execution of that material is how we tailor lessons to each group of students. We might, for example with Triple meter, play the meter on a drum for one group, engage another in Rhythm Dialogue Activity and another in Macro/Micro Beat Activity. We might use toddler hammers with one group and pom pons with another, or do a string of activities in the meter with yet another.

We select a week from our sets of RTS for any given class, choose specific rhythm and tonal narratives, songs, and activities, and decide how we want to implement each, arranging each set of RTS to most efficiently sculpt energy. We put everything together in an expanded RTS chart or other format, using our own teacher shorthand that only we can understand. We keep our little chart next to us while teaching so we know at a glance what's next and what we intend to do with each activity. We can keep the notation for narratives and songs on a sturdy music stand at our side so we have everything we need to guide us in action.

Learning as We Go

Beginners offer the finest training ground for the early childhood music teacher. Novices, particularly the youngest, provide for us the most direct experience with the power of meter and tonality on the musical mind, the need for sculpting energy, and the magic of a seamless class that takes children and accompanying adults from beginning to end without verbalization or dead space. Teaching beginning classes through weeks and months teaches us to communicate with the musical mind, efficiently sculpt energy, and effectively lead highly musical classes from start to finish.

There is no need to rush into one-on-one interaction and the use of props. Children need extensive immersion in the language of the musical mind before they can meaningfully use it, and we need extensive experience capturing the musical mind with naked meter and naked tonality before we can lead meaningful one-on-one interaction. Knowing that props can distract the musical mind of beginners implores us to look beyond shiny objects that attract children and fine-hone our teaching. Simple rhythm narratives with primarily macro and micro beats and easy tonal narratives with the simplest of rhythm, through ongoing repetition, have the greatest power to hold the musical mind captive.[7]

Engaging young children in rhythm and tonal narratives in the various meters and tonalities enables communication with the young musical mind and develops a foundation for more advanced activities for children and for the teacher. Leading beginning classes in group Rhythm Dialogue Activity, Resting Tone Activity, Macro/Micro Beat Activity, and Tonal Dialogue Activity then prepares us to lead one-on-one activities in long-term classes, just as it prepares the children for one-on-one response. We grow with the children through successive years, developing our readiness as well as the children's readiness to move into the dimensions introduced in Chapters 5, 6 and 7.

Artistry in teaching demands that we consider energy with every choice we make so that we can effectively sustain and manage children's energy throughout every class. Every activity we create and each song we choose generates its own energy, as does going from one to another. We use our imagination and make our best guesses about the energy flow within each activity and from one activity to the next. We then keenly observe children as we teach, reflecting on the success of each of our choices, making more informed choices for the following week's class. We might decide that we need greater movement, lesser movement, or a song of a different energy. We might decide to order our sets of RTS the same or differently, or to order a set differently at a particular point in the class. Actively engaging our imaginations in planning lessons that can flow seamlessly stimulates greater reflection on our teaching, better choices for successive classes, and greater success in sculpting energy.

Each deliberate choice, as in a chess game, is a well-planned move dependent upon the previous move and in anticipation of response. Considering the many possibilities and reflecting on how each move might affect a response is part of the process of developing artistry in teaching. We as teachers, like the determined chess player, become better and better at making our moves.

We can shape our classes to our own liking. The more skilled we become in sculpting energy, the more we can shape every class we teach into an artistic whole. There are so many options we can play with in the way we shape a class session. We might, for example, just start singing amidst the noise of participant chatter to draw the class together, or we might choose to establish order before starting. We might make our first activity a burst of energy with everybody up and moving, or we might design our first activity with everybody sitting. We might want to build our classes to a peak or to something predictable in the middle, or we might not. We might want to begin with familiar material, start with new material, or create our first rhythm and tonal activity with consideration for those who were not in attendance the previous week. We might choose a high-energy final activity before the closing, generating positive energy to go home with, or settle a class before returning them to their classroom teacher. We might shape a class differently for different levels of development or for different settings. Each week we tweak a little more to shape the class to our liking. How we choose to shape a class is not as important as the awareness that every decision we make in planning a lesson contributes to our effectiveness in the classroom.

We learn from every class we teach. Each group of youngsters brings its own joy and its own challenge, teaching us to adjust on the spot or try something different the following week. We might, for example, present a tonal narrative to a group of seated beginners that for whatever reasons get distracted or antsy rather than settling into the tonality. What do we do? We might just continue the tonal narrative, as the longer it goes on, the more the young musical mind tunes in. We might, instead, end the activity very quickly and move to the next activity or a play song without interruption or verbalization, as if the very short activity were planned that way. Then we can take the week to reflect on how we might adjust our approach the following week. We might decide to introduce tonality the next time on a recorder or other instrument and then move into singing with flowing movement in a tonal narrative. We might, instead, engage sitting children in a calm play song, followed by engaging them in flowing movement with a tonal narrative while standing. We can make every experience fresh without the baggage of a previous setback.

Every challenge we face, including limitations of the room we teach in and its safety for little children, spurs us to new growth. Thoughtfully planning lessons can head off a lot of predictable challenges, building our confidence to better handle those we encounter that we might not anticipate. A pre-K class of children, for example, may bring with them classroom behaviors that are more disruptive than children of the same age who do not know each other. We may need to sculpt energy differently with each group. We might shorten a play song to just a quick burst of energy with the more volatile group, followed by a sitting tonal activity. We might at another point engage them in flowing movement with tonal while standing and then get them seated for a play song. We might briefly try Rhythm Dialogue Activity with the group just to see how that kind of activity might affect energy, whereas the more sedate group moves comfortably through each class and into Rhythm Dialogue Activity without such special handling.

We accommodate children's musical needs, working around age and class temperament. We might, for example, engage long-term two-year-olds in one-on-one Rhythm Dialogue Activity for a couple of weeks before introducing the more intimate one-on-one Resting Tone Activity. We might, however, with pre-Ks at the same level of music development, introduce one-on-one Resting Tone Activity in the same class that we introduce Rhythm Dialogue Activity. We cannot assume, however, that a beginning pre-K class is musically ready for one-on-one Resting Tone Activity just because the children are more willing to respond individually.

We might have a class made up of both beginners and long-term students. We can meet the challenge while still effectively sculpting energy and meeting the musical needs of the children. We can provide a lot of immersion for all and engage the whole group in Rhythm Dialogue Activity, Resting Tone Activity, Macro/Micro Beat Activity, and Tonal Dialogue Activity. We can include some one-on-one activities with just a single prop that stays in our hands, inviting children to respond one-on-one. We adjust content to meet each child's level of output, knowing that the newbies will learn from the responses of the more developed children. We might include an occasional art song with mixed levels, but hold any gem songs until the beginners have had more substantial time with us. Every class we teach, whatever the level, will include children who are more advanced than others, so we are always accommodating mixed levels.

The number of children in a class can present challenges in planning lessons and in sculpting energy. Very large classes can make it difficult for one-on-one interaction with each child, yet too few children do not generate optimum energy for vibrant classes. Beginning classes with mixed ages from infants through five-year-olds, with attending adults, can work beautifully with at least twenty children. Long-term classes work best with about twelve children, allowing time to repeatedly interact with each child. A class with twelve children registered and two or three at home sick can still generate sufficient classroom energy. A class with only a handful of youngsters can diminish children's overt engagement and affect the energy of participating adults—including the teacher. We may have classes with more or fewer children than optimal, necessitating that we become even more creative in planning lessons.

We may also have classes for a shorter period of time than we'd like. Forty-five- to fifty-minute classes are optimal for classes of young children accompanied by attending adults, but schools usually schedule shorter classes. Every challenge we encounter expands our creativity in lesson planning and teaching. Etude 2 will help you to plan lessons for any situation and with each different type of activity for both beginners and long-term students. The effectiveness of our process of planning lessons determines the effectiveness of our teaching.

Brainstorming

Long-term students, even at two-years-old, have become more musically sophisticated and engage as musicians. They go along with most anything worthy of their artistry and require fewer adjustments in sculpting energy. They are ripe for an endless number of activities for immersion, Rhythm Dialogue Activity, Resting Tone Activity, Macro/Micro Beat Activity, and Tonal Dialogue Activity. Planning lessons for these youngsters is a celebration of creativity—our own and the children's.

New ideas for activities can be triggered in any setting by just observing little children. The tot in the grocery store cart using a wrapped candy bar for a cellphone, the three-year-old mowing the lawn with a toy lawnmower, or the little tyke with a flashlight dancing with the light can stimulate our own creativity. The more far-fetched the idea might seem to be, the more the unexpected prop becomes a musical instrument, without little ones' preconceived notions about how to interact with that prop. Two- and three-year-olds do not necessarily know how hula hoops or pom-poms might normally be used, so whatever we might do with them becomes the definition of the item—an instrument for practicing music. That toy lawnmower might even find its way into an activity, stimulating much the same musical behavior at home. No toy or household item is beyond consideration as an instrument for practicing music.

Creative ideas can also come from activities we have seen or used for other purposes. We might, for example, engage a group of four-year-olds or seven-year-olds in a simple rhythm or tonal folk dance. We get them in a circle holding hands, set up a meter, and start a rhythm narrative with just macro and micro beats, leading the group around the circle and shifting directions with each phrase or verse. We might lead the children into the center of the circle while chanting or tonguing micro beats, moving back out with macro beats, before repeating the original chant and circle dance. We might shift weight on macro beats for a verse or two, bounce micro beats for a verse or two, or throw in a contrasting verse with divisions, always going back to the circle dance with just macro and micro beats. We can create a folk dance spontaneously when the meter dominates the activity and we lead with movement rather than verbalization. We could similarly create a folk dance with a tonal narrative.

Generating many options for each type of activity opens an abundance of possibilities for successive lessons. We could, for example, plan to do a Rhythm Dialogue Activity every week and make it different every time. One week we might use a microphone, another week cellphones, another week puppets. We might bring in a mixing bowl and wooden spoon and take turns stirring Duple cookies in an empty bowl. We might incorporate that lawn mower, having children take turns engaging one-on-one in Rhythm Dialogue and then "mowing the lawn" while being immersed in a tailor-made rhythm narrative in the same meter. We can use the same approach with tonal for Resting Tone Activity or Tonal Dialogue Activity. Any prop can be used as long as the meter or tonality dominates the activity, and we can use a prop for either rhythm or tonal. Using a prop for both rhythm and tonal in the same class, however, diminishes its effectiveness.

Varying props also provides for a great deal of repetition of music content. We could, for example, include Macro/Micro Beat Activity in successive classes, each time with a different prop and a different meter so it's always fresh. We can also expand our repertoire of seemingly new activities by using a prop differently in different weeks. We might, for example, string a retractable rope across the floor, securing it safely, and engage children and adults in jumping into rhythm patterns for group Rhythm Dialogue Activity. We might get them straddling the rope in a different week, moving weight side to side for Macro/Micro Beat Activity, all with the meter dominating the activity. We might in other weeks use the rope for group Resting Tone Activity or Tonal Dialogue Activity, jumping into tonal response. We could also use hula hoops instead of a rope for activities like these, expanding possibilities still more.

Sitting on the floor or being up and moving increases options for each type of activity and offers more possibilities for sculpting energy. We might want to engage children in Rhythm Dialogue Activity with the preceding activity in our RTS set including full body movement with tonal, so we choose a sitting activity for Rhythm Dialogue.

We can rotate props throughout several weeks just as we rotate meters and tonalities so that every activity every week is fresh. Each type of activity, multiplied by the number of props we might use for that activity, multiplied by options for engaging with the activity sitting or standing, multiplied by five meters and seven tonalities creates an abundance of options for every lesson, and we can make every combination enchanting. We can sometimes put together a series of activities that are so effective for music learning and for energy flow that we can use the same series dressed differently through multiple successive weeks, without a hint of similarity.

We might want to play into a seasonal theme or use a prop or a type of activity as an anchor in a class, just as we might use a song. We might want to explore something in our laboratory to better understand the musical mind, or experiment with a new prop or activity we have come up with. We can build all of this into our lesson planning and create delightful classes while still maintaining the rotation and contrast of meters, the rotation and contrast of tonalities, and an appropriate balance of play songs, art songs and gem songs, whatever the level of the children.

Planning a string of two-to-five rhythm activities in a particular meter (RRTS) or tonal activities in a particular tonality (TTTSR) can create a powerful experience in the meter or tonality with long-term classes and hold the attention of the group of little children longer than we might ever have imagined possible. We might, for example, go on a "Phrygian Picnic." We start a Phrygian narrative, and with picnic basket in hand, offer scarves to each child. We all engage in fluid movement with scarves in the Phrygian narrative on our way to the picnic across the room. The scarves become picnic blankets for each child, as we pull various items out of our carefully- packed picnic basket, carrying the tonality throughout. We might find a recorder in the picnic basket and continue the tonality on the recorder in the same key. We might find a hand chime of the resting tone in our basket and give each child a turn to play the resting tone on the instrument in response to our tonal segments. We might find that Resting Tone Rabbit has come along in our basket so that each child can take a turn singing the resting tone with the puppet. Any number of items for a string of activities in our chosen tonality could be included. We speak on the resting tone to the children if there is anything we need to say, and keep the tonality flowing throughout the whole picnic without interruption or verbalization. We continue the tonality, pick up our picnic blankets, and engage with the Phrygian narrative with flowing movement all the way home—across the room to the attending adults.

Any number of "themes" could be developed into a string of activities like the picnic, as long as the theme itself, or the pretending, doesn't interrupt the meter or tonality. We could, for example, take the class across the room on a "camping trip." We take along a backpack with a variety of well-packed items that serve the camping theme, presenting each in the context of a rhythm or tonal narrative, without verbalization, and with the chosen meter or tonality dominating the experience. We might take along a parachute we have previously used for Macro/Micro Beat Activity and make it a tent.

We may not be taking the children very far away on our picnic or camping trip, but the imagination—and the musical imagination—are taking all on quite a journey. We do have to make sure that the children can see their loved ones on the journey. We might, for example, drape the parachute over some tall, sturdy music stands to create an overhead tent in which the children can see out. The parachute might also serve at Halloween, as we stand in the middle under the parachute with the children and move together as a large ghost while singing a rhythm or tonal narrative. We spread our arms, raising the height of the ghost so that little children can still see their loved ones. The activity can then simulate being scary without frightening the little ones. Our props need to only suggest the intended theme. Activities like these entice children away from their attending adults, promoting musical independence, even with the adults in the room.

We can actually enjoy the creative process of planning lessons, generating delightful classes that meet the ongoing musical needs of our students at every level, charming both children and attending adults, and exciting our teaching. We could, instead, make lesson planning the tedious process of trying to balance activity and repose, immersion and interactivity, repetition and contrast, activities with and without props, fresh and familiar experiences, meters, tonalities, easy and more difficult music content, group and solo activities, play songs, art songs, and gem songs, while trying to shape each class into an artistic whole, accommodating children of various ages and levels, creating variety yet sustaining continuity within each class and from one week to another, and moving forward in successive weeks while reinforcing earlier content. Our own wizardry can transform what could be an overwhelming task into a highly creative process that produces magic in the classroom.

Part 2

About Part 2

The first four chapters of this book provide the foundation for Part 2. Part 1 serves children from birth-to-eight years for more than two years of instruction, developing the readiness in both children and teachers for the dimensions presented in Part 2. Chapter 5 takes children two years and older into rhythm and tonal syllables, the prelude to music reading and writing. Chapter 6 takes children two and older into music reading and writing. Chapter 7 takes children in kindergarten and beyond into vocal and ensemble development in the higher singing range. The two parts of the book together provide for music instruction throughout early childhood.

5
Taking It to a Higher Level

Little children raised on the principles presented in Part 1 of this book unleash still greater capacity for music learning, pointing us forward into previously uncharted territory with such young children. These youngsters are highly developed musically, though they may not yet be fully rhythmic or tuneful. They are not yet ready for far more difficult rhythm and tonal narratives, rhythm patterns, or tonal segments, and they are not nearly old enough for kindergarten. Still, they display a depth of understanding and readiness to move forward, much like the three-year-olds who demonstrate competence with language through inarticulate speech.

We know that the richness of musical input is a greater measure of young children's readiness to move forward than the precision of little children's musical output. We know that emerging precision rhythmically and tonally is a process not to be rushed. Where, then, is forward for the young musical mind? What do we do with three- and four-year-olds who have had three or four years of our instruction? We can, of course, expand song repertoire. We can broaden the listening experience with various types of music, engaging little children in movement with recorded music of various genres or cultures, but that is not enough to tap the greater whole of the young child's capacity for music learning. The children are ready for far more. We can take the young musical mind to higher levels of music learning in its direct processing of rhythm and tonal, if we do it in a manner that is appropriate for young children.

Extensive research at the Come Children Sing Institute, informed by the work of Edwin Gordon and the process of learning language, explored with young children what Gordon considered to be higher levels of music learning with older children.[1] Classroom application of the findings of the Come Children Sing Institute can be found in *Letters on Music Learning*.[2] The material presented here applies only to children who have had many months of immersion in various meters and tonalities through rhythm and tonal narratives, and many months of one-on-one experience with Rhythm Dialogue Activity, Resting Tone Activity, Macro/Micro beat Activity, and Tonal Dialogue Activity, all as defined in Part 1 of this book. It can be applied with children as young as two-years-old with this level of experience, throughout early childhood, and beyond.

Labeling becomes an important part of language development, as it represents in language what children already know in life. It also provides for the thinking mind to reflect on what it knows without words, and to sort out and better understand what it knows. Labels articulate the thinking mind's deeper understanding.

Rhythm and tonal labels can serve the musical mind similarly, representing in language what the musical mind knows in sound. Rhythm and tonal labeling, however, must be in a language the musical mind understands, so as not to interrupt the musical mind. The meta-language for rhythm and tonal that can stimulate the musical mind to reflect on itself and propel it to more comprehensive knowing consists of rhythm and tonal syllables that are the language equivalent of rhythm and tonal processing in the musical mind.

Rhythm and tonal syllables that both reflect and reinforce the young musical mind's knowing can provide for the musical mind to become aware of, sort out, and better understand what it knows in sound. Syllables that align with the musical mind's processing of rhythm and tonal shed a direct spotlight on the musical mind's rhythm and tonal knowing as if to say, "Take a look at this. You already know this." They articulate the musical mind's deeper understanding within the context of meter and tonality, sorting into discernible categories the meters, tonalities, and beat and melodic functions that the musical mind already knows in sound. They speak directly to the developed musical mind.

Rhythm and tonal syllables that meet these criteria, when used in accordance with the principles presented in Part 1 of this book, very naturally adhere to what the children already know in sound, serving as labels for the musical mind's knowing just as "chair" and "book" label objects the children already know conceptually. Playing music with rhythm and tonal syllables is just as joyous for little children with the readiness for them as playing music without the syllables, and little children easily switch back and forth between neutral syllables and rhythm or tonal syllables. The syllables also provide the bridge to music reading and writing with little children.

Choice of Syllables

Rhythm syllables have to mirror the musical mind's processing of rhythm in order to serve music learning. They have to be the language equivalent of the musical mind's rhythm knowing in all dimensions. They have to articulate the musical mind's understanding of a variety of meters. They have to reflect the relationship between macro beats, micro beats, and melodic rhythm. They have to clearly articulate the rhythm anchors of macro and micro beats in all meters, reflect the distinction between meters, yet the sameness of beat functions across meters.

Gordon's rhythm syllables meet these criteria, as they align precisely with the way the musical mind processes rhythm, shedding greater light on the young musical mind and on the necessary features of a syllable system that serves the musical mind. Gordon's rhythm syllable system uses "du" for macro beats in every meter, with the syllable for micro beats reflecting the meter, and with a less weighted syllable articulating divisions. Figure 5.1 presents an example of macro beats, micro beats and divisions with Gordon's rhythm syllables in five different meters. A complete discussion of Gordon's rhythm syllables can be found in Gordon's *Learning Sequences in Music: A Music Learning Theory*.[3]

Figure 5.1 Gordon's Rhythm Syllables

These syllables reflect the prominence of macro and micro beats, with melodic rhythm patterns falling into place in relation to macro and micro beats. They articulate the greater weight on macro beats. They reflect the distinction between meters, with micro beats defining each meter. They articulate the similarities in beat function across meters, as macro beats, micro beats, divisions, and more difficult rhythm patterns function similarly in each meter. Rhythm syllables that mirror the musical mind's processing of rhythm directly adhere to what the children already know in sound, so that little children can naturally and effortlessly acquire rhythm syllables. Gordon's rhythm syllables reflect and reinforce the way the musical mind processes rhythm. (See Appendix E for pronunciation of rhythm syllables and more information about this rhythm syllable system.)

Tonal syllables that serve music learning have to be the language equivalent of the musical mind's processing of tonal. They have to articulate the musical mind's understanding of a variety of tonalities. They have to reflect the magnetism of the resting tone, the fifth, and the relationship of pitches to the resting tone in all tonalities. They have to clearly articulate the tonal anchors of resting tone and fifth in every tonality, reflect the distinction between tonalities, yet the sameness in melodic placement of pitches in relation to the resting tone and fifth across tonalities—the "melodic function." Traditional solfege syllables do not meet these criteria. They interrupt the musical mind rather than adhering to the sound the children know and understand. They do not become one with tonal knowing as they do not reflect and reinforce the way the young musical mind processes tonal. They are not the language equivalent of tonal knowing.

The ease with which little children acquire Gordon's rhythm syllables, in contrast to the difficulty they experience with traditional solfege syllables, highlights the inherent challenges in traditional solfege syllables. The young musical mind's processing of tonal needs a tonal syllable system that parallels Gordon's rhythm syllables, reflecting and reinforcing the musical mind's tonal knowing. Figure 5.2 presents the tonal syllable system that evolved through long-term research at the Come Children Sing Institute.[4] It is presented here in tonal preps from the same resting tone.

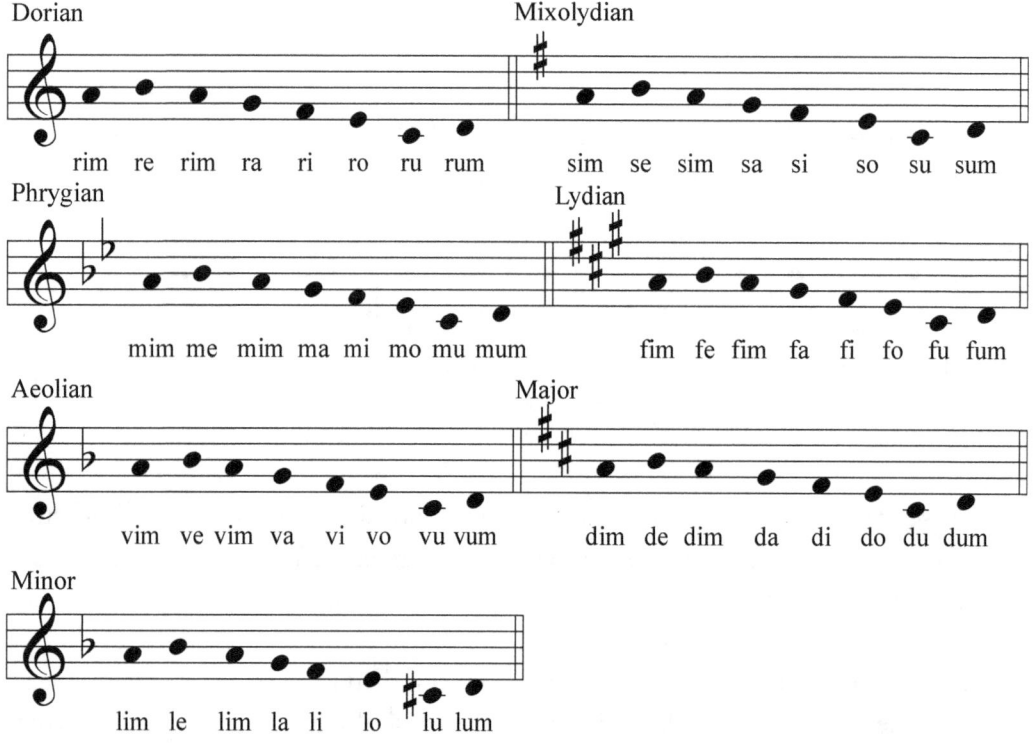

Figure 5.2 New Tonal Syllables

Notice that the consonants are unique to each tonality, while the vowels are unique to pitches across tonalities. The consonants, combined with the sound of the tonality, distinguish one tonality from another, while the vowels reflect the sameness in melodic function across tonalities. The resting tone and 5th are the same pitches across all tonalities, shaded in sound by the unique relationship of other pitches to the tonal anchors within each tonality, all leading to the resting tone. You may find that as you become familiar with these syllables in each of the various tonalities that characteristic tones that define each tonality seem to pop out, as if lighting up aurally. (See Appendix E for pronunciation of tonal syllables and more information about this tonal syllable system.)

Little children, of course, do not learn these syllables from a book, but in sound. Children demonstrate ease with the syllables, as the syllables adhere to tonal knowing. The children's comfort in acquiring these tonal syllables affirms that the musical mind distinguishes between tonalities while generalizing across tonalities. Little children confidently display their command of the melodic placement of resting tone and fifth across tonalities, their awareness of the sameness in melodic placement of the seventh in relation to the resting tone, the sixth in relation to the fifth, and the third in relation to the resting tone and fifth, whatever the tonality. Immersion in tonal syllables in the various tonalities that the children already know in sound makes the tonal syllables more accessible in each tonality, because the similarity of the syllables across tonalities reflects the way the musical mind processes tonal. This tonal syllable system, like Gordon's rhythm syllable system, is accessible to young children with the readiness for syllables. Little children's extensive experience with rhythm and tonal syllables, in turn, creates the readiness for music reading and writing.

Implementing Syllables

We present rhythm and tonal syllables to little children in the same manner that we have presented meters and tonalities—through immersion in the easiest rhythm and tonal narratives in the various meters and tonalities—now with syllables.[5] We also immerse little children in easy Rhythm Dialogue Activity, Resting Tone Activity, Macro/Micro Beat Activity, and Tonal Dialogue Activity, all in the various meters and tonalities—with syllables. We space these activities out over time, introducing rhythm syllables one meter at a time, over several class sessions, before introducing tonal syllables. We use syllables in just one meter or one tonality in a class session until the children experience all. Initial rhythm narratives with syllables are made up of primarily macro and micro beats in each of the various meters. Initial tonal narratives in each of the various tonalities include only macro and micro beats, with melodic contour that supports the musical mind tonally. The more familiar the musical material of rhythm and tonal narratives and the various types of activities, the more easily the syllables attach to sound in the young musical mind. We begin one-on-one activities with the simplest musical input with syllables and engage in the same way we have right along, responding in relation to each child's offering, now with syllables.

Using puppets to introduce rhythm and tonal syllables is very effective, encouraging children to just sit and listen, much as they do when we present meters on a drum or tonalities on a recorder. Using one puppet to introduce rhythm syllables and another to introduce tonal syllables reinforces the separate identities of rhythm and tonal.

Rhythm Syllable Activities

Rhythm is always more immediate than tonal for little children, and rhythm syllables are more easily acquired than tonal, so we introduce syllables in Duple meter. We start without rhythm syllables, with a rhythm prep and rhythm narrative familiar to the children, and then introduce a new puppet who is "visiting" from another country.[6]

"Rigatoni comes all the way from Calamari to sing with you. He's going to sing Duple meter in his language." Rigatoni starts by singing the rhythm prep with syllables, re-establishing the meter, and then begins singing a rhythm narrative, like the example shown in Figure 5.3, with rhythm syllables. He delivers only macro and micro beats for several phrases, contrasted by a section including familiar division patterns, all in syllables, and then goes back to the macro and micro beat section to reinforce macro and micro beats with syllables.

Figure 5.3   Rhythm narrative, Duple syllables

The children are mesmerized, demonstrating "deer-in-the-headlights" stares as the syllables lead the musical mind to reflect on itself, reinforcing rhythm knowing. The syllables make so much sense to the musical mind that is steeped in the various meters that the children generally sing macro and micro beats on syllables right along with Rigatoni. The following week, Rigatoni returns to sing Triple meter in his language, presenting the syllables in the same manner as described for Duple meter.[7]

We might, depending on the age of the children and the allotted time we have with them, bring Rigatoni back in successive weeks, revisiting Duple meter and then Triple, and then perhaps introducing Unusual Paired and Unusual Unpaired meters with syllables, limiting Rigatoni to one meter each week. We might, instead, go directly into Rhythm Dialogue Activity with syllables in Duple meter one week and Triple the next, directly following Rigatoni's introduction of syllables in each meter, immersing the children further in syllables in the familiar meters. Little children are very comfortable dialoguing with rhythm syllables on macro and micro beats in Duple and Triple meters. We might invite them into Rhythm Dialogue with Rigatoni, singing in his language. We might follow up with Macro/Micro Beat Activity with syllables in Duple meter, and then the following week move from immersion to Rhythm Dialogue Activity, to Macro/Micro Beat Activity in Triple meter. Each of these activities immerse children in the syllables just as they do in the various meters, and they begin to get children using the syllables that so naturally attach to what the musical mind already knows in sound. Including the unusual meters with syllables provides the necessary contrast that facilitates children's grasp of syllables in the easier meters.

Delivering a verse or two of a rhythm narrative without syllables and then a verse or two with, continuing to go back and forth in every activity, serves to reinforce meters in sound and with syllables. We always provide the full spectrum, just as conversation at the dinner table speaks to children of different developmental levels, with every child absorbing the greater whole and putting it to use in their own time frame. We continue to immerse the children in the various meters with and without rhythm syllables and engage in Rhythm Dialogue Activity and Macro/Micro Beat Activity with and without rhythm syllables. We start with the easiest rhythm patterns with syllables and move to patterns of greater difficulty that the children know in sound. We deliver rhythm patterns in Rhythm Dialogue Activity with syllables and gear our response to each child's response.

We might offer a couple of patterns with syllables and a couple of patterns without, depending on the child's response. We might move into divisions with syllables with some children, or even more difficult rhythm patterns, while with others, we do more of the simplest patterns without syllables. Rhythm activities with syllables look much like rhythm activities without syllables. Children will initially be more articulate with rhythm patterns without syllables than with, growing with syllables in the same manner that they grow without—first in Duple meter and then Triple, acquiring macro and micro beat patterns before division patterns, developing the readiness for more difficult rhythm patterns.

We present and use rhythm syllables in meters in the same way we present meters—we include regular experience with syllables in unusual meters to better secure command of Duple and Triple meters with syllables. We provide greater opportunity for Rhythm Dialogue Activity with syllables in Duple and Triple meters, but include rhythm syllables in the unusual meters in Macro/Micro Beat Activities, which can serve for immersion, movement in the meters, and chanting along with the syllables. Guidelines presented in Part1 of this book for rhythm activities without syllables and planning lessons in sets of RTS also apply to rhythm activities with syllables.

We can, after introducing a particular meter in syllables, use syllables with any rhythm activity in that meter, starting with the most basic rhythm patterns. We can include rhythm syllables with any rhythm activity that we have done without syllables. Toddler hammers, pom-poms, or any other props we might have employed for rhythm activities without syllables serve equally well with rhythm syllables in the full variety of meters. We start the activity without syllables as we always have, add a few phrases with syllables and then a few phrases without, going back and forth while gradually spending more and more time with syllables. We can then start the activity with the rhythm prep in syllables, use the rhythm syllables throughout the activity, and occasionally throw in a few phrases without syllables. Children become very comfortable floating in and out of rhythm syllables in all of the various meters. Children's fluency with syllables is always less than without, as using syllables demands a higher level of skill.

Tonal Syllable Activities

Little children's ease with rhythm syllables facilitates learning tonal syllables. Children comfortable with rhythm syllables demonstrate greater readiness and willingness to engage with tonal syllables. We present tonal syllables in the various tonalities in tonal narratives in Duple meter with just macro and micro beats. We begin with a tonal prep and narrative without tonal syllables in Dorian tonality, seating the children in the tonality, and then introduce another new puppet who is visiting from another country.[8]

"Babushka comes all the way from Begonia to sing with you. She's going to sing Dorian tonality in her language." Babushka begins by singing a tonal prep on syllables, re-establishing the tonality. She then sings a familiar tonal narrative on tonal syllables in Dorian tonality and Duple meter. Her familiar narrative provides substantial repetition of the syllables. She adds a contrasting section to her narrative, alternating between the fifth and resting tone on macro beats, as in the example shown in Figure 5.4, highlighting and reinforcing the relationship between the fifth and resting tone in syllables. She sings through the entire narrative twice, begins a third time and ends after the second line, with the fifth and resting tone back in context.

Figure 5.4 Tonal narrative, Dorian syllables

The children, once again, are mesmerized, exhibiting "deer-in-the-headlights" stares as the syllables lead the musical mind to reflect on itself, reinforcing tonal knowing. Babushka can return each week to sing a different tonality in her language, always starting with the tonal prep in syllables followed by multiple repetitions of a familiar tonal narrative with just macro and micro beats sung on tonal syllables, and including a contrasting section with a couple of repetitions of 5-1, 5-1 on macro beats sung on tonal syllables. Securing tonal anchors with syllables initially makes tonal syllables easier to acquire in all tonalities.

We might move directly into Resting Tone Activity with Babushka, now with tonal syllables, inviting the children to sing the resting tone with Babushka in her language. We might play the game Babushka says they play in her country. We all stand and engage in flowing movement with a familiar tonal narrative in syllables. We then include two repetitions of 5-1 on syllables with arms going up on the fifth and down on the resting tone. We sing the fifth a third time, extending the duration of the fifth while whirling around with arms up, breaking the whirl with a squat on the resting tone, helping to secure the syllables for the resting tone and fifth. The children are more than happy to play Babushka's game over and over in any tonality.

Securing syllables on the resting tone and fifth anchors the other syllables just as the resting tone and fifth serve as anchors for tonal knowing without syllables. The anchors set the stage for Tonal Dialogue, now with syllables. Tonal segments most appropriate for Tonal Dialogue with syllables are the same as those recommended without syllables—5-3-1, 1-7-1, 5-6-5, 5-4-3-2-1, 5-1, with the addition of 1-2-1 in Phrygian tonality and 5-4-5 in Lydian. All are presented in Duple meter with just macro and micro beats, with each tonal segment starting and ending on either the resting tone or fifth, and with macro beat weight aligned with tonal anchors. Figure 5.5 presents the recommended set of tonal segments in Mixolydian tonality with syllables, complete with the tonal prep. Once again, we can begin to expand tonal segments around the resting tone and fifth in any tonality (7-2-1, 6-4-5).

Figure 5.5 Tonal Segments, Mixolydian syllables

Young children demonstrate that the musical mind relies on the tonal anchors and understands the characteristic sound of each tonality with or without syllables. They also demonstrate that the musical mind is not yet ready to grasp the one-to-one correspondence between pitches and particular tonal syllables, whatever the tonality. They might, for example, when familiar with the descending pattern 5-4-3-2-1 with and without syllables, sing discreet pitches throughout, with the correct syllables for the fifth and resting tone, but with imprecise vowels on the other pitches, always with the appropriate consonant for the tonality. This common response indicates security within the tonality, security with the syllables on the resting tone and fifth, and security starting each pitch with the appropriate consonant. It also demonstrates that the children are not yet secure with the one-to-one correspondence of particular syllables to pitches except for the resting tone and fifth. Grasping one-to-one correspondence is a later development.

Any tonal activities we have done without syllables can be done with syllables. Scarves, microphones, or any other props we might have employed with tonal activities without syllables serve equally well with tonal syllables in all of the various tonalities. A variety of activities with tonal syllables immerse children in the syllables just as they immerse them in the various tonalities, and the syllables attach to the sound in the musical mind. We begin the activity with a prep without syllables, move into syllables, and then alternate a couple of phrases with and without syllables until gradually spending more time with syllables. We can then start the activity with the tonal prep in syllables, use the tonal syllables throughout the activity, and occasionally throw in a few phrases without syllables. Little children become very comfortable floating in and out of tonal syllables in all of the various tonalities.

Familiarity with tonal syllables in each tonality directly transfers to every other tonality. For example, if children easily handle the tonal segment 5-6-5 with syllables in one tonality, that strengthens their ability to handle 5-6-5 with syllables in any tonality. The melodic function is the same across tonalities, even with the different characteristic tones that make the tonalities sound different. The young musical mind that is well versed in the various tonalities without syllables readily transfers tonal knowing from one tonality to another with syllables unique to the sound of each tonality.

Delivering a verse or two of a tonal narrative without syllables and a verse or two with syllables, continuing to go back and forth in every activity, serves to reinforce tonalities in sound and with syllables. We always provide the full spectrum, as we did with rhythm, with every child absorbing the greater whole and putting it to use in their own time frame. We continue to immerse the children in the various tonalities with and without tonal syllables, engage them in Resting Tone Activity, and then eventually Tonal Dialogue Activity, with and without tonal syllables. We deliver tonal segments in Tonal Dialogue with syllables, and then gear our response to each child's response. We might include a couple of tonal segments with syllables and a couple without, depending on the child's response, always gearing our part of the dialogue to the level of each child. Children continue to move forward tonally with and without syllables.

Maintaining the practice of providing a few phrases without syllables and a few phrases with syllables within any activity provides for children to grow at their own level with the aural input needed. Delivering some phrases without syllables allows the more developed musical mind to attach the syllables, while providing for those who need greater input without syllables. We cannot rush the process of acquiring rhythm and tonal syllables any more than we can rush the process of developing a sense of meter and a sense of tonality.

Guidelines presented in Part 1 of this book for tonal activities without syllables and planning lessons in sets of RTS also apply to tonal activities with syllables. Rotate meters and rotate tonalities to keep them all alive in the musical mind, now with syllables. Avoid consecutive activities in two different meters or two different tonalities by separating meters with a tonal activity and separating tonalities with a rhythm activity. We can, after introducing a particular tonality in syllables, use syllables with any tonal activity in that tonality, starting with the easiest music content. Children's fluency with tonal syllables is always less than without, as syllables demand a higher level of skill.

We will before long be able to employ syllables with more than one meter or more than one tonality within a class session, and use both rhythm syllables and tonal syllables within a given class. Children at this level who have had many weeks or months of experience with rhythm and tonal syllables are ready to move on to the more difficult activities of comparing and contrasting what they know in sound, now using rhythm and tonal syllables.

Comparing and Contrasting

The young musical mind that is well-versed in the various meters and tonalities senses the difference in sound between meters and between tonalities. Syllables give voice to those differences, making them more concrete in the musical mind and providing labels with which both the musical mind and the thinking mind can relate. Proper names of meters and tonalities speak to the thinking mind. We might use them casually to label each meter or tonality as we do with the puppets, but the musical mind associates meters and tonalities with their syllables rather than proper names, as it is the syllables that adhere directly to what the musical mind knows in sound.

Syllable acquisition brings the thinking mind and the musical mind together. Syllables become the common language between them. It is through syllables that the verbal thinking mind becomes cognizant of what the non-verbal musical mind knows in sound. The collaboration between the musical mind and the thinking mind, with the musical mind leading the way through syllables, deepens musical understanding, while developing the necessary infrastructure for music reading and writing.

We can provide for the musical mind to compare and contrast what it knows in sound and syllables so that it can become "mindful" of its own sense of differences between meters, between tonalities, between beat functions, and between rhythm and tonal, while guiding the young thinking mind to reflect on the musical mind's knowing. Children have to be fully steeped in meters and tonalities with and without syllables to be musically ready for comparing and contrasting meters and comparing and contrasting tonalities. We may have to remind ourselves to avoid well-meaning verbalizations of the differences between meters or between tonalities or tips as to what to listen for, as language interrupts the very process of the musical mind's comparing and contrasting in sound.

We have up until now avoided consecutive rhythm activities with two different meters and consecutive tonal activities with two different tonalities to allow the musical mind to process one at a time rather than confusing the two. Now we deliberately design experiences with two different meters or two different tonalities presented consecutively so the musical mind can aurally compare and contrast different meters and different tonalities in sound. We can playfully put two meters or two tonalities with syllables "next to each other" in sound, stimulating the musical mind at this point in development to compare the two in sound.

Rhythm Discrimination Activity

Figure 5.6 Rhythm Discrimination Activity, Duple/Triple

We present two identical puppets (bluebirds in this example), one on each hand, and activate one at a time. "This bird is going to sing in Duple meter." The bird on one of our hands sings, "Du de du, du de du" (Duple prep). "This bird is going to sing in Triple meter." The bird on our other hand sings, "Du da di du, du da di du" (Triple prep in the same tempo as macro beats in Duple meter). The first bird starts singing several bars of macro and micro beats in Duple meter with syllables, as in the first line of Figure 5.6, followed immediately by the second bird singing several bars of macro and micro beats with syllables in Triple meter, as in the second line, maintaining the same tempo.

Taking It to a Higher Level

Both puppets now go to our ears, as if whispering to us, and we pose to the children, "I wonder who's singing?" We then sing in our regular voice a few easy bars in Duple meter, as in the third line. After a couple of measures, the bird singing Duple meter moves away from our ear and finishes the phrase, singing directly to the children on syllables, which reveals which bird is singing Duple meter. The bird visually confirms which bird was singing, while reinforcing Duple meter.

The bird goes back to our ear and we begin to sing a few easy bars in Triple meter with rhythm syllables, as in the fourth line, with a bird at each ear. The bird that is singing Triple meter reveals itself after a couple of measures by singing directly to the children, finishing the phrase. The activity goes on repeatedly, with several pairs of lines in the contrasting meters, without additional verbalization, and perhaps with divisions, as in the third pair of Figure 5.6, giving children the chance to hear Duple and Triple meters repeatedly back-to-back, so they can aurally compare and contrast the meters they already know in sound and syllables.

Children develop hypotheses about which bird is singing. The confirmation of their hypotheses, or challenge to them by the disclosure of the singing bird, guides them to discover that the two meters they know in sound are different, and brings that discovery to the thinking mind.

Children may or may not point to the bird they think is singing, and different children may point to different puppets. It is essential that the musical examples be presented successively, without verbalization, without confirmation or praise for choosing the appropriate puppet, and without children's cheers for themselves when they choose the right one. The sound of contrasting meters has to dominate the activity. Children have to hear the ongoing contrasting examples "next to each other" in sound without any verbalization in order to compare and contrast the sound of the meters. Each whispering puppet reveals itself after a couple of measures in the meter by singing directly to the children.

Alternating Duple, Triple, Duple, Triple places the meters next to each other in sound, but children might select or anticipate the bird singing by the predicable alternation between right and left. We throw in a couple of successive examples of the same meter after a couple of alternating examples to encourage discrimination of meters and deter the anticipation of the alternation. We know by children's expression those who thought the meters were distinguished by the alternation of puppets, as they obviously try to listen more closely to develop a new hypothesis. The bird on the left consistently sings one of the two meters chosen for the day and the one on the right consistently sings the other, maintaining the visual distinction while children learn to make the aural distinction.

Puppets chosen for this activity are identical and used primarily for this activity, facilitating the choice of any meters in successive weeks without children associating any given puppet with just one meter or one type of puppet response like that of Dancing Doggie. The birds always sing with rhythm syllables, whether preps or familiar rhythm narratives. The syllables reflect and reinforce the difference between the meters and invite the musical mind to tune in to the distinguishing characteristics in sound that make them different from each other, now expressed in syllables. The more familiar the rhythm narratives with and without syllables, the easier it is for children to learn to discriminate between meters. The narratives can be improvised, but rhythm patterns have to initially be primarily macro and micro beat patterns, with just occasional divisions—the patterns children know best—so that they can discover that the meters are different.

Rhythm preps are essential with the introduction of each meter to be contrasted, and can be used if needed to re-establish a meter. Subsequent examples may or may not include the rhythm patterns of the preps. Silent beats of preps are not necessary in subsequent examples on the same day, as this Rhythm Discrimination Activity is designed to contrast the meters directly. Maintaining the tempo of macro beats while contrasting Duple and Triple meters, and maintaining the tempo of micro beats while contrasting either Duple or Triple with one of the unusual meters facilitates discrimination. Contrasting the two unusual meters is a much more difficult discrimination.

Our goal with this type of activity is simply for children to discover that the two examples they know so well in sound and in syllables are different from each other. We are not looking for "correct" responses, but rather, we are providing the opportunity for children to aurally compare and contrast meters in sound by hearing two different meters back-to-back repeatedly. We are encouraging children to form aural hypotheses about the relationship between the two meters just as they might physically compare the size or colors of stacking cups next to each other. Using puppets as a visual indicator invites the thinking mind to work with the musical mind. The musical mind knows in sound that the meters are different, but now we are providing an opportunity for the musical mind to become aware of rhythm knowing, and for the thinking mind to become cognizant of that difference, enabling children to take greater command of their own rhythm knowing.

The syllables provide the link between the musical mind and the thinking mind, so it is essential that these activities always be done with syllables. Rhythm syllables highlight the fact that the meters are different, inviting the musical mind to tune in to the distinguishing characteristics in sound and syllables that make them different from each other.

We might, depending on the level of the class, give each child a turn to point to which puppet is singing through several rhythm examples, but without any verbalization as we go from one child to another. You might think that the children differentiate between meters only by the syllables, as the thinking minds of those of us who are not yet familiar with the various meters or syllables might be doing; however, at this point in the young musical mind rhythm syllables have become part of the meters in sound. They label what the musical mind knows in sound, and they become a language with which the musical mind can communicate its knowing to the thinking mind.

You might question why Duple and Triple meters were used for this activity designed for comparing and contrasting meters, when including an unusual meter would provide greater contrast. The children at this point are familiar with the syllables of the unusual meters, but they are most comfortable and competent with Duple and Triple meters, as these meters are easier for the children. An initial Rhythm Discrimination Activity with Duple and Triple meters makes it easier for the children to learn to play the "meter game." Following up the next week contrasting Duple meter and Unusual Paired Meter with the puppets adds greater contrast, as does an activity the third week contrasting Triple meter and Unusual Unpaired meter. Cycling back to Duple and Triple the fourth week, you'll find greater security in the children as they more easily discriminate between Duple and Triple meters.

Tonal Discrimination Activity

We can create the same kind of experience to discriminate tonalities, once the children are accustomed to discriminating meters. We simply place two contrasting tonalities with syllables next to each other so the children can compare them in sound, keeping the meter and tempo consistent throughout. It is best with tonal to use contrasting tonalities, one with a minor third contrasted by one with a major third, starting with Dorian and Mixolydian for ease in learning to play the "tonality game." We can follow up the next week with perhaps Phrygian and Lydian, and the third week with another contrasting pair, followed in successive weeks by mixing and matching contrasting tonalities.

Figure 5.7 Tonal Discrimination Activity, Dorian/Mixolydian

We present two identical puppets (redbirds in this example), one on each hand, and activate one at a time. "This bird is going to sing in Dorian tonality." The puppet on one of our hands sings "rim re rim ra ri ro ru rum" (Dorian prep). "This bird is going to sing in Mixolydian tonality." The bird on our other hand sings "sim se sim sa si so su sum (Mixolydian prep). The first bird starts singing several bars of Dorian tonality with tonal syllables in Duple meter, using just macro and micro beats as in the first line of Figure 5.7, followed immediately by the second bird singing several bars of Mixolydian tonality with syllables, as in the second line.

The two birds maintain the same tempo throughout and start on the same pitch for the resting tone. The puppets then go to our ears as if whispering to us, and we pose to the children, "I wonder who's singing?" We sing in our regular voice a few bars of Dorian tonality on tonal syllables, as in the third line. After a couple of measures, the bird singing Dorian tonality moves from our ear and sings to the children, completing the phrase on syllables, which reveals which bird is singing Dorian tonality. The bird visually confirms which bird was singing while reinforcing Dorian tonality.

The bird goes back to our ear and we begin to sing a few bars in Mixolydian tonality with tonal syllables as with the fourth line, with a bird at each ear, all without verbalization. The bird that is singing Mixolydian tonality reveals itself after a couple of measures by singing directly to the children to complete the phrase. The activity goes on repeatedly, with several pairs of lines of the contrasting tonalities, without verbalization and with the simplest rhythm, giving children the chance to hear Dorian and Mixolydian tonalities repeatedly back-to-back so they can aurally compare and contrast tonalities they already know in sound and syllables.

Children develop hypotheses about which bird is singing. The confirmation or challenge of their hypotheses guides them to discover that the two tonalities are different, and brings that discovery to the thinking mind.

Tonal preps are essential with the introduction of each tonality to be contrasted, and can be used as needed to re-establish a tonality. Subsequent examples may or may not include tonal preps, but they do make it easier for the children to compare tonalities in sound, at least with the first example, as they immediately flag differences between tonalities. Later experiences can contrast the tonalities directly after the puppets have introduced the contrasting tonalities with the preps. The birds always sing with tonal syllables, whether preps or familiar tonal narratives. The syllables reflect and reinforce the difference between the tonalities and invite the musical mind to tune in to the distinguishing characteristics in sound and syllables that make them different from each other.

Maintaining the meter and tempo throughout the tonal examples while contrasting tonalities helps to focus the young musical mind on the tonalities, as does using just macro and micro beats in Duple meter. Using the same pitch for the resting tone with each tonality being contrasted also helps the musical mind attend to the differences between tonalities.

Children learn to discriminate between tonalities most easily with short tonal narratives that are very familiar to them. The narratives can be improvised, but the melodic structure should support the musical mind and be what the children are accustomed to hearing. We might even improvise identical narratives in two different tonalities for an experience in discrimination, as in the third pair of Figure 5.7. We can increase the difficulty level of tonal examples by presenting both tonalities in Triple meter with just macro and micro beats, but the unusual meters draw more attention to meter than tonality. This activity is not about increasing difficulty through rhythm patterns or tonal segments but rather, for children to discover that the tonalities they know in sound are different from each other, and for the children to begin to tune in to the distinguishing characteristics in sound and syllables.

Presenting the chosen tonalities "next to each other" repeatedly gives children multiple chances to compare and contrast the tonalities and to form hypotheses about which puppet is singing. Children may or may not point to the puppet they think is singing and react happily when their choice reveals itself, but the activity goes on without the vocal interruption of praise or cheers. The whispering puppet that then reveals itself by singing directly to the children provides the confirmation of tonality. Puppets chosen for this activity are identical and used primarily for this activity, facilitating the shifting of tonalities in successive weeks without children associating either puppet with a particular tonality or a particular puppet response like that of Resting Tone Rabbit.

The sound of contrasting tonalities has to command the activity. Here again, we deliberately break children's anticipation of the alternating pattern of left and right by occasionally including successive examples in the same tonality, encouraging attention to the aural differences rather than left-right alternation. It is, however, the alternation of tonalities that provides for the children to compare and contrast the two different tonalities. Determining that two examples are the same is more difficult than discovering that they are different. The bird on the left consistently sings one of the two tonalities chosen for the day and the one on the right consistently sings the other, maintaining the visual distinction while children learn to make the aural distinction. Tonal Discrimination Activity at this level is for the musical mind to develop awareness that the tonalities it knows in sound are different, to begin to tune in to those differences through syllables, and to engage the thinking mind in working with the musical mind so that together they can move to higher levels of musical understanding.

We might, depending on the level of the class, give each child a turn to point to which puppet is singing through several tonal examples, but without any verbalization as we go from one child to another. Once again, it can be easy to conclude that the children differentiate between the two examples only by the syllables; however, at this point of development, tonal syllables have become part of the tonalities in sound, even if they might still be a challenge for us. They label what the young musical mind knows in sound, and they become a language with which the musical mind can communicate tonal knowing to the thinking mind.

Inferring and Naming

It is always tempting to see if children can tell the difference between two meters or two tonalities without syllables. Some may be ready to do that, but our role is to guide each of the children every step of the journey, and to secure what they already know in sound in order to bring all of the children to that level of readiness. The puppets might, after multiple examples of Duple and Triple meter in syllables, or two tonalities, whisper and then deliver a couple of examples without syllables just to see how children might respond, or include a couple of examples without syllables with particular children in one-on-one response.

Inferring and naming the meter or tonality without syllables are much later developments. The intent at this point in development is to lead the musical mind to become mindful of what it already knows in sound and to playfully lead the thinking mind to work together with the musical mind to propel music learning.

Children cannot be expected to name the meter or tonality they are hearing at this level of development, with or without syllables, though a few children might be ready to do that. One kindergartener in his first year of instruction, for example, when being introduced to a new song which happened to be in Mixolydian tonality, volunteered, "That's like *Wake-Up Jacob*." He was communicating that his musical mind knew that the two songs were in the same tonality. Syllables provide for the musical mind to directly reflect on and become aware of its own knowing. We can continue to use the proper names of tonalities informally when we offer, for example, "This puppet is going to sing in Dorian tonality," followed by the tonal prep in syllables in Dorian, but it is the syllables that reflect, represent, and reinforce the distinguishing characteristics of meters and of tonalities in the musical mind.

The proper names of meters and tonalities will eventually become the verbal representation of meters and tonalities in syllables, but at this point, we use them incidentally. Little children are apt to label a meter or tonality by its syllables. They will often use "du des" or "du de dus" to refer to Duple meter, and "du da dis" or "du da di dus" to refer to Triple meter. This practitioner on one occasion was trying to learn more about the young musical mind with well-developed five-year-olds. She created an activity to better understand children's ease in moving from one tonality to another with syllables. Short tonal narratives in different tonalities were presented successively with syllables, each concluding with a couple of bars of just the fifth and the resting tone. Children spontaneously joined in singing the segments with the fifth and the resting tone in each tonality with proper syllables, moving effortlessly from one tonality to another. The activity ended with a five-year-old piping up with, "You forgot rim rum." She was right. Dorian tonality had, indeed, been accidentally left out of the series of tonalities.

We can create all kinds of Discrimination Activities with little children at this level of development, helping the musical mind and the thinking mind to work together to propel music learning. The key is to present sound examples next to each other without verbalization, offering some kind of visual cue to confirm or challenge the musical mind's hypotheses. The activity becomes kind of a matching game for children with the musical readiness, as they match the sound to the object, discriminating differences in sound.

We can create Discrimination Activities with very developed youngsters to learn more about the musical mind. Doodley Duck, a beloved puppet, always needed the children to help him. An activity repeatedly presented macro and micro beats next to each other in sound, inviting Doodley Duck, with a minimum of verbalization, to sing either macro beats or micro beats. He always did the opposite of what was requested, keeping the contrast in sound between macro and micro beats foremost. When asked to sing "du du, du du," Doodley Duck would enthusiastically deliver "du de du de, du de du de," or vice versa. The meter dominated the activity, except for one time after when a four-year-old interjected, "But those were beautiful micro beats, Doodley Duck!"

We can design Discrimination Activities for more difficult discriminations, for example, putting bean bags in one bucket when we hear macro beats or micro beats, and in a different bucket when we hear divisions, as long as we present contrasting examples in syllables next to each other in sound. We might use Orff instruments to explore the young musical mind's differentiation between tonal segments. We might design activities to discriminate rhythm from tonal, just to try to better understand the young musical mind.

A group of developed five-year-olds not old enough for kindergarten may be ready to discriminate between meters in a game of "hopscotch." We set up hoops on the floor with two pairs of adjacent red and blue hoops followed by one yellow hoop at the end of the course. We demonstrate jumping from one hoop to another, as we go through the course.

> "When we jump into a red hoop, we're going to sing Duple meter, 'du de du, du de du.' When we jump into a blue hoop, we're going to sing Triple meter, 'du da di du, du da di du.' When we jump into the yellow hoop, we're going to sing Unusual Paired meter, 'du be du ba bi, du be du ba bi.'"

Each child gets a turn to go through the hoops with the teacher, with the child leading the ordering of meters by jumping into each hoop of his choice. We prompt each child as needed by starting Duple meter in the red hoops, Triple meter in the blue hoops, and Unusual Paired meter in the final yellow hoop. We let go of the proper names and any talking so that the meters are next to each other in sound, just as the hoops are next to each other. The children may surprise you as they become more and more adept at distinguishing between meters and initiating appropriate meters, perhaps favoring the red hoops because they are sure of Duple meter, or demonstrating triumph that they knew what to chant in the yellow hoop.

Little children teach us as we teach them. Our learning to communicate with the musical mind opens horizons we never thought possible with young children. We just have to make sure that we don't rush the process or try to engage children in such advanced Discrimination Activities before they have command of rhythm and tonal syllables in sound, which are meaningful only after they have command of the various meters and tonalities without rhythm and tonal syllables.[9]

Added Benefits

Four- and five-year-olds, as well as older children at this point of development, have been exposed to more difficult rhythm patterns, rhythm and tonal narratives with more difficult rhythm patterns, and tonal narratives in unusual meters, all without syllables. They are familiar with rhythm and tonal syllables and have extended experience with Discrimination Activity. They have developed the aural infrastructure to comprehend musical detail through an ongoing commentary of syllables in the context of narratives similar to familiar ones. Rhythm and tonal syllables can shine a spotlight on music in flight, highlighting and communicating meter, shifting meters, rhythm patterns, tonalities, and melodic structure to the young musical mind — aspects we would never consider approaching verbally with such young children.

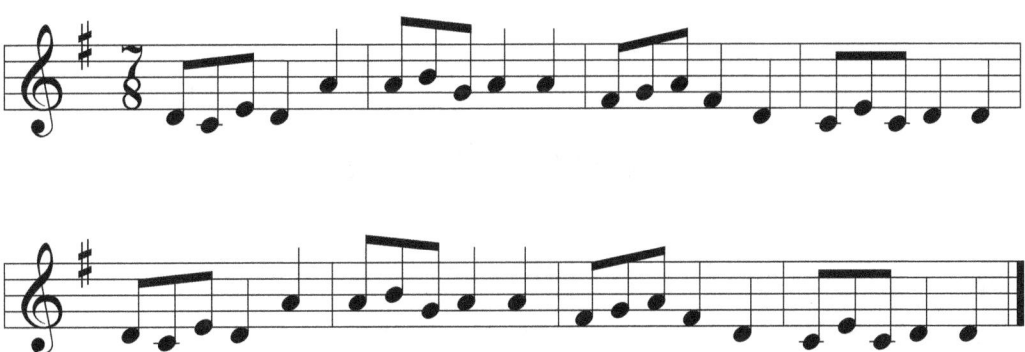

Figure 5.8   Mixolydian, Unusual Unpaired

Figure 5.8, introduced in an earlier chapter, offers a Mixolydian narrative in Unusual Unpaired meter. Let's assume that our four- and five-year-olds are familiar with similar narratives without syllables, comfortable with rhythm and tonal syllables in the various meters, and have substantial experience with Discrimination Activity with both rhythm and tonal. We sing a few verses of this tonal narrative on "too" as usual, and then without losing a beat, we sing at least four bars of micro beats on the resting tone with rhythm syllables, using the beat groupings of this narrative (3/2/2). The micro beats with rhythm syllables spotlight the meter in flight as if to say, "Notice the meter of this song. It is a meter you know that powers this jaunty song." Singing micro beats on the resting tone also highlights the relationship between macro and micro beats in the meter, while also keeping the tonality alive. We continue with a couple more verses of the narrative on "too," giving the children the opportunity to process the song with the musical mind's greater awareness of the meter. We might go back to singing micro beats on the resting tone with rhythm syllables before bringing the experience to a close with a couple more verses of the narrative on "too."

We could similarly sing micro beats on the resting tone on "bah" to spotlight the meter in the context of a narrative or song with children who have not yet engaged in rhythm syllables, but we can communicate through syllables on a deeper level with children who know syllables. We might even sing the song on tonal syllables, making the musical mind more aware of tonality and what is going on tonally before ending with a couple more verses of the narrative on "too." Nothing needs to be explained. The syllables have done the explaining to the musical mind, pointing out the meter and then the tonality in flight.[10]

You might think children would confuse rhythm and tonal syllables if we sing the melody on rhythm syllables but they do not. They simply follow the spotlight of the syllables to whatever the syllables point to, as they know the various meters and tonalities in sound and in syllables. Children are fascinated to catch onto the meter in the context of an ongoing song. Chanting rhythm syllables on the rhythm of the song without the melody takes away the dynamic of rhythm and tonal together that the children at this level of development are ready to embrace.

We can even use rhythm and tonal syllables with these children in the context of art songs or gem songs, speaking to the musical mind in flight about song complexity, and exciting children as they aurally discover meter changes. *Butterfly Dreams* (Figure 5.9) offers an example of an art song in Dorian tonality with meter shifting from Duple to Triple.

Butterfly Dreams

Figure 5.9   Dorian, Duple/Triple

We sing a few verses of the song with words with movement of the energy of the line, and then go directly into a couple of verses of singing the melody with rhythm syllables, singing micro beats throughout and shifting from Duple to Triple syllables in measure five. We continue with a couple more verses with words, perhaps a couple more with rhythm syllables, and then a couple more with words. Hearing the verses with rhythm syllables propels the musical mind to greater awareness of the shifting meter, which is then brought into the next couple of verses with words. We can if we choose add a couple of verses with tonal syllables, leading the musical mind to greater awareness of tonality, which is then brought into the song with words. The experience of this song with rhythm syllables, with or without verses with tonal syllables, brings little children to far greater musical understanding of the song than when we introduced the song at the beginning of the experience. The well-bred musical mind, now in collaboration with the thinking mind, understands the shifting meters, without our saying a word about it.

Using rhythm and tonal syllables for an ongoing commentary on musical detail can be very helpful with older children in rehearsal. The syllables can communicate far more efficiently and far more musically than anything we can verbalize. We can illuminate the dynamic of rhythm and tonal together, using syllables to spotlight each, bringing greater understanding of song in flight with children who have extensive experience with the various meters and tonalities, with and without syllables.

Rhythm and tonal syllables take children to a higher level of music learning. They cement what the musical mind already knows in sound in children who have the foundation for syllables. They serve as labels, making rhythm and tonal knowing accessible. They provide a language for aural knowing that is understood by both the musical mind and the thinking mind, inviting the two to work together to propel music learning. They offer a language that also enables us to address rhythm and tonal knowing in the context of music in flight. Rhythm and tonal syllables provide the direct link to music reading and writing, which we will see in the next chapter. (Appendix G guides teacher acquisition of rhythm and tonal syllables.)

6
Reveling in Music Reading and Writing

Little children learning language demonstrate new growth throughout their earliest years, often surprising us with their spontaneous expression, their depth of understanding, and their command of language, however inarticulate they might be. The more we learn to reach and teach the musical mind, the more little children do the same thing musically, surprising us with their spontaneous expression, their depth of understanding, and their growing command of rhythm and tonal, however inarticulate they might be.

Children two to five years old have reached an unprecedented level of music learning for children not yet old enough for kindergarten, and those in kindergarten and beyond are ready for more. These children are well-versed in meters and tonalities and well-versed in rhythm and tonal syllables, however inarticulate they might be. We once again look to the process of learning language for guidance as to where we go from here to stimulate musical growth appropriate to such young ages.

Parents and teachers stimulate language development throughout early childhood by reading to little children. They might read a simple little storybook, and they might point to the words as they read. They might read a more complex story that is within the children's level of understanding, but well beyond their day-to-day lives. They might choose a story that naturally draws children's attention to the conventions of print, and they might choose a story that invites independent reading. Children grow in the process.

Young children observe parents and teachers reading and begin to formulate concepts of print. Little children often "read" their favorite storybooks by reciting the familiar stories while turning pages of the book, imitating the reading behaviors they have witnessed. The children realize that the print has meaning. Parents and teachers also guide young children to recognize and to write letters and numbers, and to write their own names. Children witness parents jotting notes or making a grocery list and begin to understand that we can represent our own thinking in print. Little ones put marks on paper and "read" what they have written, imitating writing behavior they have observed. Those further along in the process make up their own spellings as they attempt to convey meaning in print. These common behaviors develop reading readiness as children move toward independent skill in reading and writing language. Little children develop music reading readiness and move toward independent skill in reading and writing music in much the same way.

Many years of research at the Come Children Sing Institute, informed by the way little children learn to read and write language, mindful of Edwin Gordon's higher levels of music learning with older children,[1] and empowered by little children's striking musical growth, charted new territory in music reading and writing in early childhood. All of the children were well-versed in meters and tonalities and rhythm and tonal syllables through the process offered in this book, and had at least two years of instruction. Children as young as two-years-old were included. This chapter presents the classroom application of the findings of that research.[2]

Notation for the young child is a picture of what the musical mind knows in sound. Rhythm and tonal syllables become the magic link between the musical mind and music notation, communicating to the musical mind, "You know this in sound. Here is what it looks like." The recommended rhythm and tonal syllables speak to both the musical mind and the thinking mind, and they serve as the language equivalent of the musical mind's knowing in sound. Rhythm and tonal syllables now also become the language equivalent of rhythm and tonal in print. Syllables are the intermediary between music in sound and music in print, inviting the musical mind and the thinking mind into a more dynamic collaboration. Music in print serves as a visual reflection of the musical mind's processing of rhythm and of tonal.

Little children with the background addressed in Part 1 of this book, who are also well versed in rhythm and tonal syllables (Chapter 5), have the musical readiness for us to read rhythm and tonal narratives to them on syllables. We might be tempted to read music to young children on a neutral syllable before they are familiar with rhythm and tonal syllables, but it is the rhythm and tonal syllables that speak to the musical mind about music in print. It is the syllables that provide the vehicle for the musical mind to bring its knowing to notation, whereas reading music on a neutral syllable bypasses the musical mind, forcing the thinking mind to try to decipher notation.

Reading music on syllables to young children with the musical readiness opens the world of music reading and writing for little children. The youngsters follow the notation as we point to what we are reading, developing concepts of print. The youngest children imitate our music reading behaviors as they do with language, "reading" familiar rhythm or tonal narratives as they point to music notation. They begin to realize that the marks on the page have meaning, and that they are different than the letters and numbers that they have seen in their storybooks. Children in kindergarten and beyond are necessarily tuned in to reading language, so they try to "figure out music in print."

We can develop in young children the readiness for music reading and writing and guide them as independent readers to make sense of music notation in the same way that they make sense of language in print. The process of reading either language or music is a complex process that becomes so automatic that we are not aware of our own procedure.

> .....the reader develops strategies for dealing with print—strategies that set in motion an active process of relating what he knows to what he sees. He selectively attends to the features of print that carry meaning. He scans the print, looking ahead and behind, picking up cues that trigger meaning. He compares cues with each other and compares them with his knowing. He revises his reading as he picks up new data. He relies on context to guide his reading and uses redundant cues to confirm his reading. His split-second processing creates

a system of checks and balances that leads to self-correcting reading behavior and the development of reading skill. The reader engages in a complex system of problem solving through which he constructs meaning.[3]

We are going take a look at four different types of rhythm and tonal reading materials that are similar to those used in language. The first is akin to the familiar little picture books with sparse wording that very young children recite as they imitate music reading behaviors like turning pages, pointing to notation, and "reading" expressively. The second is more difficult material that is within the realm of children's understanding, but well beyond their music reading level. This type is intended for the children to listen and "look at the pictures" while being read to, rather than for the children to read. It presents a broader view of music in print. The third type of music reading material is closer to children's reading level, drawing children's attention to the conventions of music notation and guiding their formulation of strategies with print. The fourth is appropriate to the children's reading level, fostering independent music reading.

We are also going to take a look at music writing, both rhythm and tonal. Music writing is to music reading what chanting and singing are to aural immersion in meters and tonalities. They are reciprocal processes, with each strengthening the other. Little children who watch us write music notation and read the music we have written put pencil to paper and imitate writing music; they "read" the music they have "written," and develop the awareness that they can represent in writing what they know in sound. Older children who engage in writing music as described in this chapter begin to notice the conventions of print in greater detail, which improves music reading, and in turn, improves music writing.

Music reading and writing activities are presented here as we would present them to children. We read all musical examples with syllables, but rhythm and tonal syllables are not written into the notation. You may have to suspend your grasp of music theory to engage with music notation as do children at this level who know meters, tonalities, rhythm syllables and tonal syllables in sound, without the encumbrance of music theory.

Music Reading—Rhythm

We read music to a class of young children by projecting the notation of a rhythm narrative on a large screen that all can see, using a pointer on the screen as we might use a finger, pointing to what we are reading as we go. Figure 6.1 offers a reading example in Duple meter that is immediate for very young children. They are familiar with the rhythm narrative in sound on "bah" and with rhythm syllables. Now they see the notation, including a visual prep.

Duple Meter

Figure 6.1   Rhythm Story, Duple

"Today we are going to read a story in Duple meter, and du de du, looks like this." We set up the rhythm prep visually and aurally by chanting "Du de du, looks like this" in rhythm, while pointing to macro beats in the visual cue on "du de du," and pointing to them again on "looks like this," making sure that the macro beats fall on "du," "looks," and "this." Introducing the visual cue within the familiar aural cue sets up the musical mind for the meter while setting up the thinking mind for how the meter is represented in print. Leaving two silent beats before we begin to read the "Duple story" prepares the musical mind as usual, while allowing the thinking mind to look at the visual prep as the representation of what the musical mind knows in sound.

"Du de du, du de du, du de du de, du de du. Du de du, du de du, du de du de, du du." We read the story expressively following the prep, with syllables and in rhythm, pointing in rhythm on macro beats with a gentle flick of the wrist for micro beats. We read the story at least twice through (without repeating the prep), most often with children spontaneously reading right along with us.

The notation of the familiar narrative serves like a picture book of what the musical mind knows in sound. Children two-years and older begin to become aware that what they know in sound can be represented in print. They learn by our rhythmic pointing that we read music left to right, and they begin to notice the features of music notation that carry rhythm meaning. They read right along with us, just as they "read" familiar picture books with sparse wording in language, developing confidence and enthusiasm for reading music.

The rhythm story in Figure 6.2 presents a broader picture of music in print, with rhythm patterns that the children understand aurally, but that are represented by conventions of print that are beyond the children's reading level and not nearly as accessible as that of Figure 6.1. The example in Figure 6.2 is more for the experience of being read to, for the greater exposure to music in print, and for listening and "looking at the pictures."

Duple Meter

du   de   du

du   de   du

Figure 6.2 Rhythm Story, Duple (for broader picture)

We go through the same process we did in Figure 6.1, starting with the prep, complete with two silent beats, and reading the first "Duple story" to the children twice through on syllables, using a pointer throughout. (Du de du, du ta de ta du, etc.) We move directly into the second narrative without losing a beat, chanting

"Now du de du, looks like this," pointing in rhythm to the second visual prep on "du de du" and again on "looks like this," maintaining the tempo of the first narrative so that the two preps sound identical. We leave two silent beats and then read the second narrative on syllables, in rhythm, pointing rhythmically on the now half-note macro beats with a gentle flick of the wrist for micro beats. (Du de du, du ta de du, etc.) (Appendix F includes this more difficult example with syllables in the notation for teacher reference.)

The two Duple stories of Figure 6.2 communicate that Duple meter can be represented in different ways. Our reading the two narratives in Duple meter, with each represented differently in print, tells the young child that what is in the musical mind dominates the music reading experience rather than the black marks on the page—that it is the musical mind rather than the thinking mind that leads the collaboration between the two in the process of reading music.

We might use the example in Figure 6.2 with younger children as a rhythm story parallel to the storybooks in language that offer children a taste of the world beyond where the children live, yet one they can understand aurally while looking at the captivating pictures. We might use it with older children at the same level for the same purpose, or we might use it with older, more developed children, who are closer to becoming independent readers.

Rhythm stories that children can understand, but that are beyond their rhythm reading ability, provide the notational equivalent of immersion in meter. They serve beginning readers well, as they expose them to notation with sufficient difficulty that it invites listening and watching more than it does reading or trying to "figure out" the notation. This type of rhythm story also serves well in classes with accompanying adults. It communicates to those who are familiar with traditional notation the connection between what they have experienced in class with their children and what they know in notation. Syllables are spelled out in the prep to serve as a reference as to how the meter is represented visually. Syllables are the intermediary between the musical mind and notation and are relevant only in sound.

Verbalization about the features of print in an example like Figure 6.2 would get in the way of the musical mind. Reading is a discovery process. We guide children by the music reading materials we offer so they can make discoveries about music in print and revise their hypotheses about how notation works as they develop. We lead them to see notation as a mirror of the musical mind, which leads them to develop hypotheses and develop strategies for dealing with notation. We then deliberately challenge those hypotheses, causing children to revise them and create better strategies as they discover more and more about the features of music in print that carry meaning.

Figure 6.3, for example, offers an easier example than that of Figure 6.2, guiding children's discovery that the relationship of macro and micro beats in print mirrors the relationship between macro beats and micro beats in the musical mind. Figure 6.2 presents beamed micro beats in relation to macro beats, the most immediate "picture" of the musical mind's rhythm knowing, which leads them to look for the relationship in print between macro and micro beats. Beginning readers might form the hypotheses from the example in Figure 6.3, or even 6.1, that the figure that we know as two eighth notes and a quarter note is always "du de du." The example in Figure 6.2 might confirm that hypothesis in the first half, but it challenges it in the second half, directing children to look for additional clues and develop new hypotheses that serve every example.

Duple Meter

Figure 6.3 Rhythm Story, Duple (for discovery)

We go through the same process that we did with Figures 6.1 and 6.2, presenting the visual cue with the rhythm prep, complete with two silent beats, and then reading the Duple story to the children on syllables. We use a pointer throughout and move directly from the first narrative to the second without losing a beat, sustaining the tempo. We present the second visual cue with another prep, speaking in rhythm "and du de du still looks like this." We point in rhythm on macro beats, with a gentle flick of the wrist for micro beats, whatever the melodic rhythm.

The familiarity of all of the rhythm patterns in Figure 6.3 in sound and syllables and their predictability enable the beginning reader. We read the Duple story to the children and then we might ask that the class read it with us. They will, of course, follow our lead and feel like they have read the page with us. They are, however, in the process, noticing that macro and micro beats are represented differently in print. The beaming of micro beats in particular, and even the bar lines in this example, help to group beats visually the way the musical mind groups beats aurally, so the musical mind sees its own reflection in print, facilitating reading. The example draws children's attention to visual relationships that correspond to beat relationships they know in sound, leading them to easily read the examples with us, without any verbalization about the features of print. The notation itself, through syllables, communicates with the musical mind.

We know that the musical mind processes beats in relation to each other rather than individual beats. Reading the rhythm story to the children, while pulsing the pointer on macro beats and flicking the wrist on micro beats, leads the musical mind to see the notation as a pictorial representation of rhythm knowing. The narrative naturally leads children to the features of print that carry rhythm meaning—beats in relation to each other. The narrative helps children attend to the differentiation between macro and micro beats in print, without concern for note names, durations, time signatures, or bar lines. The children will easily read the narrative along with us the second time through. The only verbalization we might use following the reading of the example in Figure 6.3 might be to marvel out loud that the children knew how to read the story, wondering how they knew.

"Gee, I wonder how you knew that this is du de du, du de du," (pointing to the notation of the first two measures of the first line) "while this one is du du, du de du" (pointing to the first two measures of the second line). We might then do the same in the second narrative, contrasting its first two measures with the first two measures of the final line, pointing to the notation in rhythm as we pose, "I wonder how you figured out that this one is du de du de, du de du, and this one is du du de, du de du. I just can't fool you, can I?"

Marveling out loud at the children's prowess empowers them as readers, boosting their confidence, enthusiasm, and success as readers, while subtly drawing the children's attention to the contrast between macro and micro beats in print that corresponds to the contrast between macro and micro beats in the musical mind. We are subtly guiding children to scan ahead and behind to pick up cues and to compare those cues with other cues and with their own knowing. Note that we are not verbally pointing out or trying to explain features of print, or asking children what they notice, but rather, we are guiding children to make discoveries that validate or challenge whatever hypotheses they may have already made about how rhythm in print works, and revise them as needed. Our marveling out loud confirms or challenges their hypotheses, gently guiding those who might not yet have recognized the features of print that are the picture of what they know in sound.

Figure 6.4 offers an example that fosters independent rhythm reading with children in kindergarten and older, inviting one-on-one response in reading music, with our scaffolding the children individually as needed.

Figure 6.4   Rhythm Story, Duple (for independent reading)

We read the entire page to the children as if one long story, starting with the meter prep in notation as described in earlier examples, and then pointing macro pulses as we go, with a flick of the wrist for micro beats. The children generally read aloud right along with us. We might, as we did with the example in Figures 6.3, marvel at how they knew that this (pointing to the first two measures of line 1) was "du de du, du de du," and this (pointing to the first two measure of line 4) was "du du, du du," reading both segments in rhythm.

138   Unveiling Artistry in Early Childhood Music

We invite the children to choose a line to read for us. Children's hands generally shoot up, excited to demonstrate their reading ability. The child calls the number of the line he chooses to read and we set up the meter and do the pointing for the line selected, sustaining the meter and tempo for all in attendance and scaffolding each child as needed in reading his chosen line, sometimes reading along with the child.

Every child's individual turn, with our support as needed, challenges or validates hypotheses each child makes about how notation works, and reinforces every child's ability to read music. You might notice some children practicing the line they want to read, or selecting a line another child just read, having practiced silently as the other child read. Some children may be able to read their line independently, while others need our support. The session becomes one of children practicing reading individually, with no pressure, no rights or wrongs, and children enthused to read the line they choose. Our scaffolding as needed assures success for all.

Note the lack of "instruction" in teaching rhythm reading. Well-designed rhythm narratives that we read to the children on syllables speak to the musical mind more than anything we could ever verbalize, leading the children to discover the connection between the notation and the musical mind. Teaching music to very young children prods us to rediscover the joy in learning through discovery. It forces us to let go of our dependence on verbalization. We'd feel foolish trying to "instruct" two-year-olds to read music, drawing their attention to features of print, or explaining mathematical relationships of note durations. We are also forced to let go of the desire to question children or ask them to reflect on their own learning. The musical mind is wordless. A collaboration between the musical mind and the thinking mind creates and revises hypotheses about beat groupings in print relating to beat groupings in the musical mind, but there is no way a three-year-old is going to know that he might be doing that, let alone be able to articulate it.

We would have a hard time trying to explain our own process in reading music or language. We read a sentence like this, having no awareness that we just read the same word twice with two different meanings and pronunciations. We learn from little children the folly of our dependence on teaching music verbally, a lesson that serves us in teaching music to any age.

We can use the four types of rhythm reading materials presented in Figures 6.1-6.4 in the various meters with all levels, with each type of example presented in accordance with the continuum of rhythm difficulty—Duple meter, Triple meter, Unusual Paired meter, and then Unusual Unpaired meter. Substantial time would be spent reading just macro and micro beats before introducing divisions in print, and reading divisions would precede reading elongations, rests, ties, and upbeats in each meter. Experience reading the unusual meters strengthens children's reading of the more usual meters. Reading Duple and Triple meters progresses far more quickly than reading the unusual meters when rhythm patterns move beyond macro and micro beats.

Rhythm reading materials are always easier on the difficulty scale than materials used for rhythm immersion, Rhythm Dialogue Activity, or Macro/Micro Beat Activity with syllables, as reading is a more difficult skill. A rhythm story that serves one group of youngsters as a story for the broader perspective might serve a more developed group for discovery. One that serves a particular group for discovery might serve another for independent reading. Rhythm stories for the broader perspective are always just a little more difficult than the children's assumed reading level. Rhythm stories for discovery are closer to the children's reading level and direct children to greater understanding of features of print at that level.

Two-to-five-year-old children who are not yet in kindergarten are best served by rhythm stories for the broader perspective like that of Figure 6.2, and the little rhythm stories like that of Figure 6.1. Children in kindergarten and beyond, with their focus in school on reading language, are ready for all four types of examples, with each type progressing in difficulty.

Rhythm stories like that in Figure 6.1 present a most delightful option with the youngest children. We read the story through several times in class, with children reading right along with us in successive repetitions, and then provide a durable copy of the rhythm story that each child can hold in his hand and take home, preferably with large print and folded in half so it can be opened like a book.[4] Sending one little "music storybook" home each week, after reading the book to the children in class with attending adults, sends little children on their way to "read" the music storybook at home, and to request that their attending adults read the book to them. The adults are fully prepared to do so from class experience with the little book.

Parents read the weekly music books to their child at home just as they read storybooks to their child, reinforcing all that we are doing in class on the road to developing independent readers. Having the children trade in the previous week's music storybook for the new storybook of the week keeps the single music storybook at home special, while better assuring that the adults are prepared to read it correctly, without the confusion of multiple books and multiple meters. Each little book looks like what attending adults know in sound from class. Technology, of course, provides for us to offer the notation and a recording of our reading the notation for home use, but there is nothing like a book in hand for a little tot with a parent reading it to and with the child. Technology is also not always as effective as a music teacher in pointing to macro beats with greater weight than the flick of the wrist on micro beats.

Let's look now at more advanced examples of rhythm reading materials to accommodate our more developed children on the older end of early childhood. Figure 6.5 offers a more difficult example that invites one-on-one rhythm reading of Triple meter with divisions, with our scaffolding each child as needed. This example could also be used for discovery of the features of print that carry meaning at this level.

Triple Meter

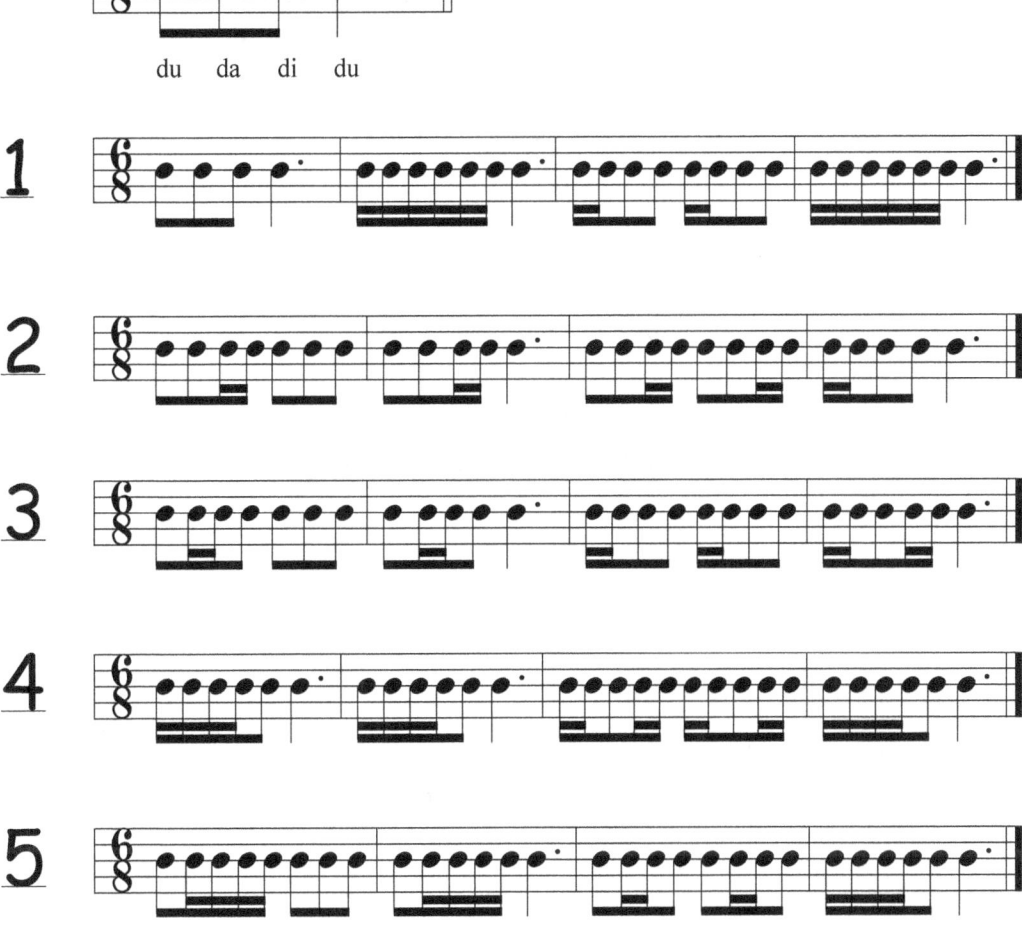

Figure 6.5 Rhythm Story, Triple (for independent reading)

We present Figure 6.5 through the same process described with Figure 6.4, including the rhythm prep and two silent beats, making sure that we speak "Now du da di du, looks like this" in Triple meter, with macro beats falling on "du," "looks," and "this." We read the page to the children on rhythm syllables, inviting them to read with us the second time through. We then pick a couple of contrasting measures, like the last two of line one, and marvel aloud that the children knew that the final figure was "du ta da ta di ta du," while this one was "du ta da di, du ta da di," pointing to each and reading in rhythm, so the children can compare the various figures in notation and become more aware that the figures they know in sound and syllables look different from each other.

Children's gradual discovery of the direct relationship between the more complex notation and the way the music sounds is the first step in their becoming aware of a one-to-one correspondence between individual sounds and notation. The one-to-one correspondence becomes more apparent in tonal notation.

Figure 6.6 offers an example in Triple meter that might eventually be used for the broader picture or for discovery. The notation itself guides children visually to look for relationships between macro and micro beats in print, however they might be represented.

Figure 6.6 Rhythm Story, Triple (for broader picture)

We read the page to the children on rhythm syllables as described with Figure 6.2, setting up the prep for each line both visually and aurally, ("Now du da di du, looks like this"). We maintain one tempo of Triple meter throughout, whether micro beats are represented by eight notes, quarter notes, sixteenth notes, or half notes. This directs the young musical mind to look for the relationship between macro and micro beats in print, however they might be presented. We do all of this without verbalization about rhythm writing styles. The notation, the musical mind's sense of meter, and the children's experience reading easier examples lead them to read the whole page right along with us.

It is the relationship between macro and micro beats in notation that carries rhythm meaning, more than it is time signatures or bar lines. Each of the examples in Figure 6.6 is in Triple meter, which the children know in sound and syllables. Theoretical constructs of time signatures or even different tempos do not change that.

Figure 6.7 moves children a bit further with a Rhythm story for discovery that is notated in two different styles of rhythm writing. We approach it just as we have previous examples.

Triple Meter

Figure 6.7   Rhythm Story, Triple (for discovery)

We read the two narratives to the children on syllables as described earlier, sustaining the tempo throughout, and then invite the children to read them with us. We might then marvel out loud, "Gee, I wonder how you knew that the two rhythm stories were exactly the same, that du da di du, du ta da ta di ta du (pointing to and reading the first two measures of the first narrative) is the same as du da di du, du ta da ta di ta du" (pointing and reading to the first two measures of the second narrative). I just can't fool you." We do this to direct children's attention so they can discover the features of print that carry rhythm meaning—the relationship between macro and micro beats, not to offer explanations or elicit answers from the children.

Figures 6.1-6.7 present rhythm patterns in notation that the children already know in sound and syllables. Each of these rhythm examples directs the collaboration between the young musical mind and the thinking mind in the process of reading rhythm. They present a mirror of how the musical mind processes rhythm. They lead the children to develop concepts of print and then challenge children's assumptions about how notation works. They provide visual clues that guide the process of music reading.

The rhythm reading materials and our approach in reading them to the children guide children to develop reading strategies—comparing what is being read with what was just read and what is ahead, noticing repetitions, and using the musical mind's tendency to predict through its own musicality and experience. The various strategies and hypotheses that children employ in the process are confirmed or challenged by the notation itself as children grow, directing the children to the finer features of print that carry precise rhythm meaning, and leading the children to new hypotheses, more effective strategies, and self-correcting behaviors.[5]

Music Reading—Tonal

Rhythm reading is more immediate for young children than tonal reading, just as rhythm is more immediate for the young musical mind than tonal. Reading rhythm to and with little children develops the readiness for the more complex tonal reading. The features of print that carry meaning rhythmically are very different from those that carry meaning tonally. Success in reading rhythm lays the groundwork for tonal reading.

Examples presented here for tonal reading, like those for rhythm reading, include little tonal narratives that the children can immediately read along with us; those that present the broader picture that are more for children's listening and watching rather than reading; those closer to children's reading level that are for discovery of the conventions of print that carry tonal meaning; and those for independent reading. Simple rhythm facilitates tonal reading just as it serves the musical mind's acquisition of tonal and directs the musical mind to tonal, so tonal reading examples are presented in context with easy rhythm.[6]

Figure 6.8 presents a tonal story that young children can read along with us. We include both tonal and rhythm preps visually for the children. The tonal prep not only sets up the musical mind for the tonality to come, but it also locates the resting tone and fifth on the staff to guide the reading of what is to come. The rhythm prep sets up the musical mind for the meter and tempo aurally, but also offers a picture of how the meter is represented in print.

Dorian Tonality

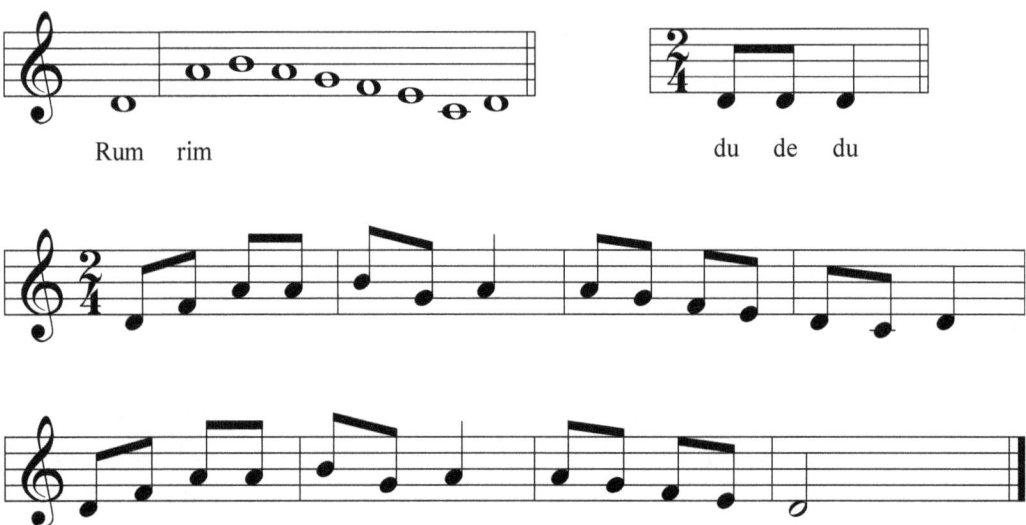

Figure 6.8 Tonal Story, Dorian

"Today we are going to read a tonal story in Dorian tonality" (speaking the statement as we display the story on a large screen for all to see). "And our resting tone is here" (singing the sentence on the resting tone while pointing to the resting tone in the prep, and then singing the resting tone on "rum" while pointing to the resting tone). "Rim re rim ra ri ro ru rum" (pointing to individual pitches of the tonal prep as we sing). "And we're in Duple meter" (singing on the resting tone and pointing to the rhythm prep). "And du de du, looks like this" (singing the rhythm prep on the resting tone, in rhythm, followed by two silent beats).

"Rum ri rim rim, re ra rim, rim ra ri ro, rum ru rum. Rum ri rim rim, re ra rim, rim ra ri ro rum." (We sing the story on tonal syllables, in rhythm, at least twice through, without repeating the preps, pointing to each pitch as we go.)

The notation serves like a picture book of the shape of the melody. Children's familiarity with the tonal narrative both on "too" and on tonal syllables compels the children to "read" aloud right along with us on successive verses, though they may be more tentative than they were with the more immediate rhythm reading examples. Note that we are pointing to pitches rather than pointing to macro beats in tonal reading. The example in Figure 6.8 in hard copy serves well as one of the little music storybooks that little children can take home with them to read and to have parents read to them.[7]

We read to the children more advanced tonal narratives for the broader perspective, just as we did with rhythm. We select material that is within their musical understanding, but that invites children's listening and watching rather than reading. Tonal reading material for the broader perspective is more expansive than rhythm reading material for the broader perspective, as it necessarily includes rhythm. Tonal materials of this type might include narratives in different keys, different meters, and even symbols like repeat signs or crescendos. Figure 6.9 presents a tonal narrative for the broader picture.

Figure 6.9 Tonal Story, Mixolydian (for broader picture)

"Today we are going to read stories in Mixolydian tonality" (speaking the statement as we display the page on a large screen). "And our resting tone is here" (singing the sentence on the resting tone while pointing to the resting tone in the first prep, and then singing the resting tone on "sum" while pointing to the resting tone). "Sim se sim sa si so su sum" (pointing to individual pitches of the tonal prep as we sing). "And we're in Duple meter," (singing on the resting tone and pointing to the rhythm prep). "And du d e du, looks like this" (singing the rhythm prep on the resting tone, in rhythm, followed by two silent beats). We then sing the first story in rhythm twice through on tonal syllables, pointing to each pitch as we go (sim si sum sum sum, su so sum, etc.)

We change keys for the second story, sustaining the tonality, without talking, and speaking on the resting tone. "And now our resting tone is here" (singing the new resting tone on the word "here" as we point to the new resting tone, and then singing and pointing to the tonal prep in the new key). "Sim se sim sa si so su sum" (pointing to individual pitches of the tonal prep in the new key as we sing). (We move the pointer to the rhythm prep) "And now we're in Triple meter, and du da di du, looks like this" (singing the rhythm prep on the new resting tone, in rhythm, followed, by two silent beats). We sing the second story in rhythm twice through on tonal syllables, pointing to each pitch as we go (sum so su, sum sim sim, etc.) (Appendix F includes this more difficult example with syllables in the notation for teacher reference.)

An example like that presented in Figure 6.9 takes the children well beyond their reading level and exposes them to a more expansive view of music notation than they have experienced previously, though it is still within their aural understanding. Reading tonal stories like this to young children serves like reading fairytales to young children for language development, taking them well beyond their little world and providing enrichment aurally, visually, and imaginatively. They understand the narrative in sound, but the complexity of the notation invites listening and watching more than reading along or trying to figure out the features of print, much as a fairytale does with language. An example like this could serve both preschool and primary grade children for the broader experience. It can also serve to jar older children out of some of their preconceived notions about music notation.

Presenting melodies in different keys leads the collaboration between the musical mind and the thinking mind to look for the features of print that carry tonal meaning in the musical mind—relationships between pitches rather than absolutes of lines, spaces, or resting tones. The musical mind processes tonal through the organization of pitches in relation to a resting tone, which remains consistent across tonalities and across keys. Notation that represents what the musical mind knows in sound has to reflect that processing in order for the young musical mind to be able to bring meaning to tonal notation.

Figure 6.10 offers a poignant example of notation representing tonal processing of the musical mind. You may have to remind yourself to suspend your grasp of music theory to engage with the notation as do children who know meters, tonalities, rhythm syllables and tonal syllables in sound, without the encumbrance of music theory. Key signatures are deliberately left out of Figure 6.10. We read this example to the children in various tonalities in two different keys. Children at this point in development, and even accompanying adults, are comfortable shifting from one tonality to another.

Figure 6.10   Tonal Story, all tonalities (for broader picture)

"Today we are going to read a tonal story in Dorian tonality" (speaking the statement as we display the story on a large screen for all to see). "And our resting tone is here" (singing the sentence on the resting tone while pointing to the resting tone in the first prep, and then singing the resting tone on "rum" while pointing to the resting tone). "Rim re rim ra ri ro ru rum" (pointing to individual pitches of the tonal prep as we sing). "And we're in Duple meter" (singing on the resting tone and pointing to the rhythm prep). "And du de du, looks like this" (singing the rhythm prep on the resting tone, in rhythm, followed by two silent beats). "Rim rum, rim rum" (singing in rhythm and on syllables the next two measures, which reinforce the visual location of the resting tone and fifth in relation to each other). We then sing the story on tonal syllables, in rhythm, at least twice through, pointing to each pitch as we go ("Rum ri rim rim, re ra rim, rim ra ri ro, rum ru rum. Rum ri rim rim, re ra rim, rim ra ri ro rum rum").

"And now our resting tone is here" (singing the new resting tone on the word "here" as we point to the new resting tone, sing it on "rum" and point to the tonal prep in the new key). "Rim re rim ra ri ro ru rum" (pointing to individual pitches of the tonal prep in the new key as we sing). "And du de du still looks like this (singing on the resting tone, pointing to the rhythm prep and delivering on the resting tone followed by two silent beats.) "Rim rum, rim rum" (singing the next two measures in rhythm and on syllables, reinforcing the new location of the resting tone and fifth in relation to each other). We sing the second story twice through, in rhythm and on tonal syllables, pointing to each pitch as we go ("Rum ri rim rim, re ra rim, rim ra ri ro, rum ru rum. Rum ri rim rim, re ra rim, rim ra ri ro rum rum").

"And now we're going to read this story in Mixolydian tonality. And our resting tone is here" (going back to the top of the page and singing the new resting tone on the word "here" as we point to the new resting tone, sing it on "sum," and then sing and point to the tonal prep in the new key and new tonality). "Sim se sim sa si so su sum" (pointing to individual pitches of the tonal prep in the new key as we sing in the new tonality). "Sim sum, sim sum" (singing the next two measures in rhythm and on syllables). We sing the story twice through, in Mixolydian tonality, in rhythm, and on tonal syllables, pointing to each pitch as we go ("Sum si sim sim, se sa sim, sim sa si so, sum su sum. Sum si sim sim, se sa sim, sim sa si so, sum sum").

"And now our resting tone is here" (singing the new resting tone of the second example on the word "here," as we point to the new resting tone and then sing it on "sum.") "Sim se sim sa si so su sum" (pointing to individual pitches of the tonal prep in the new key as we sing). "Sim sum, sim sum" (singing the next two measures in rhythm and on syllables). We sing the second story twice through, in rhythm and on tonal syllables, pointing to each pitch as we go ("Sum si sim sim, se sa sim, sim sa si so, sum su sum. Sum si sim sim, se sa sim, sim sa si so, sum sum").

We then go back to the beginning and read the page in yet another tonality, and then another, cycling through a number of tonalities, each with appropriate syllables, alternating tonalities with a major third and those with a minor third. Children often read aloud right along with us, whatever the tonality, as they begin to recognize, without any verbalization from us, the features of print that carry tonal meaning. They are not distracted by the rhythm notation, and they are not distracted as we are by music theory and conventions of notation like key signatures.

The tonal reading experience described with Figure 6.10 provides for the musical mind to see its reflection in notation. The musical mind processes pitches in relation to each other and in relation to a resting tone, using the resting tone and fifth as anchors. It focuses on tonality with the support of the simplest rhythm. Notation can make sense in any tonality, when the musical mind brings its sense of tonality to music in print.

The song architecture in Figure 6.10 spins around and between the resting tone and fifth, which are presented both visually and aurally. The two bars that precede the tonal narrative supports the musical mind and helps locate its anchors in notation. The predictability of the melodic line and its repetition facilitates tonal reading in any tonality, as does the simplicity and predictability of the rhythm, with rhythm anchors aligned with tonal anchors.

The presentation of the melody on the staff with the resting tone on a space in the first example and on a line in the second leads the reader to prioritize relationships between pitches over absolutes of lines or spaces. Singing the narrative in print in different tonalities leads the musical mind to reflect wordlessly on what it knows in sound—that it perceives relationships between pitches the same in every tonality, reinforced by the sameness of syllables across tonalities, yet distinguished by the difference in sound of each tonality, as well as the difference in the consonants in syllables across tonalities.

Reading the example in Figure 6.10 to children, whether preschool or primary grade children, provides for all in attendance to experience the command that the musical mind has over notation. The musical mind knows in sound the characteristic tones of each tonality, sings them in tune when the musical mind is in that tonality, and easily switches from reading the story in one tonality to reading it in different tonalities successively. The experience for primary grade children leads them to revise hypotheses they may have made about absolutes in notation. That experience prepares them for the next example, which draws them closer to the features of print that carry tonal meaning. (Appendix F includes the first example of Figure 6.10 in three different tonalities with key signatures so that you might observe your own process to see how differently you may or may not process this example with key signatures.)

Dorian Tonality

Figure 6.11   Tonal Story, Dorian (for discovery)

Figure 6.11 offers a tonal story for discovering features of print that carry tonal meaning, as it presents the same melodic line not only in two different keys, but also in two different clefs. They are identical melodies, with the resting tone of one on a space and the other on a line. We go through the same process as in the earlier examples, reading the first half twice through, placing resting tones aurally and visually while maintaining the tonality, and then reading the second half twice through. We sing the whole page in rhythm and on tonal syllables, pointing to each pitch as we go. We sing both examples in our own range.

The first two bars of Figure 6.11, being much the same as the opening bars of Figure 6.10, serve beginning readers much as stories in language with repeated words or phrases. The third and fourth bars in example 6.11 being quite different from those of Figure 6.10, however, make children attend more closely to the notation of Figure 6.11. Their musical minds may be predicting the melody from Figure 6.10, while the notation indicates something different—drawing children's attention to note heads, and perhaps leading them to revise their hypotheses about how tonal notation works. Our reading the story to them and with them guides their process of discovery.

The example in Figure 6.11, like that in Figure 6.10, once again reflects the processing of the musical mind, focusing the reader on relationships between pitches. The musical mind processes melody the same way, whatever the key, whatever the clef. The child with a well-bred musical mind who sees a reflection of the processing of the musical mind in print can read in any key, any tonality, and any clef, without being distracted by extraneous notational markings and theoretical aspects.

The features of print that we assume to be so important for tonal reading, like clefs and key signatures, do not reflect the processing of the musical mind, but rather, notational conventions in relation to music theory. The new clef for the children in the second example of Figure 6.11, plus the amount of ink used with all the sharps at the beginning of each line, leads the novice reader to think they are of greatest importance in reading, just as emerging readers in language think long words are more important than short ones. Drawing attention to the features of notation that are processed by the thinking mind rather than the musical mind distracts the musical mind. Theoretical considerations are a much later development, including note names and durations.

The tonal story in Figure 6.11 could be used for discovery, with our marveling out loud, wondering how the children knew that these two little stories were the same melody, even though the resting tone of the first one is on a space and the second on a line, and even though the second has all these other marks on it. Proud children beam when they feel they have outsmarted the teacher, or gone beyond the teacher's expectations of their ability. We are in the process of drawing subtle attention to the features of print that carry tonal meaning, reinforcing the musical mind's processing of pitches in relation to the resting tone and the fifth, and helping the musical mind to see its reflection in print.

Dorian Tonality

Figure 6.12   Tonal Story, Dorian (for independent reading)

Figure 6.12 offers a tonal story for independent reading with children in kindergarten and older, designed much like that of the earlier rhythm examples for reading independence. We start with the tonal and rhythm prep as described in earlier tonal reading examples, and then read the whole page to the children, singing in rhythm on tonal syllables while pointing to each pitch. We invite the children to read the page with us as we go through it again, and then invite children to choose a line to read. We read with each child, scaffolding their reading as needed. The consistency of rhythm in this example helps children attend to tonal notation. Children tend to practice silently as each individual reads, as they try to figure out the various lines.

Figure 6.12, more than previous examples, directs children's attention to the one-to-one correspondence between pitches and notation. Some begin to realize that tonal notation is even more a picture of what they know in sound than rhythm notation, with each melody having its own shape on a background of lines. They begin to notice that each line and space of that background has meaning, though they may not yet have discovered their significance. Witnessing kindergarten and first grade children read tonal so effortlessly sheds greater light on tonal processing of the young musical mind, mirrored in notation and reflected in the tonal syllables that give voice to tonal knowing.

Note the difference in recommendations for reading rhythm and reading tonal to children. We point to macro beats when reading rhythm, using the flick of the wrist for micro beats. We point to individual pitches while reading tonal. This and notation itself reflect the difference between the way the musical mind processes rhythm and tonal. Developing a sense of meter creates an aural structure that processes rhythm linearly in time, which is reflected in rhythm notation. Developing a sense of tonality creates an aural structure that processes tonal more spatially, which is reflected in tonal notation.

Every music reading experience we provide for young children has to support the musical mind both aurally and visually through song architecture. There will always be more difficult rhythm and tonal stories to read to children for the broader picture, for discovery, and for independence. We can take more developed children into reading multiple parts, stylistic considerations, and other dimensions beyond the scope of this book. (Developmental music reading materials can be found in the Come Children Sing Institute *Music Reading Library.*[8])

Learning to read music with rhythm and tonal syllables that mirror the musical mind strengthens children's developing sense of meter and sense of tonality. Tonal and rhythm reading examples that provide for the musical mind to *see* its reflection in notation serve to build a direct link between the musical mind and notation. A solid link becomes a sturdy bridge which can then support the use of any syllable system that might be encountered in future instrumental or choral settings.

We learn a great deal about the process of music reading by teaching very young children and by teaching to the wordless musical mind. The young musical mind speaks to us most directly about music reading through music writing, which offers a picture of what is going on inside.

Music Writing—Rhythm

Very young children begin to write music the same way they start to read music. They watch us writing music, imitate music writing behaviors, and then "read" what they have written. Little children's initial attempts to write music or language may initially look like just marks on a page. The child, however, is very quick to "read" what he "wrote." Looking more closely at a child's deliberate marks on the page in writing music can reveal the features of print that the child feels carries rhythm or tonal meaning.

We initiate music writing with a demonstration. We project staff paper on a screen that all can see and proceed to write music, narrating our process out loud as we engage in music writing. We begin with rhythm writing, as it is more accessible than tonal writing. We select a line on the staff on which to consistently write rhythm, so as not to distract children with features of print that carry tonal meaning. We could write rhythm on any paper, but the children are accustomed to our reading music on a staff, so to the children, staff paper indicates that we are writing music.

"Today we are going to write music. Let's see, I think I will write a story in Duple meter, and make du de du, look like this." (We write the rhythm prep, initially with two eighth notes and a quarter note for the greatest clarity.) "I think I'll write du de du (narrating/chanting while writing), du de du, du de du de, du de du." (We sketch out the notes for four bars of a very familiar chant in Duple meter, using only macro and micro beats, beaming eighth notes together, and then adding bar lines to include two macro beats in a measure.)

"Now let's see, what did I write? (We read in rhythm the four measures we just wrote, pointing as usual when reading a line of rhythm to children.) "I wrote, du de du, du de du, du de du de, du de du. Now I'm going to write du de du de, du du, du du de, du de du." (We sketch out the notes for bars five through eight, narrating and chanting while writing, beaming eighth notes for the greatest ease in reading, and then filling in bar lines.) "Let's see, what did I write this time?" (We read in rhythm the four measures we just wrote, pointing as usual.) "I wrote du de du de, du du, du du de, du de du." (We can then add a time signature.) "Let's read my Duple story together." (We lead the class in reading the two lines we have written, reading in rhythm and on syllables just as we do with rhythm reading activities. We start with our prep and then read what we have written, pointing to macro beats with a flick of the wrist on micro beats.)

The children have just witnessed our process of writing music. They have seen that it is the writer who decides what meter to write, how to represent that meter in print, and what to write in that meter. They have seen, whether or not they have yet noticed, that rhythm cannot easily be written in rhythm, that it takes additional time to create what is being written, but that it can then be read in rhythm. They have seen that a rhythm story that has been handwritten looks very much like rhythm stories they have read but not so perfectly formed as music in print, as the teacher might, for example, use only slashes across lines for note heads.

Rhythm Writing Sample

Establish Duple meter in the basic rhythm writing style.

Sketch rhythm and bar lines for the first 4 bars of an 8 bar chant with macro and micro beats. Read the first 4 bars.

Sketch rhythm and bar lines for the last 4 bars. Read the last 4 bars.

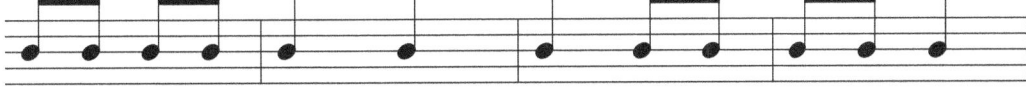

Add time signature to complete the chant. Invite children to read our rhythm story along with us. We point to the notation while reading, as in the earlier rhythm reading examples.

Figure 6.13   Rhythm Writing Demonstration, Duple

Figure 6.13 shows our process with each step notated and written in italics, though the children will see only the first line and the final two lines of notation—the compilation of the process we narrated. We leave our Duple story on the screen during the next segment of this music writing experience. We continue to chant in Duple meter on syllables to keep the meter going in the musical minds of the children, while passing out wide-space staff paper and pencils, plus a firm surface to write on.

"Now we can all write a story in Duple meter. You might write du de du, du de du, (chanted in rhythm), or you might write du de du de, du de du, or you might write du du, du, du." (We chant familiar rhythm patterns with just macro and micro beats in Duple meter, without additional talking, so the meter dominates the experience of the children's rhythm writing. The Duple story on screen that we had written serves as reference for the little composers as they write, while we continue to chant occasional rhythm patterns with just macro and micro beats in Duple meter.)

Each child "reads" his story to the teacher upon completion, with the teacher scaffolding each child's reading as needed to help the child deliver what he is attempting to read. This might include setting up the meter, helping a child deliver what he has actually written, or simply helping the child recite the most familiar Duple narrative, which may be what he was trying to write. The child comes away feeling that he expressed his own music in writing. The child has also created a graphic account of what he feels are the features of print that carry rhythm meaning.

Notice that throughout the writing experience, there was no attempt to teach notational conventions, but rather, to demonstrate and then invite the children to write their own music. The children's writing teaches us more about the knowing of the young musical mind and the process of children transferring that knowing to print. It shows us what features of print the children attend to—those they think carry meaning, and it guides us in our ongoing demonstrations of music writing. We don't "instruct" how to draw music notes, but rather, simply demonstrate music writing to stimulate children's music writing. We witness in the process how children who have had music read to them, as addressed in this chapter, begin to bring meaning to print, attend more and more to the conventions of print over time when being read to, and progress accordingly in writing music.

Little children are very deliberate about their music writing. They most often write whatever their own musical mind has to say rather than copying whatever the teacher wrote. Their writing may or may not resemble the conventions of notation. They make up their own spellings, so to speak, just as they do with language, and read what they have written with the authority of a musician.[9]

A dedicated puppet on a stand for the children to read their stories to can be very effective, with the teacher scaffolding the child's reading to the puppet as needed. The teacher defines the "Little Ole Song Keeper" as the one who keeps all the songs that the children write, as he just loves the music they write. The beloved puppet's presence assures acceptance and appreciation of all music writing of the children. The teacher might set up a special mailbox for the Little Ole Song Keeper and give each child a piece of staff paper to take home, making more available online, and encouraging children to write music at home and bring what they write to the next class to mail to the Little Ole Song Keeper. The children read what they have written to the teacher before mailing it to the Little Ole Song Keeper, or they read it directly to the puppet before mailing it for the Little Ole Song Keeper to keep.

A child reading his own music generally delivers whatever is on his musical mind at the time. He may, for example, have written something at home in Triple meter, but reads it to the Little Ole Song Keeper in Duple meter. Children's music writing, over time, creates a picture of the developmental process. The more children engage with music reading and writing as described in this chapter, the more they begin to use the conventions of notation in their own writing.

A two-year-old's rhythm writing may initially look like scribbles, but as children grow they demonstrate awareness that vertical lines and beaming has meaning in print, and they may or may not yet attend to note heads. Three- and four-year-olds document through their rhythm writing, and their reading of what they have written, the point at which they become aware of the difference in print between meters and between macro beats, micro beats, and divisions. They document when they realize that the dot has significance with the macro beat in triple meter in 6/8 time, when they realize that divisions are represented with double beams, and when they feel that bar lines have significance. They also show through their rhythm writing that bar lines and time signatures are not nearly so important in expressing the musical mind as are stems and beams.

Figure 6.14 (p. 166) shows four-year-old Allison's writing in Duple meter.[10] Notice that she seems to be aware that note heads carry meaning, but only in contrast to beamed groupings. There is no attention yet to bar lines or double beams.

Figure 6.15 (p. 167) offers an example of three-year-old Jeffrey's writing in Triple meter.[11] He wrote this example in class in a writing session in Triple meter as described earlier in Duple meter, beaming micro beats together in contrast to macro beats, and beaming six divisions together in contrast to both macro and micro beats. Jeffrey did not copy the teacher's example, and he read precisely what he wrote in Triple meter to the Little Ole Song Keeper. He shows that he has not yet attended to bar lines, dots with macro beats, nor double beaming for divisions. Compare the precision of his music writing on the staff with the more typical three-year-old writing of his name. Only the "L" in his attempt to write his last name bears any resemblance to the five letters in his last name. Both Allison (Figure 6.14) and Jeffrey (Figure 6.15) demonstrate that the horizontal lines of the staff don't carry rhythm meaning. (Additional examples of children's rhythm writing documenting the developmental process can be found in *Letters on Music Learning*.)[12]

We present rhythm writing to young children in an ongoing manner, introducing Duple meter before Triple meter, and Triple meter before the unusual meters. We use only macro and micro beats initially, slowly moving into divisions, first in Duple meter. Children learn to read rhythm patterns before they learn to write the same patterns, just as their ability to read language is greater than their ability to write language. You may find that children writing music at home and reading it to us in the next class document their discoveries during the week. A child might, for example, write part of a page in Duple meter and part in Triple meter and correctly switch meters when reading it whether or not the patterns are precisely written or precisely read. That child demonstrates that he has cracked the code of depicting the differences between the meters in print.

Five-year-old Justin, not yet in kindergarten, wrote the example in Figure 6.16 (p. 168) at home and brought it to the next class.[13] He read the whole page precisely in Combined meter, complete with divisions and the appropriate rhythm syllables, with the first two measures as "du de, du da di." His mother, however, reported privately that when Justin wrote his rhythm story at home, he read the whole page in Unusual Paired meter. The mother, who was not a musician, didn't know the names of the different meters, but knew the difference in sound and in syllables from attending classes with her son, and offered the syllables "du be du ba bi" to explain his reading at home. Justin heard Unusual Paired meter a while later and when asked to read his composition to the Little Ole Song Keeper at that time, he read it precisely in Unusual Paired meter with appropriate syllables even on divisions.

The mother also volunteered that Justin was not at all interested in reading or writing language. Yet he wrote paired macro beats, with one divided into two micro beats and the other into three, complete with double beamed divisions, and read his composition in each of the two meters that have paired macro beats with one divided into two and the other into three micro beats. Justin had discovered the one-to-one correspondence between rhythm notation and sound, whatever the meter.

Music Writing—Tonal

Substantial experience in writing rhythm develops young children's readiness for writing tonal. The children know that their own music can be represented in print, and that they can read what they write. They have witnessed that rhythm is in the musical mind, that the act of writing rhythm is not done in rhythm, but that what is written can be read in rhythm. They know that staff paper serves music writing. Children at this point of development have also had substantial experience with tonal stories in print read to them. They now have the readiness to move into tonal writing. The teacher displays a piece of staff paper on screen for all to see and adds a treble clef.

"Today I'm going to write a story in Dorian Tonality. Let's see, I think I'll put my resting tone here. (We visually mark the selected line or space for the resting tone while singing the resting tone on the word "here" and then on "rum.") "Rim re rim ra ri ro ru rum." (We mark the pitches of the visual tonal prep using just note heads while singing the prep.)

"I think I'll write in Duple meter, and I'll make du de du, look like this." (Singing on the resting tone and notating the meter prep on the chosen line or space of the resting tone. We deliberately use only macro beats and beamed micro beats in our initial writing demonstrations, with macro beats aligning with the resting tone and fifth, and a melodic contour that supports the young musical mind. We also use Duple meter for greatest ease in attending to tonal writing. Our Dorian story should sound familiar to the children even though we create it "spontaneously" in writing.)

"I think I'll write rum ri rim rim re ra rim, rim ra ri ro rum ru rum." (We mark only note heads for each pitch we sing while singing in rhythm. We then go back and read what we just wrote, singing on the resting tone anything that we might otherwise speak.) "Now let's see, I wrote, rum ri rim rim re ra rim, rim ra ri ro, rum ru rum." (We sing on tonal syllables what we have just written, singing in rhythm and making sure we wrote what we intended.) "And I wanted du de du de, du de du, du de du de, du de du" (singing our melody this time on rhythm syllables, adding stems, beaming micro beats, and adding bar lines while singing, slowing down or breaking the meter to accommodate the writing.) "Now let's see what I have written." (We sing the line of music we have just written, now on tonal syllables and in rhythm, pointing as we've done with tonal reading.)

"Now I think I'll write rim rim re ra, rim ri rum ro, ri ro rum ru, rum rum." (We mark only note heads while singing this line of our story in rhythm and continue to sing on the resting tone anything that we might have to say.) "Let's see, I wrote, rim rim re ra, rim ri rum ro, ri ro rum ru, rum rum." (We sing on tonal syllables the second line of our composition, singing in rhythm while checking to make sure we wrote what we intended.) "And I wanted du de du de, du de du de, du de du de, du du." (We sing our melody this time on rhythm syllables, adding stems, beaming micro beats, and adding bar lines while singing, slowing down or breaking the meter to accommodate the writing. We can then add a key signature if needed and desired, or we can wait until a later point in time to add a key signature to our demonstrations.) "Now let's see what I have written." (We sing our entire story on tonal syllables in rhythm to make sure the notation came out just as intended, pointing to each pitch as we do with tonal reading.)

"Now let's read my story together. My resting tone is here" (singing the resting tone as before). "Rim re rim ra ri ro ru rum" (pointing to the pitches of the tonal prep while singing.) The children join us in reading the story we have just written, as we point to each note and sing on tonal syllables just as we have in tonal reading activities. Children's familiarity with what we have written will aid them in reading our story with us and in better understanding our demo.

Tonal Writing Sample

Establish resting tone and tonality sequence for Dorian tonality.
Establish Duple meter on the resting tone in the basic rhythm writing style.

Sketch tonal for the first 4 bars of an 8 bar song with macro and micro beats while singing.
Read in rhythm with tonal syllables.

Sketch in rhythm and bar lines for the first 4 bars (singing rhythm syllables).
Read the first 4 bars (singing tonal syllables).

Sketch tonal for the last 4 bars. Read in rhythm with tonal syllables.

Sketch in rhythm and bar lines for the last 4 bars (singing rhythm syllables).
Read the last 4 bars (singing tonal syllables).

Add time signature. (Add key signature if needed and desired.)
Invite children to read our tonal story along with us.

Figure 6.17 Tonal Writing Demonstration, Dorian

Figure 6.17 shows our process, with each step notated and written in italics, though the children will see only the first line with the preps and the final two lines of notation—the compilation of the process we narrated. We leave our Dorian story on the screen during the next segment of this music writing activity for reference, though the children may locate their resting tone on a different line or space. We keep singing simple lines in Dorian tonality and Duple meter on tonal syllables, keeping the tonality and meter alive in the musical minds of the children, while passing out wide-space staff paper and pencils, plus a firm surface to write on.

> "Now we can all write a Dorian story in Duple meter. You might write rim ri rum, or ru ro rum, or maybe rim rum, or rim re rim, or rim ra ri ro rum." (We keep singing the familiar short tonal segments so the children continue to hear the tonality and meter while writing, without verbalization that interrupts the musical mind. We sing on the resting tone anything we might have to say. The tonality has to dominate the experience of children's tonal writing.)

Each child writes and then "reads" his own Dorian story to us or to the Little Ole Song Keeper upon completion. We scaffold each child's reading as needed to help the child deliver what we think he is trying to deliver. This might include setting up the tonality or setting up the meter on the resting tone, helping a child deliver what he has written, or simply singing familiar tonal segments, which may be what the child was trying to write. We might position the Little Ole Song Keeper away from the rest of the class so as not to interrupt the musical mind of the little composers while an individual child reads his composition. Each child puts his song in the mail box after reading his composition, knowing that the Little Ole Song Keeper loves all the songs that the children write. Each child feels the satisfaction of having expressed his own music in writing as well as pleasing the Song Keeper, who collects each child's documentation of the features of print they think carries tonal meaning.

Children reading their own writing will initially sing whatever is on their musical mind, which may or may not relate to their writing, until they begin to attend more to the conventions of music in print. Keeping the tonality alive in the children's musical minds while they are writing feeds children's writing. It keeps the tonality foremost in the musical mind, so children will compose in that tonality and most often "read" what they have written in that tonality.

Children learn a great deal by observing our writing music, as we narrate our own process through successive demonstrations. They see that we can locate the resting tone on a line or on a space. They observe that it is the writer who decides the tonality and meter, where the resting tone is placed, and how the meter is to be represented in print. They observe that the writer decides what to write in the chosen tonality and meter. They observe that we cannot write music in rhythm; that we come closer to writing tonal in rhythm than we do writing rhythm in rhythm; and that music notation includes both tonal and rhythm. They discover that they can read our handwritten stories even if we write slashes on lines and spaces for note heads, beams that aren't perfectly formed, and bar lines and clefs that don't look exactly like the printed stories we have been reading.

The process of writing tonal is much more complex than that of writing rhythm. Children become aware that the lines and spaces of a staff carry significance and that the positioning of note heads is important. They also become aware that tonal and rhythm are notated differently and perhaps separately, but that music notation generally includes both.

Discovering the difference in print between tonal notation and rhythm notation is a big step for young children. Some might document this new discovery by writing multiple pages at home, several pages with just rhythm writing and several with just tonal writing.

Figure 6.18 (p. 169) presents an example of the music five-year-old Kelsey wrote at home without staff paper.[14] Kelsey documented her new discovery of the difference between rhythm writing and tonal writing, and articulated that new awareness by referring to her rhythm notation as "du da di dus," and her tonal notation as "rims and rums."

Figure 6.19 (p. 170) presents one example from a volume of pages that kindergartner David delivered to the mailbox of the Song Keeper.[15] He seemed compelled to work out in print his discovery that the placement of note heads on the staff meant something different than note heads with stems and beams. He wrote a few pages of rhythm and many with only circles on a staff, seemingly exploring the contrast between rhythm notation and tonal notation. The example in Figure 6.19 documents David's apparent conclusion that rhythm and tonal notation are different from each other—that rhythm and tonal knowing are represented differently.

The more children engage with reading and writing tonal as described here, the more they attend to the conventions of print. They become aware that the placement of pitches on the staff has significance, that there is a one-to-one correspondence between note heads and pitch. They also begin to tune in to the shape of the melody—the melodic contour—noticing its relation in print to the resting tone and fifth and the placement of pitches in relation to each other. They notice in print the characteristics of tonal that have served aurally to support tonality in the musical mind.

Figure 6.20 (p. 171) presents seven-year-old Hal's developing notions of print.[16] The teacher sang a four-bar melody to children in second grade and older, writing the first two bars as in the tonal writing example of Figure 6.17 (p. 164). She asked the children to copy those two bars and then complete writing her melody, which she sang but did not write. She kept the tonality going, singing her melody several times. The last two bars of her melody consisted of a descending passage of micro beats from the fifth to the resting tone, with the final measure going from the resting tone to the seventh on two micro beats, followed by the resting tone on a macro beat. The melodic line was familiar to the children with and without tonal syllables.

Hal's writing of measures three and four demonstrates a sense of melodic contour, a sense of direction to and from the resting tone, and a sense of placement of pitches in relation to each other. He shows developing awareness of the one-to-one correspondence of pitch to line or space but without precision. Hal also shows some awareness of rhythm writing, whether or not it is precise, and includes bar lines. This experience would lead Hal to attend differently to the lines and spaces in the next music reading activity, stimulating greater attention to note heads in relation to staff lines. We can design our music writing demonstrations, followed by children's music writing, to explore what we as teachers are trying to understand about the young musical mind's process as children develop.

Children's Notation

Figure 6.14 Allison—4 years, 6 months (actual drawing width 7.2 inchs).

Figure 6.15 Jeffrey—3 years, 8 months

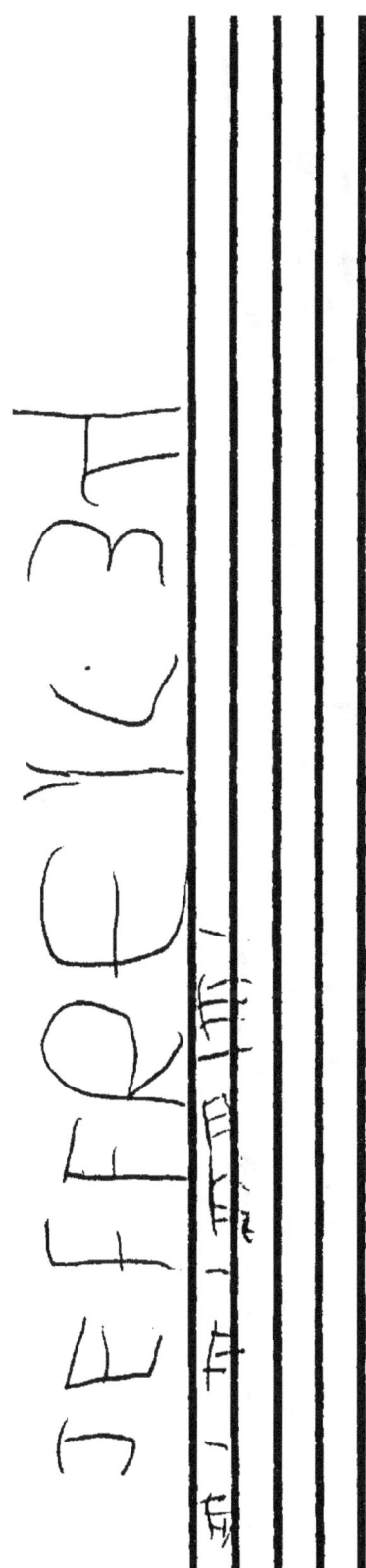

Reveling in Music Reading and Writing 167

Figure 6.16 Justin—5 years, 6 months

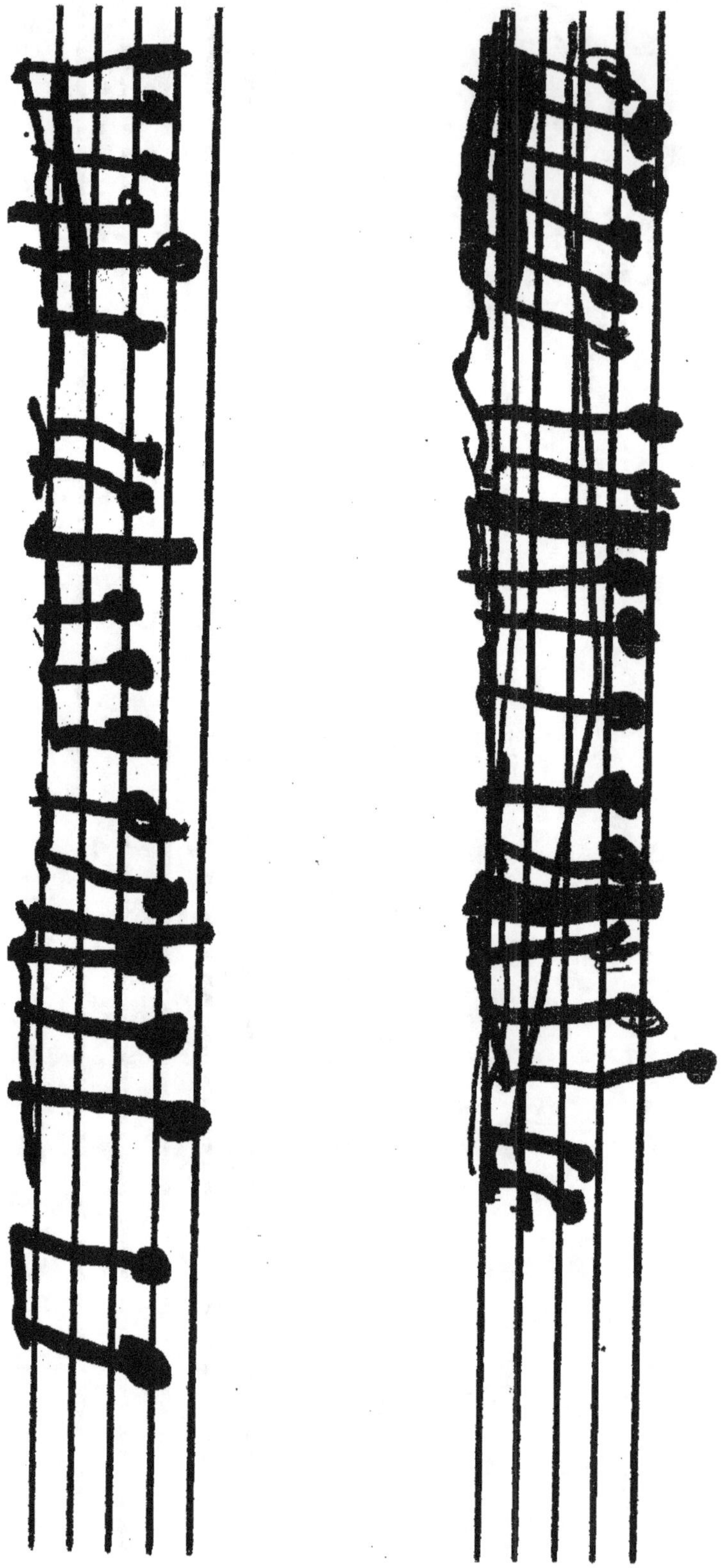

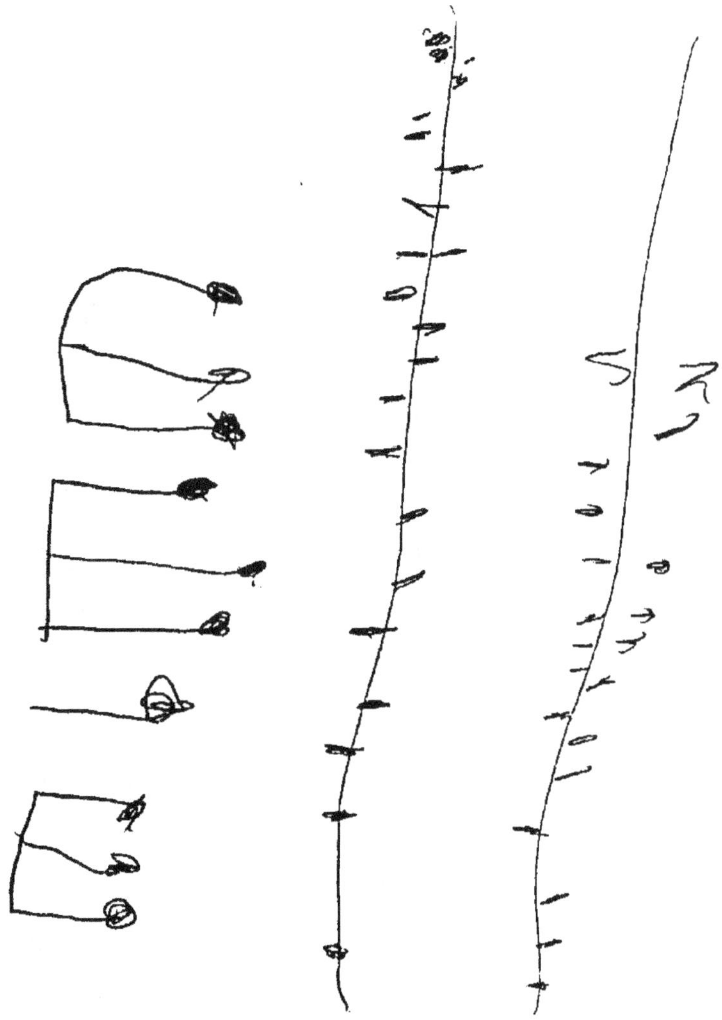

Figure 6.18   Kelsey—5 years, 9 months

Reveling in Music Reading and Writing   169

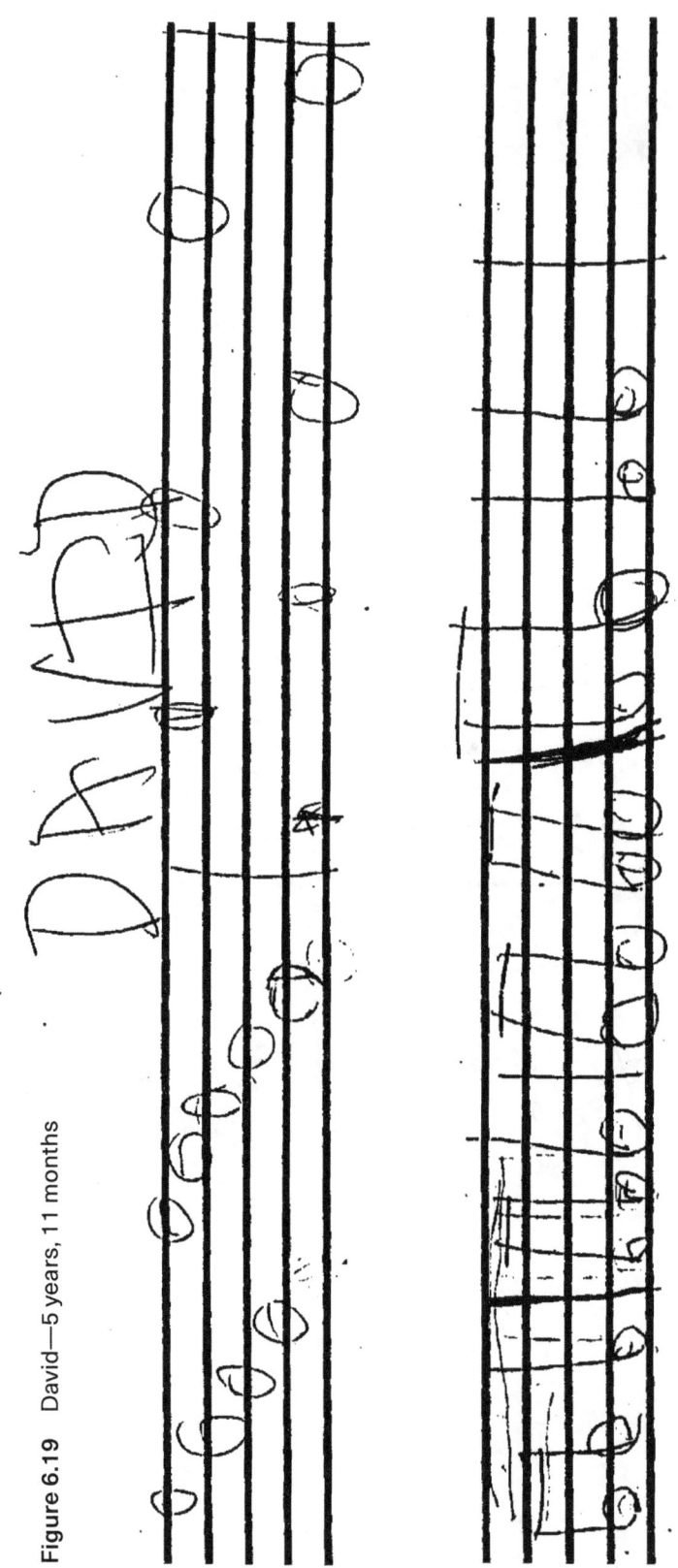

Figure 6.19 David—5 years, 11 months

170 Unveiling Artistry in Early Childhood Music

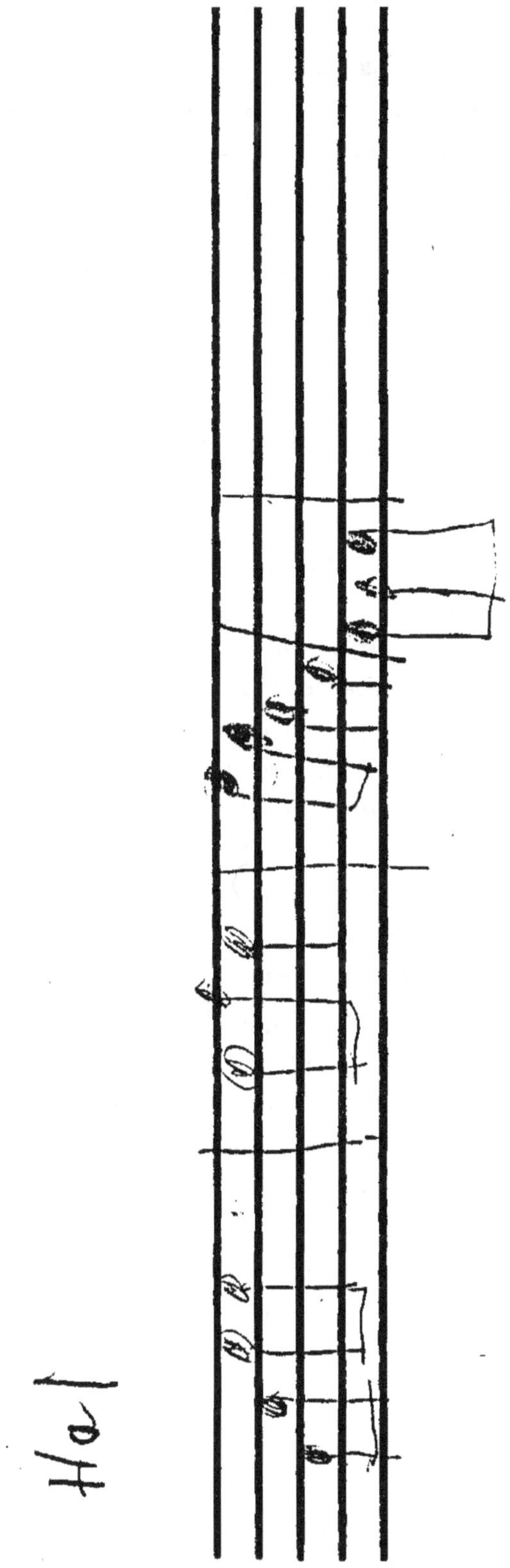

Figure 6.20 Hal—7 years, 5 months

Progressing, Pacing, and Planning

Learning to read music is an ongoing process of discovery. We set up music reading activities so that children can experience success throughout as they make the necessary discoveries about music in print. We provide reading experience in the context of familiar narratives in the various meters and tonalities, drawing upon context as well as children's musicality to guide their reading. We choose materials to read to and with the children that direct their attention to the features of notation and the problem solving that reveals musical meaning in print.[17] We lead children to discover the many ways in which music notation offers a snapshot of what the musical mind knows in sound.

The musical mind knows that macro beats, micro beats, and divisions function the same across meters, but children have to discover that each meter looks different in print. Beamed, eighth-note micro beats in each meter, contrasted by a single quarter note, with or without a dot, provides the most representative picture of the musical mind's processing of rhythm, helping children to see the direct reflection of their rhythm knowing. The mirror image of rhythm knowing in print makes rhythm reading accessible for young children, helping them to discover "how to read" rhythm. We broaden their experience in the various ways that the relationship between macro and micro beats can be represented through reading examples like that presented in Figure 6.6. Children's catching on to what macro and micro beats look like in one meter in print transfers indirectly to the other meters, as do divisions and more difficult rhythm patterns. Children's experience of our reading a familiar meter to them, when it is represented in print in different ways, helps the young musical mind look for the relationship between macro and micro beats in notation, however they might be represented.

There is a more direct transfer in tonal reading across tonalities because the sameness of melodic function across tonalities is represented in print. Every experience of reading in a tonality therefore directly facilitates reading in every other tonality. The resting tone, fifth, and every pitch in relation to those two anchors function the same across tonalities in the musical mind; and with the same resting tone, they also look the same in print in every tonality, with the exception of the raised seventh in minor tonality. Key signatures, of course, will look different, but the relationship of pitches to each other in print looks the same in every tonality, whatever the key or clef. A resting tone on the first line, for example, defines the location of the fifth (or working tone) as the third line, just as a resting tone on the first space defines the location of the fifth as the third space, whatever the tonality and whatever the key signature. Tonal notation, too, with the simplest rhythm, is a reflection of the musical mind's way of knowing, helping children discover "how to read" tonal.

Standard notation of the raised seventh in Minor tonality can distract young children, as accidentals draw attention to themselves. The other tonalities serve best for children learning how to read tonal. The children can then bring that knowhow to reading minor tonality. Key signatures can also be distracting initially, as they use a lot of ink and take up a lot of space, even though they do not change the relationship of pitches to the resting tone visually, and it is that visual relationship that aligns with melodic function in the musical mind. The more complex conventions of print can be added later.

We cannot rush the process of developing skill with music in print, and we have to make sure that the children have the readiness at every step. It takes a long time for little children to learn to read and write in language what they know so well in sound and use daily, and it takes a long time for them to learn to read and write what the musical mind knows so well in sound and syllables.

Recommendations offered in this book for rolling out content for immersion and one-on-one activities apply equally to content for music reading and music writing. We rotate meters and rotate tonalities in print just as we do aurally, taking into consideration rhythm difficulty and melodic contour, and we read narratives that most support rhythm and tonal acquisition. We cycle through the various meters and the various tonalities in successive classes, featuring just one meter or one tonality in print during a class session, until the children are ready for reading examples like that in Figure 6.9 with different meters or Figure 6.10, with multiple tonalities. We engage children in extensive music reading experience before introducing music writing, and we present rhythm reading before tonal reading and rhythm writing before tonal writing.

Reading music to young children serves to immerse children in music in print, while inviting children to read music elicits one-on-one response. The demonstration of writing music for young children immerses them in the process of music writing, while inviting the children to write music elicits one-on-one response. Reading music feeds the process of writing music, which in turn, feeds the process of reading music.

Music reading and music writing activities can take longer to do in class than some of the other rhythm or tonal activities, and they generate their own kind of energy. Making just one rhythm activity or one tonal activity each week a music reading or writing activity and placing it between activities with full-body movement in a set of RTS serves both music reading and sculpting energy. Reading just one meter or tonality within a class session keeps the musical mind on track and speaks most clearly to the musical mind about music in print.

Planning to do either a music reading activity or a music writing activity in class rather than both is most effective. Music writing sessions necessarily include music reading, as we engage the class in reading what we have written as part of our demo, and the children read what they write in our presence. An activity of music writing can take longer than expected. Our little artists can be so musically developed that we forget just how young they are and how long it takes them to write their own name.

There are many ways to make reading and writing music a regular part of young children's experience with music—if the children have the readiness. We might, for example, in a sixteen-week term with one activity each week devoted to music reading, read rhythm to the children for two to four weeks and then tonal for two to four weeks; or we might alternate rhythm and tonal reading each week after reading rhythm for just a couple of weeks. We might engage the children in reading after several weeks of reading to them, or we might invite them to read along with us in the first couple of weeks. We might engage children in music writing only in the last two weeks of each term, with perhaps rhythm writing at the end of the first term and tonal writing at the end of the second term. There are many options and many variables that influence our choices.

There are also cues we can pick up along the way that can guide our planning. We always look for children's musical response, but we can also look for their enthusiasm for reading and writing music. Little children tune out, shut down, or get antsy only when we do not meet their needs—musical or emotional.

The youngest children bring with them another source of guidance—the comfort and confidence of their accompanying adults in reading the little rhythm and tonal storybooks in class and at home with their children. We are teaching many adults to read music as well as the children. Our reading the weekly rhythm or tonal storybook to the children serves as "rehearsal" for attending adults to read the book to the children at home. Sending home a rhythm story for a number of weeks before sending home a tonal story, even though we may be reading tonal stories in class, develops parents' readiness for tonal reading at home. They have to be able and confident to read at home what we send without our prompting or setting up the meter or tonality.

Children's music writing also guides us, influencing our planning of music reading activities as well as music writing activities. Their graphic accounts tell us where each child is on the path and what they might need to move forward. Children's age, of course, also guides us. The youngest children engage in the discovery process, taking it all in. Children in kindergarten and older, on the other hand, want to figure out how music in print works. We might choose rhythm or tonal stories to read to these children to deliberately disrupt presumed notions about music in print.

We engage these older children in the discovery process with music reading examples that lead them to develop hypotheses about music notation and then to revise those hypotheses as they tune in to the features of print that carry meaning. We choose music reading examples that lead them to scan ahead and behind to pick up cues and to compare those cues with other cues and with their own knowing. The discovery process that is music reading is one of constructing meaning as children develop strategies with music in print. (Additional discussion about music reading and writing at the Come Children Sing Institute can be found in *Letters on Music Learning*.[18] Developmental materials for music reading can be found in the Come Children Sing Institute *Music Reading Library*.[19] Appendix G guides teacher acquisition of rhythm and tonal syllables.)

Expect the unexpected when engaging with young children in music reading and writing. You might be surprised by little children's focus and enthusiasm to read and write music. You might be surprised to witness a little child writing music more easily than they do their own name. You might be surprised when kindergarteners and first graders that you have taught in previous years sight-read a rhythm narrative in Unusual Paired meter in the first month of the school year. There is no end to the brilliance of children's artistry. We just have to shake ourselves out of previously conceived notions about young children's capabilities and rise to the level of children's artistry in order to uncover it.

7
Soaring in Song

We have only begun to uncover the power of song in early childhood music classes. We know that play songs serve in sculpting energy, generating participation, and eliciting joy. We know that art songs for tender ages draw children into the beauty of the art itself while drawing the artistry out of every child. We know that gem songs captivate the musical mind while enchanting children. Song has still greater power with children in kindergarten and beyond, as it becomes the impetus for vocal development, the vehicle for artistic expression, and the inspiration for children's artistry.

Songs that give voice to children's artistry hold the magic to transform our little musicians into a chorus of unison voices with quality sound, artistic expression, and vocal technique. We may not yet see our young singers as choristers, but their musical minds have grown through meters, tonalities, and one-on-one activities and they have engaged with the choral art in an ongoing manner through art songs and gem songs. Physical development has propelled the voices of our children in kindergarten and beyond into vocal instruments. Our young singers are budding choral artists ready to bloom in song.

Taking children into the higher singing range and ensemble singing is an exciting process. Children who reach kindergarten with the appropriate background move into these new dimensions with the musicality and poise of choral artists. They need very few props for playing music or even play songs, as singing beautifully becomes the play for these youngsters. We continue to offer rhythm and tonal input of increasing difficulty in the initial singing range with these long-term students, while adding songs in the higher singing range that compel the musical mind, prompt artistic expression, and enable vocal technique.

Tuneful and rhythmic beginners in kindergarten and beyond still need immersion in the various meters and tonalities in the initial singing range to develop the musical mind. Rhythm and tonal narratives, one-on-one activities, and art songs and gem songs in the initial singing range serve both the musical mind and vocal development. Focusing on the vocal instrument rather than the musical mind might be tempting with older children, particularly beginners, but everything we do to develop the musical mind develops the voice. The well-bred musical mind propels the voice far beyond anything we might do to develop the voice alone. Rhythm knowing fosters rhythmic precision, momentum, and energy in song, while tonal knowing fosters tuneful singing, in-tune singing, and quality sound.

The young musical mind develops most efficiently in the vocal range from middle C (C_4) to the B above, with a tessitura between D and A. This range speaks directly to the musical mind and initiates the musical mind's natural vocal response. The musical mind learns to speak in this range, finding its own voice, so to speak. The natural vocal response in this range, in turn, feeds the musical mind, which grows in the give and take process.

The musical mind directs the voice, so developing the musical mind in the initial singing range develops the voice in the higher range. Kindergarteners with the background described in this book easily navigate the voice break around the B above middle C (B_4), singing in tune without any prompting of head voice. Our long-term students' smooth transition through the voice break up to a ninth above middle C (D_5) assures a quality sound above the voice break, where the child voice rings. The optimal singing range for children's voices is from middle C to G a 12th above (G_5), with a tessitura between E_4 and E_5. Young singers with the appropriate background easily produce the quality sound of a fine children's chorus in this range. The initial singing range serves the development of the musical mind, and then the higher singing range, along with the developed musical mind, serves the development of the vocal instrument.

The higher singing range and ensemble singing add more blocks on top of the musical mind's tower of blocks. The whole structure of macro and micro beats, melodic rhythm, tonal, and text, becomes more tenuous when the higher singing range and ensemble singing are added. We continue to feed the musical mind, accepting, encouraging, and scaffolding children's musical output. We continue to strengthen and broaden the foundation of rhythm and tonal with all levels of development, keeping the various meters and tonalities alive in the musical mind and including contrasting meters and contrasting tonalities in every class. We continue to gradually increase the difficulty of rhythm content, tonal content, and songs to challenge the musical mind in an ongoing manner throughout childhood.

We can plan lessons for children in kindergarten and older as classroom music, as a choral rehearsal, or as a mix of the two—sustaining sets of rhythm activity, tonal activity, and song (RTS) in each context, whether beginners or long-term students. We might place rhythm and tonal activities with little art songs at the beginning of the class as warm-ups or we might intersperse them throughout the class. Songs worthy of children's artistry take on a greater role at this point, as songs become the stimulus for vocal development, ensemble development, and children's artistry.

We lead our choristers into the higher singing range and ensemble singing through song and movement, using our voices for singing rather than talking about it. Our singing and movement serve as models and scaffold our young choristers' singing and movement as they grow as independent singers and as an ensemble.

Sculpting energy takes on new meaning in leading a group of singers, as unison singing in ensemble necessitates both musical energy and physical energy from every child—and from the teacher. We have to make music come alive in order for children's artistry to come alive in vocal ensemble. Children's artistry finds sheer musicality irresistible, but it can easily withdraw, masked by an ensemble of voices. Songs that do not compel the musical mind as well as songs that are beyond its musical maturity can shut down children's artistry. Well-meaning comments that diminish children's efforts can deflate children's artistry, as can our own lack of energy. Leading singers in making exciting music, whether it's with professionals or kindergarteners, demands energy.

Our own vibrant energy and musicality ignites the life force of children and scaffolds their collective vibrant energy and musicality in making exciting music together. Add to that well-bred musical minds; and then add songs that compel the musical mind at children's level of development, prompt artistic expression appropriate to children's age and musical maturity, and enable vocal technique for that expression—and young voices soar.

Moving Forward

We continue to engage singers in kindergarten and beyond in flowing movement, macro/micro beat movement, and movement with the energy of the line. Adding tonguing as needed with macro/micro beat movement helps to secure meter. Children who have reached the primary grades are physically ready to leap into more difficult macro/micro beat movement.

> Start with a rhythm prep and easy rhythm narrative in Duple meter with children standing and swaying macro beats with knee-bouncing micro beats. Move into leaping into macro beats while lively stepping micro beats. The thrust of the body weight on macro beats with regular body weight on micro beats more powerfully activates and embodies the musical mind's developing sense of meter, leading to greater mastery of meter.

The difficulty of the various meters increases the difficulty of this "fancy footwork," with success in Duple meter leading to success in the more difficult Triple meter, with the unusual meters offering the most exciting challenge. Children delight when getting their fancy footwork in sync with the more difficult meters, much as they do when navigating a jump rope with peers. Using this fancy footwork with a rhythm narrative in a different meter in each class session makes a wonderful warm-up for singers of all ages, drawing all into happily practicing meter while fusing the musical mind and body.

We have previously engaged children in movement to develop the musical mind, generate energy, and communicate musicality, and have just added movement for greater mastery of meter. Movement now takes on the additional role of propelling vocal development. *Musical movement mentors the voice as the instrument of the musical mind when singers are moving and singing simultaneously.*

The body's sheer musicality in movement evokes the same musicality in the voice, despite a lack of training in vocal technique. Movement offers a tangible means for our young singers to connect with musical nuance and an immediate way for singers to deliver musical nuance with the voice.

Singing with movement throughout rehearsal serves all dimensions of vocal development, as vocal delivery mirrors body movement. Overt movement in rehearsal leaves an imprint on the body, which remembers the physical feel of building a line, delivering crisp articulation, or shifting musical energy with changing meters. That feel propels the voice even when movement might be more covert.

We have traditionally engaged in movement as conductors while our children sing, but our singers grow far more when they are engaged in musical movement while they sing. We can apply movement to every dimension of the choral art, communicating and eliciting musical delivery from our singers. We can apply movement differently in every song we choose and in every rehearsal, as each song offers its own kind of musical expression and each rehearsal determines what needs to be rehearsed. We might apply macro/micro beat movement while rehearsing a song, propelling momentum with appropriate weight distribution between macro and micro beats. We might engage children in movement with the energy of the line to create greater drama in the building of a line, or to articulate text with arms and hands to improve vocal delivery. We might have children literally step into a line, create a crescendo with outstretched arms or forward motion, or "place" pitches with arms and hands while singing. We can apply movement to any aspect of singing and the voice will do whatever the body does.

Movement while singing also provides a visual indicator of each child's musical grasp of a song. A child may sing tunefully while their movement demonstrates a lack of security with the meter. A child's movement might show a lack of energy to power the voice, a lack of awareness of the energy of the line, or a lack of crisp articulation. Children's movement helps us to better understand the musical needs of each child and of the ensemble, guiding us in rehearsal and in planning lessons.

Movement is a powerful tool with singers. Motionless singers are unmusical singers. Choristers engaged in musical movement make music come alive. Musical movement propels all singers to greater artistry.

Choristers All

The choice of songs in the development of children's artistry is critical. Song itself directs the musical mind and the voice. We have seen how song architecture impacts the musical mind. Rhythm and tonal difficulty, tonality and meter presentation, and the alignment between rhythm, tonal and text all affect the musical mind, as does melodic contour and vocal placement. Song architecture also impacts vocal development, as it guides artistic expression and summons vocal technique. Song architecture that supports the musical mind, prompts artistic expression, and propels vocal technique enables children's artistry at every level.

Where Are My Roses?

Figure 7.1 Aeolian, Triple

Where Are My Roses? (Figure 7.1), in Aeolian tonality and Triple meter, gently moves children with a substantial background into the higher singing range without prompts for a singing voice, head tone, or intonation. Kindergarteners turn into choral artists in front of our own eyes, despite the irrelevance of parsley in the text from the ancient Greek. Children receive the text and its setting as artists. Starting the song with tonal and rhythm preps prepares the musical mind, and our movement and singing invites children to move with us until they are ready to sing while moving. Successive repetitions provide extended time with the tonality, multiple chances for children to explore in movement how rhythm, melody, and text interact, and the opportunity to practice singing. The song then works its magic—supporting the musical mind, guiding artistic expression, and enabling vocal technique.

The song architecture of *Where Are My Roses?* promotes artistry in our fledgling singers. The tonality and meter support the musical mind, as both are securely established in the first couple of measures and reinforced throughout. The melodic contour spins around and between the resting tone and fifth in a primarily stepwise manner, and it includes all characteristic tones of Aeolian tonality, supporting the musical mind's sense of tonality. Rhythm anchors, tonal anchors and text align, reinforcing each other. The relatively easy rhythm directs the musical mind to tonal, which becomes manifest in vocal sound as well as intonation.

The first line starts in the initial singing range, moving children over the voice break with effortless ease. The octave jump in the second line, in tandem with the greater intensity of the expression of text, generates vocal energy and breath for the higher D, powering vocal technique and artistic expression with the peak of the song, and then gracefully resolves to the resting tone. Song architecture, which includes vocal placement, evokes a lovely sound from kindergarten and first grade voices.

Children with substantial background are ready to rehearse this song to make their delivery still more musical. Engaging in macro/micro beat movement, bouncing and swaying with appropriate weight distribution while singing this song, imprints on children's bodies the feeling of the underlying meter, creating the momentum necessary for musical delivery. Triple meter becomes more challenging in song with all the added layers on the musical mind's tower of blocks, so overt movement of the meter with appropriate weight distribution in rehearsal leads the musical mind to become "mindful" of the meter while singing.

Rehearsal with our long-term students, now an ensemble of singers, demonstrates readiness for the addition of a piano accompaniment with introduction and interlude between repetitions of the song. Piano accompaniment, however, is added only after children can sing the song beautifully, as intimacy with the single melodic line in both singing and movement is essential for the development of the musical mind and for full command of the song.

A piano accompaniment adds yet another block to the musical mind's tower of blocks. It requires the fledgling musical mind to keep the tower in balance with macro and micro beats at the base and melodic rhythm, tonal, and text on top—plus the expanded vocal range and ensemble singing piled on top of that, now with the addition of a piano accompaniment. Offering instrumental accompaniments prematurely masks what the unstable musical mind lacks rather than facilitating the development of needed skills. The well-bred musical mind that is fully secure in a song accompanied only by movement will sustain itself when piano accompaniment is added. (Piano accompaniment for *Where Are My Roses?* and many other songs in this chapter can be found in the Come Children Sing Institute SONG LIBRARY.[1])

Rehearsal with piano accompaniment readies these children for performance, which adds yet another block on the stack of blocks. Vulnerable block towers can be easily distracted and derailed in performance, while those of the well-bred musical mind sing with the confidence, competence, and the poise of choral musicians. The heavenly sound evoked by *Where Are My Roses?* floats like a halo over the angelic faces of our young choristers.

Our young singers have made the quantum leap into the higher singing range and the process of rehearsing and performing as a choral ensemble with piano accompaniment. The setting of the text of *Where Are My Roses?*, which is appropriate to the children's age and range of expression, meets their musical needs. The song also challenges our young singers with the expanded range and expressive line. Children at every level need songs that meet their musical needs—songs that both support and challenge their level of development rhythmically, tonally, and vocally. They need songs with age-appropriate texts that are well-set, with rhythm and melody the musical translation of text, guiding expression and stimulating vocal technique. Songs that support the musical mind, prompt artistic expression, and enable vocal technique give voice to children's artistry.

Our little artists are still just five and six years old, learning to use their shiny, new vocal instruments. They do well in one-on-one tonal response in the lower range and function well in ensemble rhythmically and with recorders, but a few may not yet be ready to move into the higher singing range so effortlessly. Their music development and their physical vocal development are not yet in sync. These children, like the tot on the ladder, need a little boost crossing the bridge to choral singing. We can choose songs and even tonal narratives that scaffold all children at this level to develop greater command of their budding vocal instruments.

I Have a Funny Clown

2. I have a funny clown.
He jumps and jumps all day.
Ha, ha, ha, ha, ha, ha, ha,
Ha, ha, ha, ha, ha, ha, ha,
Ha, ha, ha, ha, ha, ha, ha,
Goes my funny clown!

Figure 7.2   Major, Duple

The playful *I Have a Funny Clown* (Figure 7.2), in contrast to the more artistic *Where Are My Roses?*, energizes and propels little voices as they move into the higher singing rage. The setting in Major tonality and Duple meter facilitates navigating the voice break, as the laugh of the clown stimulates appropriate vocal production generated by the joy of the song. The second verse invites children to sing and jump with the clown on each "ha." The song then charges the whole body in support of the voice and frees the voice with the playfulness of the song.

The jumping body on each "ha" powers the vocal instrument. The added energy of the jump makes the voice pop into the higher range, giving young children the experience of what it feels like to power the voice over the voice break. The voice has a hard time staying in the lower singing range when the musical mind directs it higher and the energized support of the jump empowers the muscles and breath to simulate and stimulate supported singing. The feeling of the body powering the voice can then be taken into other song literature. Introducing the song with tonal and rhythm preps sets up the musical mind for the song and the jumping propels the voices of our young choristers. Holding the hands of individual children while jumping communicates still more to each child's musical mind/body connection that powers the voice.

Figure 7.3   Minor, Duple

Figure 7.3 offers an example of a tonal narrative in Minor tonality and Duple meter that invites children into the higher vocal range through call and response. It also invites one-on-one response with our scaffolding each child as needed. We sing the first two measures of each line in solo, cue a breath and then sing the next two measures with the children, all with movement and all on the syllable "too." The tonality commands the experience, with the musical mind directing the voice through multiple repetitions. The energy of the line, the deliberate breath, and our singing and moving with the children scaffold children's voices both individually and in ensemble. We gradually pull back to singing only the first two measures of each line, just moving and breathing with each child before the child's solo response of the next two measures. The energy of the line leads expression, generating breath for our young artists' response to our call, with the musical mind leading the way.

We set up the tonality and meter with preps and engage children in singing, using movement energy to scaffold the breath leading to response. Song architecture of the tonal narrative both supports and challenges the musical mind. Tonality and meter are both established early, with all characteristic tones present. Minor tonality compels the musical mind, while the easier Duple meter with relatively easy rhythm patterns directs the musical mind to tonal, manifesting in quality sound and intonation. Melodic contour with its stepwise passages supports the musical mind, while skips over the voice break challenge it. The call and response without any text speaks directly to the musical mind, inviting it into the higher range and empowering the vocal instrument.

This type of call and response in various tonalities is particularly helpful with children who might be slower than the rest of the class to move into the higher singing range. We scaffold each voice as needed, accepting whatever comes out without judgement. A teacher's well-meaning verbal or non-verbal response to a child's fledgling vocal independence can shut down children's artistry and the energy needed for vocal production. Engaging musically with individual voices as they move into the higher singing range is an intimate exchange. Budding voices need a very accepting, positive environment in which to bloom.

A seven-year-old long-term student who lags behind the other children in moving over the voice break may be reluctant to sing in the higher range because of shyness or a personality that is afraid of being exposed by having one's voice be heard. These children, despite the musicality they have demonstrated in movement and in the lower singing range, are generally not aware that they are not singing on pitch, whether in solo or ensemble. Their stack of blocks seems to be threatened by the presence of their peers or a lack of confidence. Putting our focus on the music and movement rather than on the child or pitch gives these children the space and time they need to mature, while we include songs that support the musical mind and encourage confident singing. These children might surprise you by how beautifully they sing a few months later.

2. I'm the king! I'm the king!
I'm the king of the land!
I'm the king! I'm the king
Of the castles in the sand!

3. I'm the king! I'm the king!
I'm the king of the sea!
I'm the king! I'm the king
Of the ships that sail to me!

Figure 7.4 Phrygian, Duple

I'm the King! (Figure 7.4) offers a gem song that elicits energy and confidence from young voices. Phrygian tonality compels the musical mind, while the text and setting in Duple meter guide expression. The declaration of being the king, with the bodily stance and expression of such importance, encourages the musical mind to deliver confidently over the voice break with the stature of being in command of the voice as well as the kingdom. Subsequent verses encourage confident singing throughout, even if challenging singers with multiple verses.

We begin with tonal and rhythm preps and engage children in movement and singing. The meter is established right away and sustained throughout, with the upbeat pattern offering a bit of challenge. The simple rhythm directs the musical mind to tonal, and with the text, to expression. Phrygian tonality is established early and sustained with the characteristic lowered second, and melodic contour supports tonality in the musical mind. Rhythm anchors, tonal anchors, and text are aligned, with the simplicity of this song both rhythmically and tonally providing for greater attention to expression. Song architecture provides for young voices to sing this song with confidence, which can then be taken into songs that we choose more for the development of sound. Adding a piano accompaniment with introduction and interlude and having children sing this song in concert builds still more confidence in our young singers. Those few self-conscious children who are afraid to have their voices heard might forget themselves in becoming royalty.

Artistry in Motion

We used play songs to serve many purposes with younger children while we captured the musical mind with rhythm and tonal narratives. We engaged children in playing music—practicing music—with props serving as musical instruments. We introduced the occasional art song throughout, and as children developed we introduced gem songs, which served as more musically sophisticated play songs. Now art songs and gem songs grow in musical complexity and vocal challenge as the children grow, replacing props and providing for the ongoing development of children's artistry throughout childhood. The musical and vocal challenges in song become the play for our young singers, as children's artistry revels in making exciting music.

We might choose songs for their rhythm challenge, tonal challenge, or vocal challenge, further blurring the distinction between play songs, art songs and gem songs, while offering great variety in style, energy, and expression, and still keeping all tonalities and meters alive in the musical mind. Songs that give voice to children's artistry take on a greater role with young singers as they also guide artistic expression and vocal technique.

Firefly

Figure 7.5 Lydian, Triple

Firefly (Figure 7.5) offers a song in Lydian tonality and Triple meter that elicits a lovely sound from young singers. Kindergarten and first graders navigate the challenges with artistry. Lydian tonality and Triple meter compel the musical mind. They are both established early and are sustained throughout. The simplicity of the melodic rhythm focuses the musical mind on tonal, leading to quality sound and intonation. Rehearsal with macro/micro beat movement with appropriate weight distribution in triple meter leads singers to become mindful of the underlying meter and the momentum it generates, improving musical delivery.

Rhythm anchors, tonal anchors, and text align, supporting the musical mind. The somewhat melismatic treatment of text presents a challenge for the young voice, particularly in the first two notes of the second and third measures with macro beat weight on the B rather than the D. The same figure in reverse would yield greater vocal energy in navigating the voice break. This song supports the musical mind while challenging the voice. Tonal and rhythm preps prompt the musical mind, and the musical setting of the child-like text invites children to be their sensitive, expressive selves. Adding a piano accompaniment with introduction and interlude between repetitions for concert provides for the lovely sound elicited by this song to light up the room like fireflies.

Engaging singing children in macro/micro beat movement with appropriate weight distribution, as suggested with this song and with *Where Are My Roses?* (Figure 7.1) may at first sound unmusical with such deliberate weight. The feeling of that weight while singing, however, makes the musical mind more mindful of the underlying meter of the song while singing and leaves an imprint on the body, guiding vocal delivery without the exaggerated weight and leading to highly musical delivery.

We can apply movement in rehearsal with any song to scaffold momentum, expression, or vocal technique. We might use movement in *Where Are My Roses?* or the call and response tonal narrative to generate greater energy for the D a ninth above middle C. We might use movement to encourage greater authority with the repeated declaration in *I'm the King!* Applying movement directly to anything that needs rehearsal improves delivery.

Soaring in Song   185

Singing a song twice through in concert, with a piano accompaniment that includes an introduction and interlude, builds children's confidence as singers and provides for them to revel in their own artistry. It also showcases young children's artistry, providing extended time for parents to savor the wonder of their own children's artistry.

Cricket

Figure 7.6 Major, Unusual Paired

Cricket (Figure 7.6) offers a playful song in Major tonality and Unusual Paired Meter. The challenge of this song is the meter, but song architecture makes the song effortless for our young singers. The melodic line and the words are both easy and repetitive. The words of each verse are aligned with rhythm and tonal anchors, reinforcing the meter in the musical mind and enabling ease in singing the "doo" section without the support of word pronunciation. The simplicity and repetition of the words and melody as well as the unusual meter lead the musical mind to attend more to rhythm.

Children steeped in the various meters find delight rather than challenge in singing the unusual metered song of the cricket. Note the 3/2 beat grouping in Unusual Paired meter. The rhythm prep following the tonal prep would be with that grouping. (See Appendix B for beat groupings in this meter.) Macro/micro beat movement sets the stage for the musical mind as our little songsters join the cricket singing precisely in tune and in rhythm. A piano accompaniment with an introduction and interlude between repetitions of the song can make *Cricket* a nice addition to a concert.

Engaging kindergarteners and first graders together in songs presented here can further spur the vocal development of kindergarteners. The more developed sound of the first graders, like sourdough bread starter, envelops the fresh entries, creating a rich mixture to grow on.

Snowflake

Figure 7.7 Aeolian, Duple

Snowflake (Figure 7.7) serves like a vocalise. It gives the young voice a musical workout in Aeolian tonality and Duple meter with its bouncing back and forth around the voice break. Rhythm and tonal preps will prepare the musical mind, and meter and tonality work together to support the musical mind. The melodic contour, with most of the melody below the resting tone, makes the song more difficult for the musical mind than if it were above the resting tone as in the final measures. Melodic rhythm challenges children to articulate text with vocal energy.

The song supports the musical mind while propelling vocal skill. Engaging children in movement with the energy of the line and articulating text with arms and hands transfers to singing. This song, like the more playful *I Have a Funny Clown*, works the young voice over the voice break. *Snowflake*, however, is both musically and vocally more sophisticated, evoking a light sound around the voice break and eliciting greater artistry. A piano accompaniment with an introduction and interlude between repetitions makes this song suitable for performance.

Dancing Voices

Singers that we have nurtured throughout early childhood can be musically so developed at this point that we have to remind ourselves that they are still little children. Those now singing beautifully in ensemble may be the same children we were on the floor with a year ago making Duple cookies. Their musical sophistication far outstrips their maturity. They need songs that meet their advancing musical needs at every level, but with texts appropriate to their tender age and range of expression.

Hop, Mother Annika!

Figure 7.8 Minor, Triple

Hop, Mother Annika! (Figure 7.8), with the words of a delightful Swedish rhyme set in Minor tonality and Triple meter, propels children's expression in song. The rhythm is somewhat tricky, though supported by tonal and text. Elongations, rests, and ties add rhythmic difficulty, as do the long notes, requiring young singers to maintain the meter throughout their duration. The setting of the text reinforces weight on the macro beats. (The name Annika in this setting is pronounced ah-NEE-kah.) Rhythm and tonal preps lead the way, and rehearsal with macro and micro beat movement drives the meter with appropriate weight distribution.

The melodic contour of the song supports the musical mind tonally with ample stepwise passages and skips within the tonic function, but the characteristic seventh doesn't appear until the final measure, challenging singers to sustain the tonality throughout after hearing just the tonal prep. The repeated opening statement with its eighth-note "hops" followed by quarter-note rests offers great contrast to the more legato line that follows it. The sustained note leads to the contrasting final four-measure statement that builds energy with each percussive delivery of the word "dance," building momentum to the ending triumphal dance. Song architecture, which includes vocal placement, elicits a nice sound from young voices as well as joyous expression. Children sing this song with vocal energy and delight, convincing any teacher, if we might borrow words from the song, that when they are big they'll be singing still.

Dance To Your Daddie

Figure 7.9 Mixolydian, Triple

Dance to Your Daddie (Figure 7.9) offers a highly musical experience for our young singers. The setting of the simple Scottish rhyme in Mixolydian tonality and Triple meter matches the musical sophistication of our long-term youngsters, while also matching their innocence as little children.

Meter and tonality are established and sustained throughout, as the characteristic lowered seventh secures Mixolydian tonality. Rhythm anchors, tonal anchors, and text align, supporting each other. Melodic contour supports the musical mind with its many stepwise passages and skips within harmonic functions that define the tonality. (See Appendix D for harmonic functions.) Vocal placement is in the range that serves the young vocal instrument, and the repeated figures throughout contribute to the ease of singing the song. The song's sweet simplicity belies its musical complexity.

The rhythm of this song, though securely in Triple meter and supported by text and tonal, take *Dance to Your Daddie* to a level of musical sophistication well beyond *Hop, Mother Annika!* The divisions, elongations and upbeat patterns add some difficulty, but the rhythmic figure with ties to macro beats creates not only upbeat patterns into the next macro beats, increasing song difficulty, but also unweighted macro beats, requiring singers to maintain macro beat weight in the musical mind. The figure makes each of the first two measures feel like there is only one macro beat with two micro beats, each divided into three. The contrast between that in the 6/8 section and the single macro beat in the 3/8 section with its direct weight, makes it feel like the two different sections are in two different tempos in Triple meter. The subtlety supports the expression of text, propelling our young singers to artistic delivery well beyond their years. Starting the song with rhythm and tonal preps prepares the musical mind, and rehearsing with macro and micro beat movement in Triple meter secures triple meter throughout, with more of a stylistic difference between the two sections. *Dance to Your Daddie* draws a lovely sound from young voices and showcases the advanced musicality yet innocence of our young artists.

Children who sing a song like *Dance to Your Daddie* beautifully deserve to sing the song twice through in performance with piano accompaniment that includes an introduction and interlude between repetitions. Singing the song a second time through in concert allows children to bask in their own artistry while parents marvel at their wonder.

Figure 7.10   Mixolydian, Unusual Unpaired

Winter Sweetness (Figure 7.10) presents the lovely little poem of Langston Hughes in Mixolydian tonality and Unusual Unpaired meter. The challenging meter invites children to bring their rhythmic prowess into song. The unusual meter draws attention to itself rather than focusing the musical mind on tonal, so now our young singers have the challenge of sustaining the tonality amidst the busyness of the rhythm, while sustaining the unusual meter through the long notes and delivering the poetry. The prep for Mixolydian tonality supports the musical mind, as does the prep for Unusual Unpaired meter with the beat grouping of 3/2/2. (See Appendix B for beat groupings in this meter.) Song architecture also supports the musical mind. Meter and tonality are clearly established early in the song. Vocal placement is within the appropriate range for children's voices. Melodic contour spins around and between the resting tone and fifth with skips within the harmonic functions that define the tonality. (See Appendix D for harmonic functions.) The natural rhythm of the words is maintained in the unusual meter. Rhythm, tonal, and text are aligned, supporting the musical mind and making the song easier to sing, despite the challenges for our young singers. This song yields a lovely sound from children who have the musical readiness for the song.

Children have to be quite secure in Unusual Unpaired meter to command this song, as the tempo is so quick that it is difficult to fully engage in movement with both macro and micro beats while singing. The weight of macro beats drives the song, with just a hint of micro beats, but micro beats as well as macro beats have to be secure in the musical mind in order for children to deliver this song competently. Chanting a few measures of micro beats on the resting tone, between verses of the song, helps the musical mind to become more mindful of the meter throughout. Children, of course, can learn to sing a song like *Winter Sweetness* without a background in meters and tonalities, just as they might learn to recite a poem in a language they don't understand. The well-bred musical mind's comprehension of meter and tonality, however, provides for *Winter Sweetness* to build on the greater depth of young children's artistry and propel it to new heights.

This little song through multiple repetitions is irresistible, and it is effective in concert with piano accompaniment and interlude between repetitions. It's even been known to draw in jamming dads with string bass and harmonica. The delight of the poem floats over the unusual meter as our young artists deliver the song with great ease, artistic expression, and lovely sound, offering a peep into the vast window of children's artistry.

Song Matters

Songs are the vehicle for the expression of children's artistry. They are the driving force that unleashes children's artistry. Songs worthy of children's artistry that are age-appropriate and meet children's musical needs inspire children's artistry and are essential to its development throughout early childhood and beyond.

> Children's artistry deserves increasingly difficult song repertoire at every level—songs that give voice to children's artistry and develop the readiness for more advanced song literature. The merit of songs for the development of children's artistry is not in their historical, cultural, or social considerations, but in their musical considerations that give rise to children's artistry.[2]

The Leaves Fall

Figure 7.11 Minor, Duple

The Leaves Fall (Figure 7.11), in Minor Tonality and Duple meter, raises children's voices to a high E, more fully defining and refining their developing choral sound in the higher register. The initial line of this text was a "story" written by first grader David Pinzino to accompany a picture he had drawn. Song architecture supports the musical mind, with the simplicity of rhythm directing the musical mind to tonal, which manifests in sound and intonation. The initial statement of the text moving to a higher and more intense repetition of the text stimulates breath and expression as it builds the line to the peak of the song, returning to its original statement and then resolving to the end. The simplicity of text and rhythm coupled with the drama of the melodic line building intensity in the higher range stimulates vocal resonance, moving children into a higher level as choral artists. Multiple repetitions elicit full vocal production in the optimal vocal range for children's voices, drawing artistry out of our young choristers. Tonal and rhythm preps prepare the musical mind, while movement with the energy of the line scaffolds such lovely expression and choral sound. Children love coloring the long "ee" sound on the high E with a bit of "ooh" and to minimize the "l" and "r" in the words "fall" and "work" to produce a more beautiful sound.

Songs that give voice to children's artistry stand on their own musicality, accompanied only by movement. Those that are age-appropriate and meet the musical needs of our youngsters propel the development of children's artistry, whether we use them just once or rehearse them for performance. We might, for example, choose *The Leaves Fall* just to move kindergarten and first grade voices higher, stretching their vocal range and expressive range as well. We might choose a song for its tonality, rhythm difficulty, or vocal challenges. We might choose a song to develop sound, vocal energy, or expression.

Songs that give voice to children's artistry propel children's artistry in both the music classroom and children's chorus.

The Leaves Fall, as well as many of the songs in this chapter, can also serve as warm-ups for more developed singers, as can rhythm and tonal narratives in the various meters and tonalities. Rhythm Dialogue Activity, Resting Tone Activity, Macro/Micro Beat Activity or Tonal Dialogue Activity can also offer rich experience as warm-ups, while providing the opportunity to introduce more difficult rhythm and tonal content in an ongoing manner. The "fancy footwork" addressed earlier in this chapter to command meter is a powerful warm-up, as it fully charges the body, musical mind, and spirit, readying all to make exciting music. The little art songs with haiku texts presented in earlier chapters, transposed up a third, make wonderful warm-ups with singers of all ages, as they awaken the musical mind, body, and voice and engage singers in the choral art. They also provide a lovely way to keep all tonalities alive in the musical mind while serving the voice and the choral art. Vocal warm-ups can provide the opportunity for rhythm and tonal growth in addition to engagement with the choral art through songs that feed the musical mind, prompt artistic expression, and enable vocal technique with singers of all ages.

Wild Flowers

Figure 7.12 Aeolian, Duple

Wild Flowers (Figure 7.12), in Aeolian tonality and Duple meter, supports the musical mind throughout, while offering greater challenge rhythmically, expressively, and vocally. The rhythm reflects the rhythm of the words by poet Peter Newell, but the rhythm of the words includes elongations, ties, and upbeats, requiring some skill in the meter. Rhythm anchors, tonal anchors and text align in support of the musical mind, but the high E on an upbeat increases song difficulty both rhythmically and vocally. The lovely little text and its musical translation give young children the opportunity to play the role of the teacher, narrator, and the frightened child, with the melodic contour supporting expression and that expression generating vocal technique. Rhythm and tonal preps prepare the musical mind. Movement with the energy of the line can be used in rehearsal to improve the articulation of melodic rhythm and text. It can be used to improve vocal energy with the peak of the song and the expression of the line. It can be used to improve the expression of text with its multiple personas.

Singers become actors on stage with this song, as the song itself supports dramatic delivery. The setting of the text guides performance, as the melody and rhythm demonstrate and live the expression of the text.

> Songs that give voice to children's artistry evoke artistic expression. Their rhythm and melody mirror the drama of the words, illuminate the text, and compel the musical mind, making the song and its expression irresistible for children. The song, itself, becomes like the parent reading a bedtime story with vocal inflection and intensity depicting characters and dramatizing storyline, drawing the child into the middle of the narrative through evocative delivery, and demonstrating how to be expressive in the narrative.[3]

The song architecture of songs that give voice to children's artistry leads children to sing expressively, as the expression is built into the song. The rhythm and melody rise and fall, twist and turn, slow and hasten as does the text, inviting children on the journey of its expression. A song's artistic expression then inspires appropriate vocal technique, empowering the voice.

Children are thrilled by the experience of such musicality in ensemble. Singing the song in concert with piano accompaniment that includes an introduction and interlude between repetitions demonstrates the wonder of children's artistry, even from those "timid creatures."

Bumblebee

Figure 7.13   Aeolian, Unusual Unpaired

Bumblebee (Figure 7.13), in Aeolian tonality and Unusual Unpaired meter, challenges children still more to bring their advanced rhythm development into song. The difficulty of the meter is increased by the fast tempo, but children competent in the meter can usually handle the meter at any tempo. The fast tempo in this song, however, makes it difficult to move both macro and micro beats to embody the meter. The weight of macro beats in movement has to propel the meter with micro beats sustained in the musical mind, requiring skill with this meter as musical readiness for the song. Unusual Unpaired meter draws attention to itself, focusing the musical mind on rhythm rather than tonal. The greater difficulty of rhythm requires children's readiness to maintain the tonality amidst the distraction of meter in addition to skill with the meter. Beat grouping in Unusual Unpaired meter is 3/2/2. (See Appendix B for beat groupings in this meter.) Set up the rhythm prep following the tonal prep with that beat grouping, preparing the musical mind to buzz with the bee. Tonality and meter are established within the first few measures, and rhythm anchors, tonal anchors, and text align, supporting the musical mind. Melodic contour is generally cooperative, but the upbeat starting each phrase adds difficulty.

The childlike nature of questioning the bumblebee and becoming more intense when it doesn't answer is reflected in the melodic line, which along with the driving rhythm of the song prompts artistic expression. The higher singing range in the second half of the song adds to the increased intensity of the ongoing questioning of the bumblebee. The urgency of the questioning text as well as the compelling meter and tempo drive the bumblebee to its final measures, charging the voice as well as expression. *Bumblebee*, like *I'm the King!*, promotes energy and confidence in singers, but on a more sophisticated level both musically and vocally, making *Bumblebee* suitable for older singers as well. Children of all ages become so engrossed in expressing the song with its driving rhythm that they deliver vocally with very deliberate vocal and musical energy, creating a compelling presence in concert with piano accompaniment with introduction and interlude. The buzzing nature of the bee, the song, and the children come together in exciting delivery.

Bumblebee, though in the same meter as the easier *Winter Sweetness*, requires considerably more of singers in sustaining the meter not only amidst the tonality and quick tempo, but also amidst a more expressive musical line and a more driving storyline. We once again scaffold children's mastery of songs in unusual meters with tempos too fast to move both macro and micro beats by our singing a verse or two of the song and then singing a few bars of micro beats on the resting tone on "bah," followed by a couple more verses of the song, sustaining the tempo, meter, and tonality throughout. Our chanting micro beats on the resting tone with appropriate weight distribution in song is like shining an aural spotlight on the meter, saying to the musical mind, "You know this meter. It's under the fury of this bumblebee." The back and forth, between the song as written and the occasional highlighting of the meter, helps the musical mind to become more mindful of the meter in the context of the song. We do this in most songs through movement, but in unusual meters in which the tempo is too fast to move macro and micro beats, we can still speak to the musical mind non-verbally about meter and about appropriate weight distribution between macro and micro beats.

Singing micro beats on the resting tone with rhythm syllables highlights for children who are familiar with rhythm syllables not only the meter, but also the relationship between macro and micro beats within the meter, and that relationship within the context of the song. We can communicate still more in syllables with these children in more difficult songs with shifting beat groupings or shifting meters.[4]

Artistry in Flight

Children that reach this level sing beautifully as an ensemble whether in the classroom or choral context. They sing with expression and appropriate vocal technique as they deliver the unique musicality of each song. They receive the text of songs that serve children's artistry as poets and artists. Young artistry knows when the melody and rhythm of a song is a musical translation of the text, and it enacts the musical drama of each text through singing and movement.

Unison songs that support the musical mind, prompt artistic expression, and enable vocal technique are the most powerful generators of children's artistry at this level. Unison songs of increasing difficulty throughout childhood grow with the children both musically and vocally, meeting their musical needs at every level. The pure unison line, rather than multiple vocal parts, offers children the most intimate experience with the choral art, with their own artistry, and with their young community of artists, developing both the individual and the ensemble.

Ant

[musical notation]

Lit - tle Ant, Lit - tle Ant, Why don't you rest?
Why don't you rest? You work so hard, you've no time to play.
Why don't you rest? Why don't you rest?

Figure 7.14 Phrygian, Triple

Ant (Figure 7.14) offers a song that invites children to soar as artists. It's setting in Phrygian tonality and Triple meter mesmerizes the musical mind, while the simplicity and child-like nature of the text implore children to be their inquisitive, musical selves. Rhythm and tonal preps prime the musical mind for the meter and tonality, both of which are established early and maintained throughout. Rhythm, tonal, and text anchors align, supporting the musical mind. The relative simplicity and repetition of the rhythm and text direct the musical mind to focus on tonal. The haunting repetition of Phrygian's characteristic lowered second in relation to the resting tone supports the musical mind, as does the melodic contour spinning around and between the resting tone and fifth with its abundant stepwise passages.

The shape of the line of *Ant* is most compelling for young singers, drawing young artistry into a quality sound and expression beyond what has been demonstrated in earlier songs. The opening figure with its repetition intensifies with the next figure and its repetition, building to the peak of the song with open-hearted and open-voiced wonder, and resolving gently into the final figure and its repetition, which echoes its earlier statement. Children's sincere marveling at the ant, with the shape of the line leading to such musicality, expression, and breath supported high E, puts us in awe of the children as well as the ant.

The lovely sound and heart-felt expression that this song elicits in only eight measures serves as a model or template to take into all song literature. It becomes the model for songs with distracting rhythm as well as for more advanced choral literature. Rehearsing with macro and micro beat movement with appropriate weight distribution can assure momentum in triple meter, while stepping into the peak of the song with outstretched arms can make the musicality of the song more tangible. The exaggerated macro/micro beat movement with the song might sound unmusical, but it imprints on the body the underlying meter, resulting in mindfulness of the meter and momentum in performance. A piano accompaniment with introduction and interlude makes *Ant* a lovely addition to any concert.

Songs worthy of children's artistry direct the well-bred musical mind beyond in-tune singing into quality sound. Developing the musical mind serves not only intonation, momentum, and rhythm precision, but also ensemble sound. Songs in Phrygian tonality and songs in Lydian tonality, in particular, seem to lead to greater awareness and ownership of a beautiful choral sound whether in the music classroom or chorus. Children then revel in shaping the sound to make it even more beautiful. Aiming toward the open "ah" sound on the word "why" in *Ant* and minimizing the "r" in "work" delights our young singers as they sing even more beautifully. Our young artists are developing vocal technique in the process of being their musical selves.

The song architecture of *Ant* supports the musical mind and incites embodied expression, motivating breath energy and appropriate vocal technique. Songs that give voice to children's artistry enable vocal technique, leading to quality performance.

> The architecture of songs that give voice to children's artistry supports the vocal instrument just as it supports the musical mind and artistic expression. Head voice is prompted and sustained by vocal placement and melodic contour. Breath and energy are charged by expression of appropriate text mirrored in rhythm and melody. Line and tone come alive through tonality, melodic contour, the energy of the line, and the melodic translation of text. Articulation is fostered by secure meter and the rhythmic and melodic translation of text. Intonation, momentum, and rhythmic precision are secured through support of the musical mind. The vocal, musical and expressive dimensions of songs that give voice to children's artistry lead children at every level to experience the vocal technique needed to sing the songs beautifully.[5]

Ant elicits quality sound in singers, whether well-bred kindergarteners and first graders or college singers. Song architecture can serve older voices in the process of developing artistry just as it does with young children. A lovely children's song, like a lovely children's poem, is ageless.

Penguin

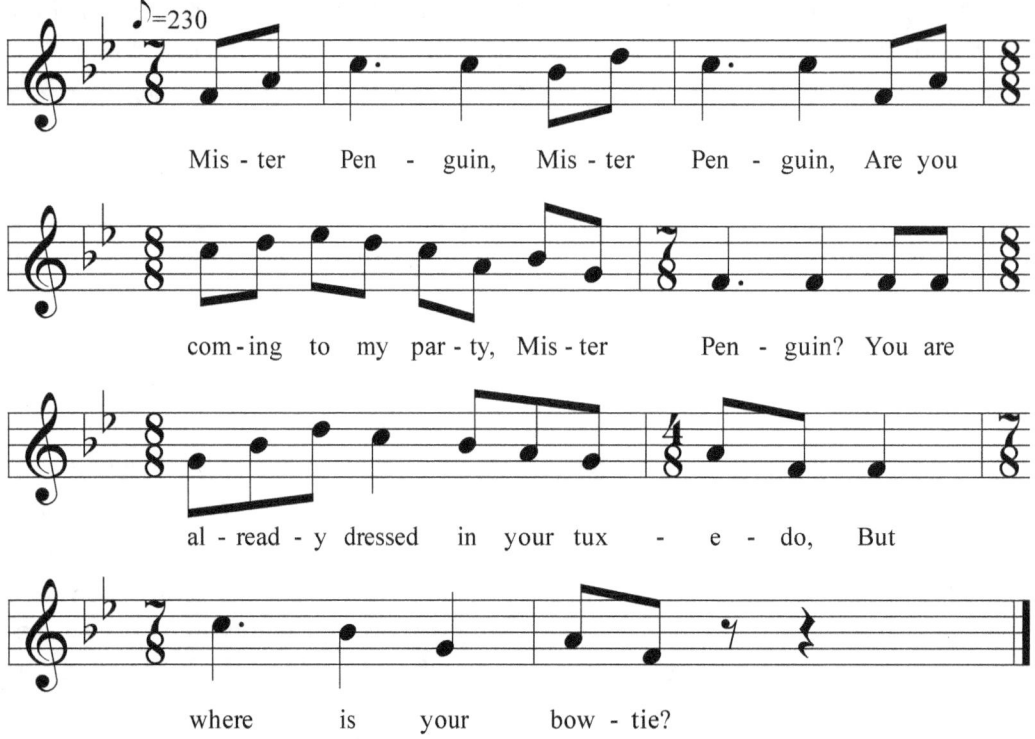

Figure 7.15   Mixolydian, Unusual Unpaired/Duple

Penguin (Figure 7.15), in Mixolydian tonality and Unusual Unpaired and Duple meter, offers quite a contrast to *Ant*. *Penguin* focuses the musical mind on rhythm rather than tonal, which obviously requires rhythm readiness, but it also requires tonal readiness, as singers have to be able to sustain Mixolydian tonality amidst the shifting meters. Rhythm is the greatest challenge of *Penguin*, yet text and tonal anchors align with rhythm anchors, supporting the musical mind. The delightful text and complex rhythm are suitable for older singers with the musical readiness for the song, and can be well in the realm of well-trained kindergarten and first graders.

The melodic contour wraps around and between the resting tone and fifth with plenty of stepwise passages and skips within the harmonic functions that define the tonality. (See Appendix D for harmonic functions.) Addressing the formality of the penguin's black and white attire tickles a child's sense of humor while the playful rhythm tickles the musical mind's sense of humor. The melodic line amidst shifting meters encourages expression of text, which stimulates appropriate vocal technique in delivery of the song, making the difficult rhythm flow without effort.

Singing and rehearsing with movement energy helps to propel the song. Tonal and rhythm preps format the musical mind for the tonality and meter, with the rhythm prep presenting the 3/2/2 beat grouping that begins the song. (See Appendix B for beat groupings in this meter.) Children with some competence in Unusual Unpaired meter are comfortable with the shift of beat groupings in Unusual Unpaired meter. We can sing an occasional verse of micro beats on the resting tone, with or without syllables, as described earlier. We could even sing the melody on rhythm syllables with children who have the readiness, with the syllables pointing out to the musical mind the changes in meter. Adding a piano accompaniment with introduction and interlude between repetitions of the song makes *Penguin* suitably dressed for any concert, showcasing the delight, innocence, and artistry of young singers.

Figure 7.16   Minor, Triple

Autumn Thought (Figure 7.16), with the lovely words of Langston Hughes set in Minor tonality and Triple meter, brings the quality sound achieved in *Ant* and the command of rhythm displayed in *Penguin* into a song whose rhythm and tonal challenges are fairly well-balanced. *Autumn Thought*, however, offers additional challenge in the words and in expression. The poetry is more sophisticated than *Ant* or *Penguin*. Its translation in rhythm and tonal is more musically sophisticated than *Ant* and more challenging expressively than *Penguin*. Meter and tonality are established and sustained throughout. Melodic contour supports the musical mind, though the leap of a sixth adds a bit of tonal challenge, and rhythm and tonal anchors align with pronunciation of text. Rhythm is a bit challenging with its divisions, elongations, and ties, though it mirrors the rhythm of the words. Rhythm and tonal preps prepare the musical mind for the song. Rehearsing with macro and micro beat movement in Triple meter propels momentum. Rehearsing with movement with the energy of the line propels expression. Quality performance, whether in rehearsal or concert, demands both.

The opening statement sets the stage, and the somewhat higher second phrase builds energy. The long note in the fourth measure demands artistry in building intensity and volume, followed by a deliberate breath to the peak of the song, which then melts into a graceful dance of the petals. Movement with the energy of the line demonstrates children's artistry in building the line through the long note, generating intensity and breath for the peak of the song, and then moving from such intensity to graceful hand movement articulating the petals' dance. Voices mirror such musical movement. Children are happy to shade the long note on the word "away" with a little bit of "ee" coloring and to aim for "ah" sound on the word "dry" to create a more beautiful sound. Adding a piano accompaniment to *Autumn Thought*, with introduction and interlude between repetitions of the song, demonstrates in concert young children's ability to become the song in all its nuance, doing justice to the beautiful little poem. Children, indeed, are artists.

Piano accompaniments that serve the development of children's artistry, like the songs they accompany, have to clearly define meter and tonality, supporting the musical mind throughout. They reflect the expression of line and style, enhancing the drama of the song and reinforcing children's expression, further empowering vocal technique. Harmonic functions are essentially those that define the tonality, and they align with rhythm, tonal, and text. (See Appendix D for harmonic functions.) Complex accompaniments distract the musical mind, and rhythm or harmonic flourish can confuse children's developing sense of meter or tonality. An appropriate piano accompaniment shines a spotlight on the wonder of the children and children's artistry rather than overpowering or upstaging young voices. (Piano accompaniments for many of the songs in this chapter are available in the Come Children Sing Institute SONG LIBRARY.[6])

What Does Little Birdie Say? (Figure 7.17) offers a delightful poem of Alfred Lord Tennyson set in Dorian tonality, with meter shifting between Duple and Triple. This song invites children to be the narrator, the bird, and the mother as they make this song come alive. The architecture of the song both supports and challenges the musical mind. Melodic contour includes many stepwise passages as it moves around and between the resting tone and fifth, with skips primarily within the tonic function. The characteristic 6th of Dorian tonality, however, doesn't appear until the second line, requiring some skill with Dorian tonality. A tonal prep will set the musical mind in Dorian tonality at this level, with a Duple prep to set the initial meter. Rhythm patterns include the challenge of ties and upbeats, but the greater difficulty is in the ongoing shifting meters. Rhythm anchors, tonal anchors and text align, supporting the musical mind, but the expression of text with its three characters requires children to maintain Dorian tonality through shifting meters, while attending to expression.

The musical translation of the text prompts its expression, with its shifts in the various characters and the nature of each of those characters. The opening in Duple meter sets the

What Does Little Birdie Say?

Figure 7.17 Dorian, Duple/Triple

stage for the narrator, while Triple meter presents the bird's longing for independence. Moving back to Duple meter provides for the overly protective mother to interrupt the bird's dreaming of freedom with words of wisdom, with the neutral voice of the narrator then leading to the final two measures in Triple meter giving the bird her freedom.

The setting of this song coaches artistic expression and vocal technique with its characterizations of the narrator, the bird, and the mother, and the musical detail throughout. The ties provide for catch breaths to better express the imploring bird and protective mother. Even the short 3/8 measure with the marked breath allow for the concerned mother to jump in with motherly advice in Duple meter, followed by the narrator finishing the story, with the shift back to Triple meter enabling sufficient breath for singers to set the bird free. The song, itself, prompts expression, enabling vocal technique; and with its vocal placement in the optimal range for children's voices, the song elicits a lovely sound from our young singers, freeing the voice as it frees the bird.

Movement is the magic ingredient with children who have the musical readiness for this song. Macro/micro beat movement helps to secure each meter throughout the song, while movement with the energy of the line sets the stage for expressing the three different characters, capturing the birdie's yearning, the mother's caution, and the narrator's neutrality. Invite children to literally take a step into each different role to better capture the three different characters. Use hands for articulation in the Duple meter sections, contrasted by sweeping arms in the Triple meter sections. Teaching songs worthy of children's artistry through artistry—engaging children in movement and singing without the encumbrance of notation or wordy instructions—makes artistry come alive. Children revel in delivering the drama of this song with the beautiful sound it generates. Presenting this song with a piano accompaniment that includes an introduction and interlude between repetitions of the song makes a lovely addition to any concert. The children soar with the bird, as their voices take flight.

Children who have reached this level are ready to move on to more and more difficult songs that give voice to children's artistry. The foundation we have provided transfers to all future choral repertoire, as our young singers bring to new material the experience of singing in-tune with precise rhythm and momentum, singing expressively, and with appropriate vocal technique. They know how to become the song, how to produce a beautiful sound, and how to work together as a choral ensemble for even greater artistry. We just have to continue to provide songs of increasing difficulty throughout childhood that support the musical mind, prompt artistic expression, and enable vocal technique.

Etude 3 presents additional songs in the higher singing range for kindergarten and primary grade children. The book, *Giving Voice to Children's Artistry: A Guide for Music Teachers and Choral Conductors* by Mary Ellen Pinzino, addresses the development of children's artistry from kindergarten through seventh grade, offering many more songs of increasing difficulty for children as they grow throughout these ages.[7] Still more songs of increasing difficulty for all levels, many with piano accompaniments, can be found in the Come Children Sing Institute SONG LIBRARY.[8]

Songs that give voice to children's artistry illuminate the wonder of children's artistry at every age. They provide intimate experience with the choral art that can be taken on to more advanced choral repertoire and that can transfer to instrumental music and a lifetime of music making. Children deserve songs worthy of children's artistry, with ongoing difficulty that meets their musical needs at every age and level of development. They deserve songs that compel the musical mind, prompt artistic expression, and enable vocal technique through early childhood and beyond. Children deserve songs that inspire children's artistry.

Part 3

Etudes

You are about to embark on the exciting journey of unveiling young children's artistry. These Etudes are designed to accompany you on your journey, supporting you in the classroom with materials and guidance while also providing professional development. They are designed for direct implementation in any early childhood music classroom, and they offer hands-on experience with additional materials and the process of teaching early childhood music. Use these Etudes as needed for your own growth and that of the children.

"Etude 1-For Getting Started" is designed to help you reach and teach the musical mind—yours and the children's. It offers rhythm and tonal narratives in the various meters and tonalities and little art songs in each tonality. You can use the materials of this Etude in the classroom, or use them without the children to develop your own competence and confidence with the various meters and tonalities.

"Etude 2-For Planning Lessons" invites you to engage in the creative process of planning lessons. It guides you in meeting children's musical needs, sculpting energy, and creating seamless classes. It supports you in the process at various levels of development. Insights gained from this Etude prepare you to create effective lesson plans for any group of young children.

"Etude 3-For Choosing Songs" offers a wide variety of songs for early childhood, including play songs, art songs, and gem songs for all ages, plus songs in the higher singing range for children in kindergarten and older. This Etude offers guidance with each song and supports you in choosing songs that meet children's musical needs at various levels. It helps you to balance song repertoire for each group of children. The many songs of this Etude, plus the host of songs offered in this book, prepare you for all ages and levels of development in early childhood music.

Engaging with these Etudes, informed by this book, offers practical experience, professional development, and a multitude of materials to use in the early childhood music classroom. Additional materials that meet the criteria of these Etudes can be found in the Come Children Sing Institute SONG LIBRARY,[1] where the songs and materials are printable and searchable by tonality, meter, and other parameters.

# Etude 1

For Getting Started

A full array of tonalities and meters provides the key to uncovering young children's artistry. It can also open new horizons for our own artistry. Many of us have moved into teaching early childhood music with limited experience in the various meters and tonalities. This Etude will fill the gap, as not only does it provide materials and guidelines for classroom use, but also for professional development.

This Etude is designed to guide your thinking mind to provide for your musical mind to absorb meters and tonalities just as the children do—through sound. We cannot think our way into competence with meters and tonalities, but we can create a sound environment so that our own musical minds can grow without the children as well as with the children. Immersing ourselves in the various meters and tonalities prepares us to use them with children.

Etude 1 is designed in ten-minute segments, alternating rhythm and tonal throughout the ten minutes. You will be working with two meters and one tonality (RTR) or two tonalities and one meter (TRT) in each ten-minute segment. Separating contrasting meters with a tonality and contrasting tonalities with a meter provides for the musical mind to learn most efficiently. Plan about ten minutes a couple of times a week for your own immersion in this Etude, focusing on meters one day (RTR) and tonalities (TRT) the next. Meters in this Etude are ordered by difficulty and tonalities are ordered as recommended in this book. Rotate through all meters and all tonalities, even if you feel competent in some of them. It is the contrast between meters and between tonalities that will enlighten your musical mind as well as the children's.

Consider recording your sessions with each tonality and meter as described in this Etude, and use the recordings to immerse your musical mind while driving the car or when your thinking mind is otherwise engaged. You could even play the recordings in the classroom, singing along and moving along with the children, even if you have to ask a colleague who is more experienced in the various meters and tonalities to create the recordings for you. You could also make the recordings accessible to parents and children to use at home between class sessions.

You will find yourself and the children making great progress in the first few weeks. Expect an occasional surprise visit of a meter or tonality when you least expect it, as your musical mind continues to practice while your thinking mind is engaged elsewhere. You will be practicing every time you engage with these materials, whether alone or in the classroom. Arrows ➜ will guide you throughout this Etude.

Meters

You will engage in one of the meters below for two to three minutes, followed by a two to three minute tonal segment as described in the next section, and then another two to three minute segment in a contrasting meter. Each meter offers an eight-bar rhythm narrative that includes only macro and micro beats, followed by an eight-bar narrative that includes divisions. Try to let go of the notation as soon as possible so your musical mind can take over. Start each meter with a prep and chant the rhythm narrative expressively on "bah." Security with macro and micro beats and the division patterns presented here in each meter provides the foundation for more difficult rhythm patterns in each meter, both in children and teachers. Similarly, security with one beat grouping in each of the more difficult meters provides the necessary readiness for competence with other beat groupings in those meters.

→ **Select a pair of contrasting meters**

- Include an unusual meter in each pair to provide the greatest contrast.
- Create a tonal segment as described below to insert between your chosen meters (RTR).

→ **Go through the four steps below with each chosen meter**

Start with a rhythm prep. Keep the rhythm narrative going throughout each rhythm segment as described without losing a beat, providing an extended time in each meter.

1. Chant the first eight-bar rhythm narrative in the meter twice through, engaging in flowing movement throughout. Use hips, knees, shoulders, and outstretched arms without regard to macro and micro beats.
2. Chant the first eight-bar narrative in the meter again followed by the second eight-bar narrative in the meter, now with more gentle flowing movement that reflects greater awareness of macro and micro beats.
3. Chant the sixteen bars again, this time engaging in macro and micro beat movement. Shift weight side to side on macro beats, while bouncing micro beats with the knees. Use full body weight, putting greater weight on macro beats.
4. Chant the sixteen bars in the meter one more time, leaping into macro beats with full body weight while lively stepping micro beats throughout.[2]

In the Classroom:

- Implement without verbalization.
- Use more basic movement with Step 4 with beginners and children younger than kindergarten.
- Intersperse songs as needed to create sets of Rhythm, Tonal, Song (RTS) as described in Chapter 4.

Duple Meter

Figure 8.1   Duple, macro/micro

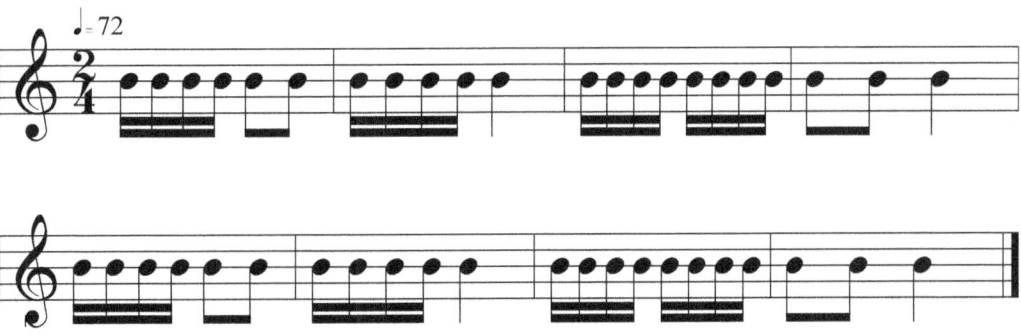

Figure 8.2   Duple, with divisions

Triple Meter

Figure 8.3   Triple, macro/micro

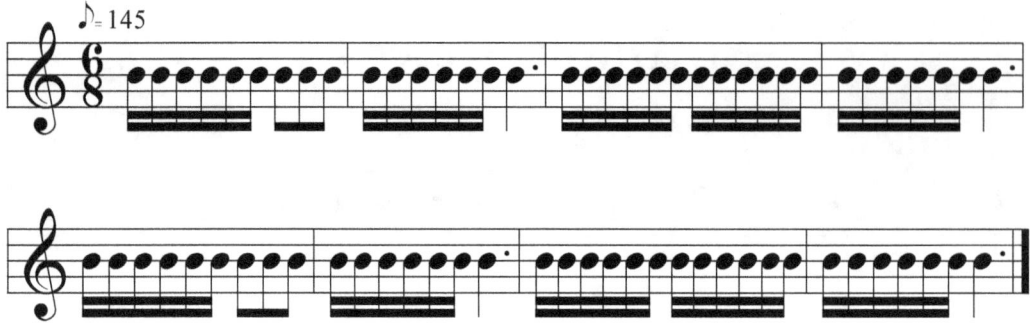

Figure 8.4 Triple, with divisions

Unusual Paired Meter

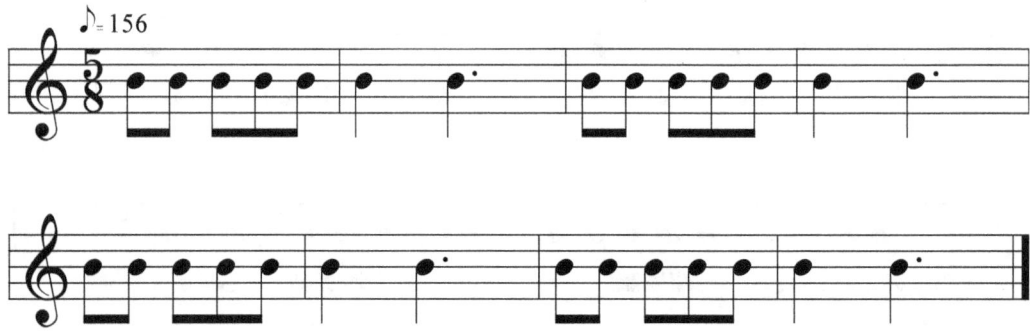

Figure 8.5 Unusual Paired, macro/micro

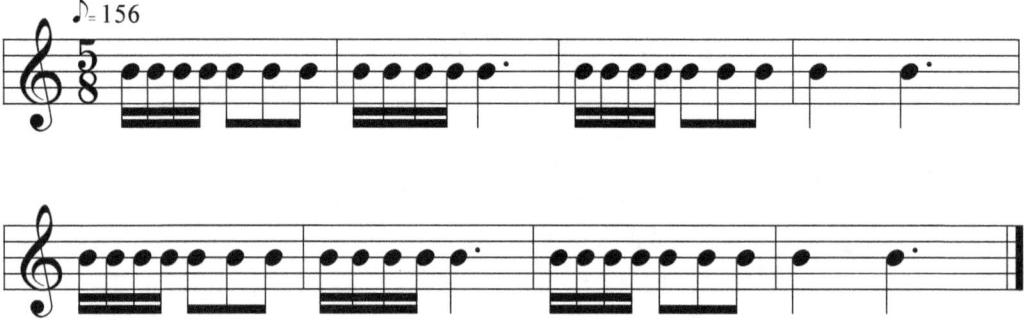

Figure 8.6 Unusual Paired, with divisions

Unusual Unpaired Meter

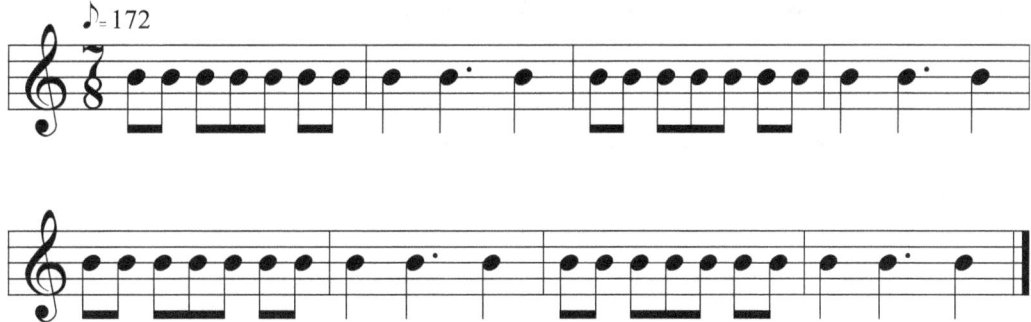

Figure 8.7   Unusual Unpaired, macro/micro

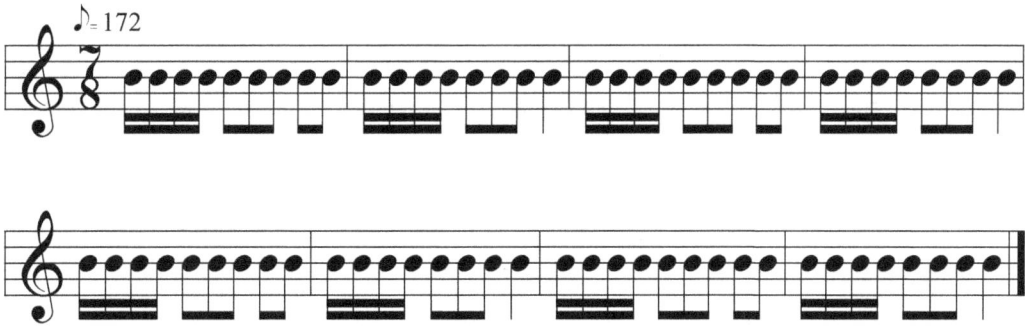

Figure 8.8   Unusual Unpaired, with divisions

Combined Meter

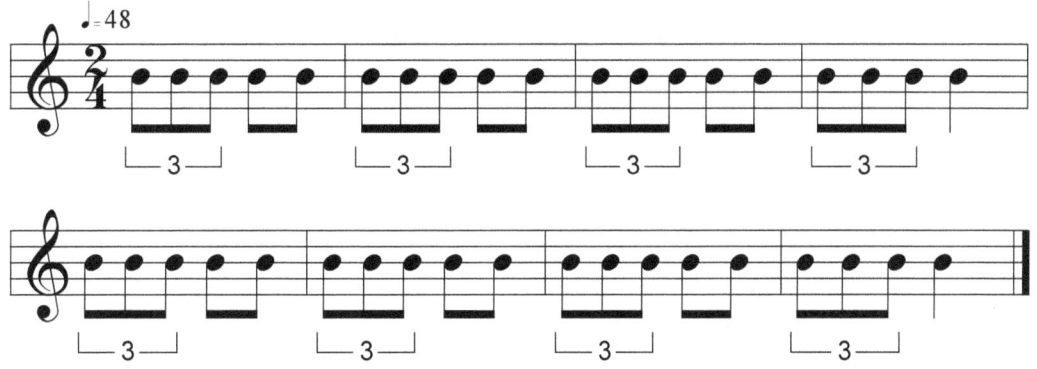

Figure 8.9   Combined, macro/micro

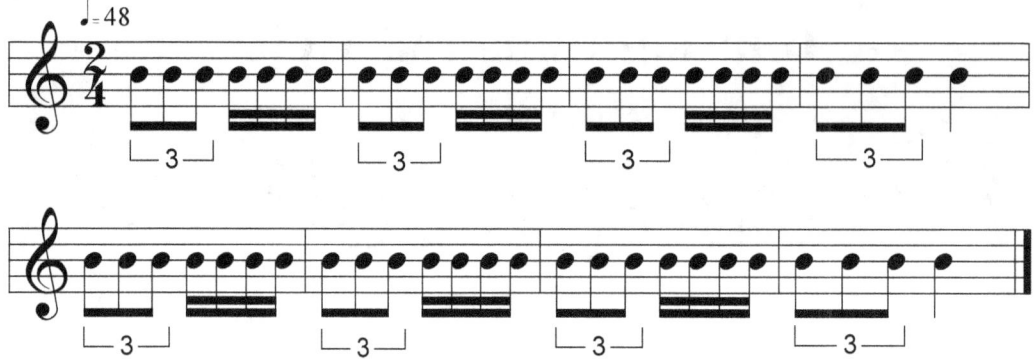

Figure 8.10 Combined, with divisions

Tonalities

You will engage in a tonal narrative and song in the same tonality for two to three minutes, followed by a two to three minute rhythm segment described in the previous section, and then another two to three minute tonal narrative and song in a contrasting tonality. The text of each song is a translation of a Japanese haiku. Start each tonality with a prep and let go of the notation as soon as possible so your musical mind can take over.

This Etude will help you to better understand the characteristics tones of the various tonalities, as all of the tonal narratives share a resting tone, so you will create the unique prep for each tonality from a single pitch. Corresponding songs should grow out of each tonal narrative seamlessly. Each of the tonal narratives and songs end on the resting tone, making it easy for you to set up each tonal prep by locating the resting tone and creating the prep (5-6-5-4-3-2-7-1) in accordance with the key signature.

All of the tonal narratives and songs in this Etude are in the initial singing range to serve the musical mind, and the song architecture of each supports the musical mind—yours as well as the children's. The tonal narrative and song in each tonality, except for one, share the same key, meter, and resting tone, facilitating a seamless transition from narrative to song, even if the tonal narrative and song are in different tempos.

Special Challenge: Aeolian tonality presents a song in a different key than the narrative in Aeolian tonality, inviting hands-on experience with seamlessly changing keys within a tonality while maintaining the tonality. This may interrupt your musical mind, giving you first-hand experience in how a focused musical mind can easily be derailed by thinking, and making you more mindful of the need to create a seamless key change without interruption for the young musical mind. (See p. 91 for how to change keys and sustain the tonality.)

→ **Select a pair of contrasting tonalities**

- Include one tonality with a major third and one with a minor third to provide the greatest contrast. (The ordering of tonalities here provides for that contrast.)
- Create a rhythm segment as described in the earlier section to insert between your chosen tonalities (TRT).

→ **Go through the three steps below with each chosen tonality**

Start with a tonal prep. Keep the tonality going without interruption through these three steps as described, providing an extended time in each tonality.

1. Sing the tonal narrative at least twice through on "too," (more repetitions with children), engaging with flowing movement throughout. Use hips, knees, shoulders, and outstretched arms without regard to macro and micro beats.

2. Move seamlessly into singing the art song at least twice through with flowing movement. (Change keys for the second song if necessary, using a tonal prep without interruption as described on p. 91.)

3. Continue singing the art song at least 2 to 4 additional times, now exploring the energy of the line in movement. Capture the drama of the song with all its musical nuance. Continue to use flowing movement while using body weight as needed for weight in meter. Use arms and hands for building intensity, articulating words, or shifting styles. Continue movement through any rests, reflect the energy in the rhythm of the words, and explore the change in energy with any change of meter. Uncover greater musical nuance in movement with each repetition. Continue singing and movement until you alone, or you and the children get lost in sheer musicality.[3]

In the Classroom:

- Implement without verbalization.
- Simplify movement with the energy of the line as needed in Step 3 to accommodate age.
- Intersperse songs as needed to create sets of Rhythm, Tonal, Song (RTS) as described in Chapter 4.
- Many more verses of a tonal narrative would be necessary with children if presented without the song in the tonality.

Dorian Tonality

Figure 8.11 Dorian, Duple

The Frog and the Cherry Petal

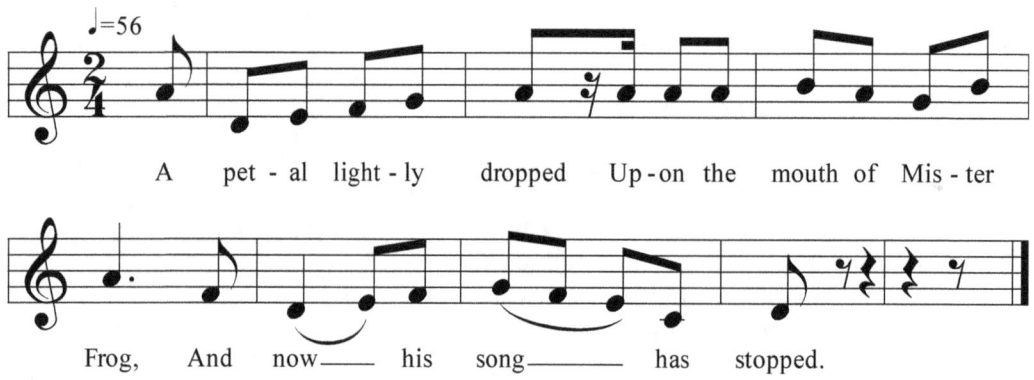

Figure 8.12 Dorian, Duple

Mixolydian Tonality

Figure 8.13 Mixolydian, Triple

Fish in the River

Figure 8.14 Mixolydian, Triple

Phrygian Tonality

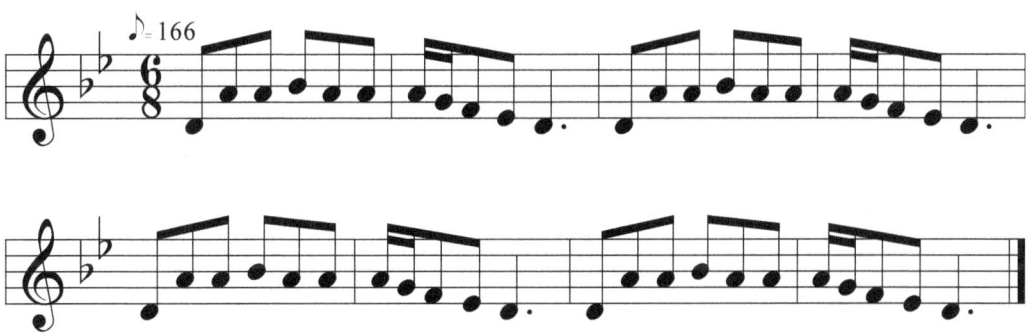

Figure 8.15 Phrygian, Triple

The Little Fly

Figure 8.16 Phrygian, Triple/Duple

Lydian Tonality

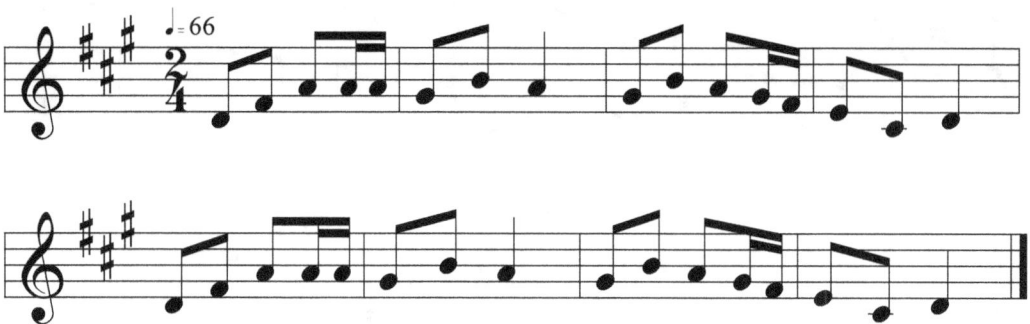

Figure 8.17 Lydian, Duple

Never in a Hurry

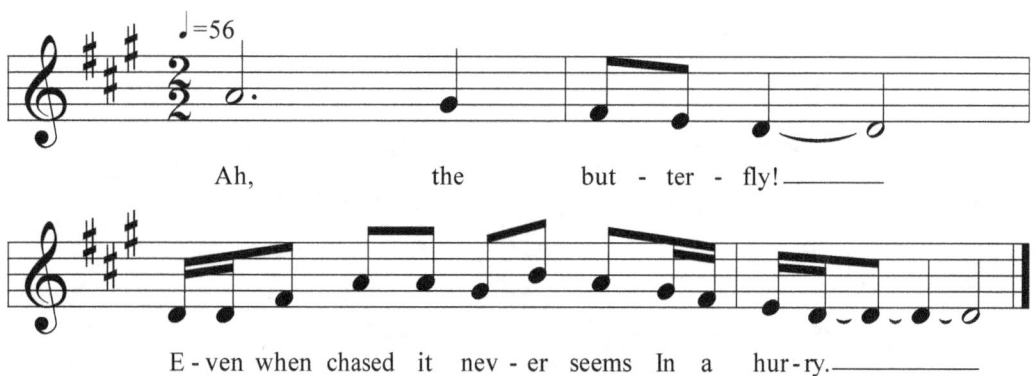

Ah,   the   but - ter - fly! ____
E - ven when chased it nev - er seems In a   hur - ry. ____

Figure 8.18 Lydian, Duple

Aeolian Tonality

Figure 8.19 Aeolian, Duple

Fluttering Butterflies

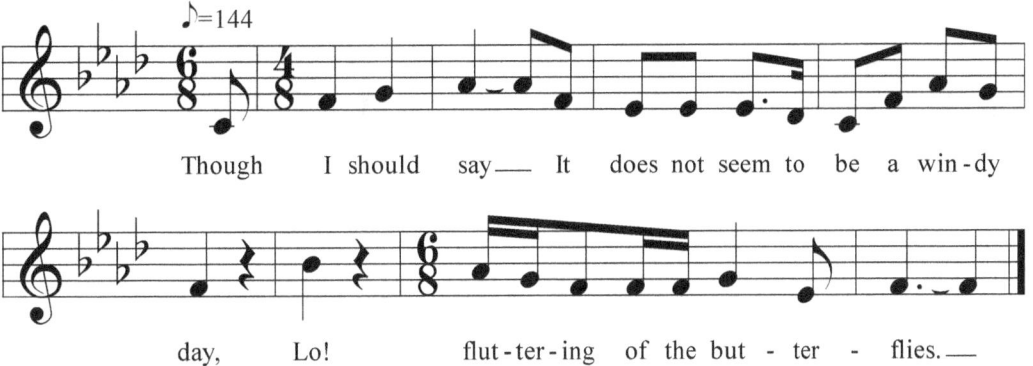

Figure 8.20   Aeolian, Duple/Triple

Major Tonality

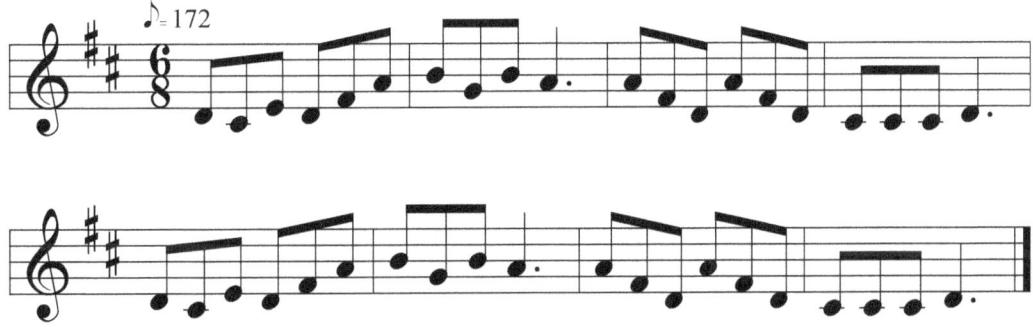

Figure 8.21   Major, Triple

The New Year's Here Again

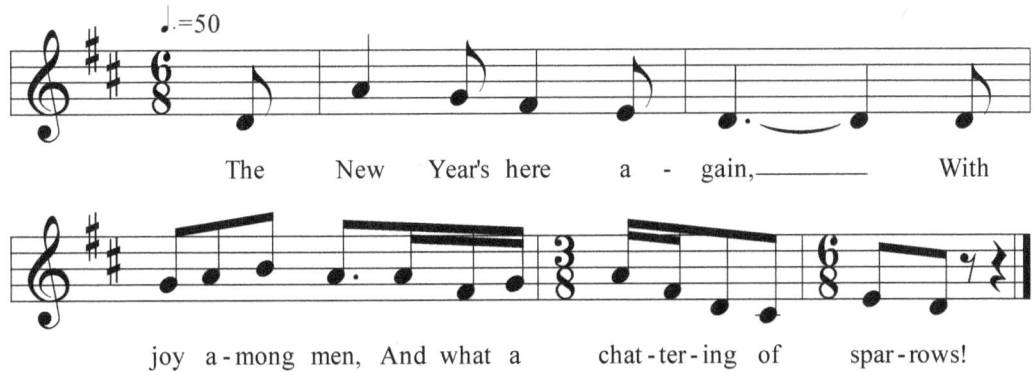

Figure 8.22   Major, Triple

Minor Tonality

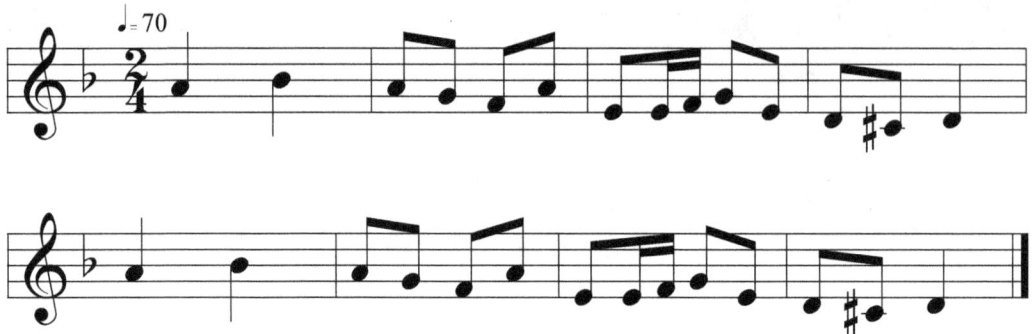

Figure 8.23 Minor, Duple

The Pheasant

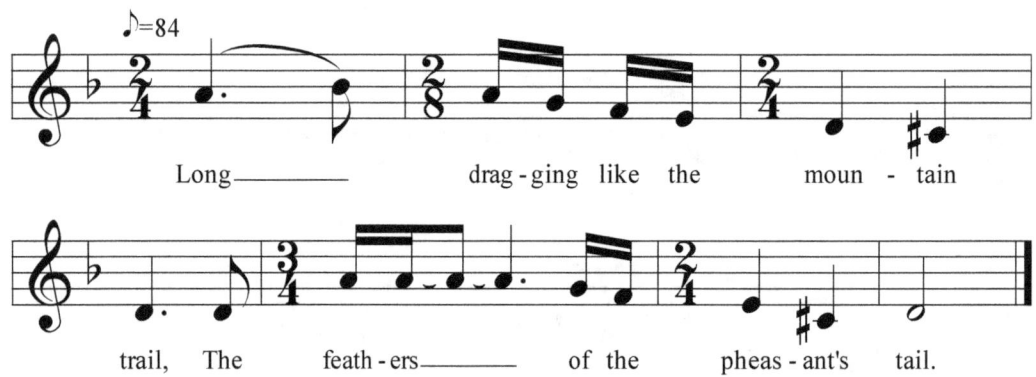

Figure 8.24 Minor, Duple/Triple

Etude 2

For Planning Lessons

We can plan lessons that are so musical and so delightful that we can hardly wait to engage with the children. Thoughtful planning can assure appropriate music content and ease in sculpting energy, assuring greater music learning and more effective classes. This Etude guides you in the process of planning lessons that serve children's artistry, enchant children, and charm attending adults.

Etude 2 is designed to take you through the process of planning lessons, whatever the age or development of the children, with or without attending adults. You will be engaged in selecting music content and types of activities as well as in sculpting energy to create seamless classes for young children, both for beginning and long-term classes at the ages of your choice. (Review pp. 93-98 as needed.)

- **Classes for Beginners**—designed for immersion in the various meters and tonalities through rhythm and tonal narratives, with the addition of group involvement in Rhythm Dialogue Activity, Resting Tone Activity, Macro/Micro Beat Activity, and Tonal Dialogue Activity to immerse children in smaller rhythm and tonal units in the context of meter and tonality. Play songs are most appropriate at this level, with perhaps an occasional art song.

- **Classes for Long-term Students**—designed for abundant one-on-one interaction in the various meters and tonalities through Rhythm Dialogue Activity, Resting Tone Activity, Macro/Micro Beat Activity, and Tonal Dialogue Activity, with ongoing immersion in the various meters and tonalities through rhythm and tonal narratives. Art songs and gem songs are appropriate for this level, with an occasional play song. Fewer songs are needed as rhythm and tonal activities expand.

This Etude will guide you in planning lessons with contrasting meters and contrasting tonalities in each class, rotating meters and tonalities through successive classes, and balancing rhythm activity, tonal activity, and song (RTS). Thirty- to fifty-minute classes allow for three to five sets of RTS within each class, with enough time to also include your chosen opening and closing songs with each class and an extra song or two. This Etude guides hands-on manipulation of activities through two sets of RTS. You will, in the process, develop insights that can be applied to all levels and any number of RTS sets to create highly musical and appealing classes.

This Etude invites your unique creativity, sense of humor, and playfulness in planning lessons for your children. It is designed to guide music content and music activities at each level, keeping you on track with music learning throughout. The Etude will assist you in sculpting energy by posing various combinations of activities that you will encounter as children develop from beginners into long-term students, so that you can better anticipate the challenges you might face in sculpting energy as well as stimulating music learning.

An arrow → invites you to engage with the corresponding challenge. Your young artists' response to each of your decisions in planning lessons will guide you further so that you can consistently create classes that capture the musical mind, bring the children into the palm of your hand, and give voice to children's artistry.

WEEK	1	2	3	4
Rhythm Activity	Duple	Triple	Un Pr	Un Unpr
Tonal Activity	Dorian	Mixolydian	Phrygian	Lydian
Song				
Rhythm Activity	Un Pr	Un Unpr	Duple	Triple
Tonal Activity	Mixolydian	Phrygian	Lydian	Aeolian
Song				

Figure 9.1 Four weeks, meters and tonalities

Figure 9.1 presents two sets of RTS that have been laid out for four weeks. Each week includes a pair of contrasting meters, with one unusual meter in each pair, and a pair of contrasting tonalities, one with a minor third and the other with a major third. Rhythm activities are separated each week to avoid successive activities with different meters and tonal activities are separated to avoid successive activities with different tonalities. The first rhythm and tonal activity each week rotate meters or tonalities in accordance with their recommended order. Each successive week also includes a meter or tonality introduced one of the previous weeks (after Week 1) as well as presenting something new. Three to five sets of RTS would, of course, provide for including more meters and tonalities within each class and for greater rotation of meters and tonalities through each class and set of classes. The more sets of RTS we can include in our classes, the more we can reach and teach the musical mind. We allow about ten minutes for each set of RTS, but it is a good idea initially to prepare a couple more RTS sets than we think we will have time for, so we are prepared if the sets go more quickly than we had expected.

Classes for Beginners

Design: Classes for beginners are designed primarily for immersion and engagement. Rhythm and tonal narratives in the various meters and tonalities provide the sound environment for music learning, while play songs serve all other purposes. Flowing movement and macro/micro beat movement are used with rhythm and tonal activities, and rhythm or tonal preps precede each activity. Rhythm Dialogue Activity, Resting Tone Activity, Macro/Micro Beat Activity, and Tonal Dialogue Activity are offered through group activity. Play songs fill out the sets of RTS and an occasional art song might be included. Multiple repetitions of the easiest rhythm and tonal narratives and rhythm and tonal segments at this level capture the musical mind without props. Beginning classes can serve children for a term, a year, or longer, depending upon the length of each term, the time allotment for each class, and the particular combination of ages and logistics in scheduling.

Music Content: Rhythm content includes rhythm narratives and rhythm patterns with primarily macro and micro beats in four meters, some division patterns, and an occasional more difficult rhythm pattern thrown in for spice. Tonal content includes tonal narratives and basic tonal segments in seven tonalities, all with the simplest rhythm. Song architecture of tonal narratives serves the young musical mind, spinning around and between the resting tone and fifth in primarily stepwise passages, with rhythm and tonal anchors aligned. Basic tonal segments in every tonality include 5-3-1, 1-7-1, 5-6-5, 5-4-3-2-1, and 5-1, with the addition of 1-2-1 in Phrygian tonality and 5-4-5 in Lydian tonality to include all of the characteristic tones of each tonality. All tonal segments begin and end on either the resting tone or fifth, and all are presented with just macro and micro beats in Duple meter, with rhythm anchors and tonal anchors aligned. Play songs are used for sculpting energy and for overt engagement. An occasional art song grows out of a tonal narrative in the same tonality.

→ **Select Meters and Tonalities**

Select any one of the weeks in the layout presented in Figure 9.1, with its two sets of RTS.

→ **Plan Rhythm Activities**

Select the appropriate rhythm narratives from Etude 1 for each meter in the week you have chosen from Figure 9.1. Assume that for each of the rhythm activities you will have the children standing and involved in full body movement. Your movement will be gentle macro/micro beat movement, with knees bouncing on micro beats and body swaying with macro beats, modeling comfortable movement for all. You'll start with a rhythm prep and use just the first eight-bar rhythm narrative through at least eight repetitions, perhaps switching to flowing movement in a couple of repetitions, and perhaps throwing in an occasional second eight-bar narrative, always followed by the narrative with just macro and micro beats.

→ **Plan Tonal Activities**

Select the appropriate tonal narratives from Etude 1 for each tonality in the week you have chosen. Assume that for each of the tonal narratives you will have the children sitting, engaging the upper body in flowing movement. You, too, will be sitting, leading flowing movement with the upper body. You'll start with a tonal prep and take the children through each tonal narrative with at least eight repetitions, immersing children in the tonality (without the art song). You might include more repetitions just to see how long the tonality can compel the young musical mind.

→ **Plan Songs**

Use the two play songs presented in Chapter 1 for your RTS sets, with children up and moving with *Who Can Walk Like a Duck* and sitting with *David Has a Dirty Face*. These songs would be in addition to your opening and closing songs. Either of these play songs can be used in either RTS set. (Additional Play songs are offered in Etude 3. If you do not find contrasting play songs in this book that you feel are appropriate for your group of youngsters, define the type of play song you would like to use and include the names of songs you know that you think would fit that description.)

✶ **Energy Considerations**

- Review the musical energy of each rhythm narrative, tonal narrative, and song and how you think each might affect children's energy.
- Review the difference in energy between flowing movement and macro/micro beat movement, between sitting and standing, and between their various possible combinations with rhythm and tonal narratives. For example, a tonal activity with flowing movement is generally more calming than a rhythm activity with macro/micro beat movement, and sitting is generally more calming than standing. However, engaging standing children in full body flowing movement with tonal changes the energy dynamic.

✶ **Tips**

- Trust the young musical mind. The more repetitions of each rhythm and tonal narrative, the more the narrative will compel the musical mind, calming children's energy and focusing the musical mind.
- Vary successive activities so that children go from sitting to standing and vice versa rather than being in one position too long.
- Remember that sitting on a two-step folding stool or stepladder with children on the floor can create a very comfortable distance for the youngest children, with or without accompanying adults.
- Remember that presenting a meter on a drum or a tonality on a recorder or other instrument can be an option for immersion activities.

> **Brainstorming: Beginning Classes**
>
> ★ How might you lead children into position for each of the RTS activities without any verbalization?
>
> ★ What are the fewest number of words you can use to give children and attending adults any instructions you might want them to have?

→ **Put It All Together**

Lay out each RTS set and the sequence of sets to create a series of activities that you feel will best serve music learning while sculpting children's energy. Plan to include rhythm and tonal preps with each activity. Try to alternate sitting and standing activities. Consider this to be your basic lesson plan, and then adjust that basic lesson plan to accommodate each of the modifications below.

→ Add a bit of group Rhythm Dialogue Activity to one of the rhythm activities so that Rhythm Dialogue grows out of the rhythm narrative. Consider how this variation might change children's energy. Rearrange activities as needed within and between each RTS set to accommodate the change.

→ Add a bit of group Resting Tone Activity to one of the tonal activities. Engage children in the tonal narrative for several verses and then move into the Resting Tone Activity in the same key, sustaining the tonality throughout. Consider how this option might change children's energy. Rearrange activities as needed within and between each RTS set to accommodate the change.

→ Add a bit of group Macro/Micro Beat Activity to one of the rhythm activities. Your basic lesson plan engages you in gentle macro/micro beat movement. Now exaggerate that movement to engage children and accompanying adults in macro/micro beat movement, and move into "tonguing" (p. 28). Consider how this addition might change children's energy and rearrange activities as needed.

→ Use just one play song and in place of the other, use the art song from Etude 1 that is in the same tonality as one of the tonal narratives you have chosen. Rearrange activities as needed so the art song flows directly out of the tonal narrative. Consider how this change might affect children's energy and rearrange activities to accommodate the change.

→ Add rhythm sticks for each child to one rhythm activity for immersion and consider how that might change children's energy. Plan how you are going to pass out and collect the rhythm sticks within the ongoing meter to best sculpt energy.

You have now been through the process of starting with sets of RTS, putting in musical content, and thinking through the sculpting of energy with each different type of activity, preparing you to create your own lesson plans. Now you can put together your own sets of RTS to fill the time frame you have with beginners, choose your own rhythm and tonal narratives and songs, and choose the activities for each lesson, assured that you can sculpt energy with whatever you choose. The same process serves three, four, or five sets of RTS through months of classes, so you are equipped to plan seamless classes for beginners through multiple sets of RTS and through multiple weeks. Just add your opening and closing. Your efforts with beginners prepare you to create classes for long-term students just as they prepare your beginners to become long-term students.

Classes for Long-term Students

Design: Classes for long-term students are designed to include an abundance of one-on-one activities, with ongoing immersion built into the one-on-one activities. Difficulty increases in immersion activities and in one-on-one activities as children develop. Rhythm and tonal narratives in the various meters and tonalities continue to provide the sound environment for music learning, with Rhythm Dialogue Activity, Resting Tone Activity, Macro/Micro Beat Activity, and Tonal Dialogue Activity, all of which were introduced in group activity in beginning classes, growing out of the narratives or group activities into one-on-one activities. Success with Rhythm Dialogue Activity one-on-one paves the way for success with one-on-one Resting Tone Activity; success with both serves one-on-one response with Macro/Micro Beat Activity; and success with the more difficult Tonal Dialogue Activity one-on-one is most easily achieved when children are comfortable with the other three activities one-on-one. Flowing movement and macro/micro beat movement continue to be used with rhythm and tonal activities, and movement with the energy of the line is added with art songs and gem songs. Rhythm and tonal preps continue to precede each activity.

Art songs and gem songs in the various meters and tonalities serve long-term students, with an occasional play song added. Fewer songs are needed than with beginners because of the increased time with one-on-one activities. Props become a regular addition with long-term classes, serving as musical instruments for children to practice music. Rhythm and tonal activities may go on quite long, with a sequence of several activities in one meter or one tonality. Assume for the purpose of this Etude that you have access to the following props:

- A hoop for each child and one for yourself
- A pair of pom-poms for each child and a pair for yourself
- One puppet.
- One toy microphone.

Music Content: Rhythm content includes rhythm narratives and rhythm patterns with macro and micro beats and division patterns in at least four meters, with one-on-one activities starting with just macro and micro beats. Division patterns are included as children develop and more difficult rhythm patterns are occasionally used in each meter. Combined meter can be included in the rotation of meters as children develop. Tonal content includes tonal narratives and tonal segments in seven tonalities with simple rhythm and song architecture that serves the young musical mind. Tonal segments for one-on-one activities grow out of tonal narratives and capture all of the characteristic tones of the tonality. Tonal segments include 5-3-1, 1-7-1, 5-6-5, 5-4-3-2-1, 5-1, with the addition of 1-2 1 in Phrygian tonality and 5-4-5 in Lydian. We can begin to expand tonal segments around the resting tone and fifth (7-2-1, 6-4-5) when children demonstrate readiness for more. Tonal segments are presented with just macro and micro beats in Duple meter, with all segments starting and ending on either the resting tone or fifth, and with rhythm and tonal anchors aligned. Groups somewhat competent with Resting Tone Activity or Tonal Dialogue Activity in Duple meter may be ready for those activities in Triple meter, but always with the same tonal and rhythm parameters. Art songs and Gem songs often grow out of tonal activities in all tonalities and meters, and an occasional play song is included.

One-on-one activities are introduced as addressed in Chapter 2 (pp. 32-40), in the recommended order of meters and tonalities. Difficulty of rhythm and tonal can increase in immersion activities, but one-on-one activities have to be at the very basic level, scaffolding each child as needed and growing in difficulty with the child.

→ **Select Meters and Tonalities**

Choose any one of the weeks in the layout presented in Figure 9.1 with its two sets of RTS.

→ **Plan Rhythm Activities**

Select the appropriate rhythm narratives from Etude 1 for each meter in the week you have chosen from the chart. Assume that for each of the rhythm activities the children will either be standing and involved in full body movement as with the class for beginners, or engaged with a prop for immersion, Rhythm Dialogue Activity, or Macro/Micro Beat Activity, any of which could be standing or sitting. You choose.

→ **Plan Tonal Activities**

Select the corresponding tonal narratives from Etude 1 for each tonality in the week you have chosen. Assume that for each of the tonal narratives you will have the children either sitting, engaging the upper body in flowing movement as with the class for beginners, or engaged with a prop for tonal immersion, Resting Tone Activity or Tonal Dialogue Activity, any of which could be standing or sitting. You choose.

→ **Plan Songs**

Select art songs or gem songs in the same tonalities as the tonal narratives, choosing the songs from Chapter 1, Chapter 4, Etude 1, or Etude 3. Add one play song (Chapter 1, Etude 3) with or without opening and closing songs. (Note: If you are working in a choral context with children in kindergarten and older, Chapter 7 and Etude 3 present songs in the higher range for children who have the background for vocal and ensemble development. Include *I Have a Funny Clown* [p. 181] for your play song just to witness the difference in children's vocal sound when jumping.)

※ **Energy Considerations**

- Review the musical energy of each rhythm narrative, tonal narrative, and song you have chosen and how each might affect children's energy.
- Review the Brainstorming sidebar and then consider how each of the props and various ways to use them might affect children's energy.
- Review your energy concerns with beginners for group Rhythm Dialogue Activity, Resting Tone Activity, and Macro/Micro Beat Activity and think about how moving to one-on-one activity with each might shift energy.

※ **Tips**

- Use a chosen prop for either rhythm or tonal within one class session rather than for both.
- Vary the props so as not to use the same props in every class session.
- Remember that every activity with a prop can be multiplied by 4 meters or seven tonalities, expanding options for activities, and that children can engage in every meter and tonality through multiple props.

> **Brainstorming: Long-term Classes**
>
> ★ How many different ways can you come up with to use each of the four props for rhythm activities? How many different ways might you use each of the four props for tonal activities? Think out of the box. For example, hoops can define individual space, they can serve for children to move in, out, around, and through, and they can be held and bounced with two hands or moved side to side. How might you apply any of these options for immersion, Rhythm Dialogue Activity, Resting Tone Activity, Macro/Micro Beat Activity and Tonal Dialogue Activity?
>
> ★ How many different ways might you use props that you may already have access to or those that you might want to acquire?
>
> ★ How might you adapt some of your ideas to accommodate holidays, seasons, or other special occasions?

→ **Put It All Together**

Lay out each RTS set and the sequence of sets to create a series of successive activities that you feel will best serve music learning while sculpting children's energy. Plan to include rhythm and tonal preps with each activity. Try to alternate sitting and standing activities as well as balancing activities with and without props. Consider this to be your basic lesson plan, and then adjust that basic lesson plan to accommodate each of the modifications below, while also including some immersion with each one-on-one activity.

→ Plan one rhythm activity with props as a Rhythm Dialogue Activity, starting as a group activity and then moving into one-on-one Rhythm Dialogue. Plan how you are going to hand out and collect the props with the meter running, or how the single prop that stays in your hand is going to appear and disappear while you sustain the meter. Plan how you are going to move from one child to the next for one-on-one interaction while sustaining the musical mind of all. Make the other rhythm activity more for immersion than for one-on-one engagement and use movement rather than props. Rearrange activities as needed within and between each RTS set to accommvodate the changes.

→ Plan one rhythm activity as group Macro/Micro Beat Activity with props for each child and one-on-one interaction. Plan how you are going to hand out and collect the props with the meter running. Make the other rhythm activity more for immersion than for one-on-one engagement and use movement rather than props. Plan how you are going to move from one child to the next for one-on-one interaction while sustaining the musical mind of all. Rearrange activities as needed within and between each RTS set to accommodate the changes.

→ Plan one tonal activity as a Resting Tone Activity, starting as a group activity and moving into one-on-one resting tone response. Plan how you are going to hand out and collect the props while sustaining tonality, or how the single prop that stays in your hand is going to appear or disappear within the tonal narrative. Plan how you are going to move from one child to the next for one-on-one interaction while sustaining the musical mind of all. Make the other tonal activity more for immersion than for one-on-one engagement and use movement rather than props. Rearrange activities as needed within and between each RTS set to accommodate the changes.

→ Plan one tonal activity as a Tonal Dialogue Activity, starting as a group activity and moving into one-on-one Tonal Dialogue. Plan how you are going to hand out and collect the props with the meter running, or how the single prop that stays in your hand is going to appear or disappear within the meter. Plan how you are going to move from one child to the next for one-on-one interaction while sustaining the musical mind of all. Make the other tonal activity more for immersion than for one-on-one engagement and use movement rather than props. Rearrange activities as needed within and between each RTS set to accommodate the changes.

→ Use an art song in one set of RTS and a gem song in the other. Select the art song and gem song in the same tonalities as the tonal narratives. Rearrange activities as needed so the songs flow directly out of the tonal narratives. Be mindful of how the chosen songs might affect energy. Art songs and gem songs can be found in Chapter 1, Chapter 4, Etude 1 and Etude 3. (Chapter 7 and Etude 3 include songs in the higher range for children in kindergarten and older who have the background for vocal and ensemble development.)

You might enjoy playing with expanding activities within one meter or one tonality once you have experience with each of the various options. For example, you might start a tonality with a tonal narrative, moving into Resting Tone Activity and then into an art song in the same tonality, with one tonality dominating the sequence of activities. You might also like to try your hand at creating a playful sequence of activities under one theme.

Remember that if you are working in a choral context with children in kindergarten and older, everything you do to develop the musical mind develops the voice, so continue to feed the musical mind while also serving the vocal instrument. You might with these children move from a tonal narrative into an art song in the tonality in the initial singing range, changing the key if necessary as described in Chapter 4. You might then change the key once again, sustaining the tonality, and move into a song in the same tonality in the higher singing range. (Chapter 7, Etude 3). Remember, too, that you can always transpose one of the little art songs or gem songs up a third to serve the vocal instrument. (It might be best to use some art songs in the initial singing range and others in the higher singing range rather than transposing songs the children know in the lower range.)

You have now been through the process of starting with sets of RTS, putting in musical content, and thinking through the sculpting of energy with each different type of activity for long-term students, preparing you to create your own lesson plans. Now you can put together your own sets of RTS to fill the time frame you have with your long-term children, choose your own rhythm and tonal narratives and songs, and choose activities and props for each lesson for both group and one-on-one activities, assured that you can sculpt energy with whatever you choose. The same process serves three, four, or five sets of RTS through months of classes, so you are equipped to plan seamless classes for long-term students through multiple sets of RTS and through multiple weeks, with or without an opening and closing. The process you have gone through also prepares you to create lesson plans for more and more developed youngsters as they move into rhythm and tonal syllables, music reading and writing, and vocal development with ensemble singing, as addressed in Chapters 5, 6, and 7.

Etude 3
For Choosing Songs

Songs can transport young children into joyful engagement, sheer musicality, and vocal development throughout early childhood. Choosing songs that meet young children's musical needs is an ongoing process with every group we teach, and every successive term adds new challenge. This Etude offers a selection of twenty additional songs for early childhood, divided into groups of play songs, art songs, gem songs, and songs in the higher singing range. Each set of five songs includes songs for a variety of ages and musical maturity. This Etude guides you in selecting age-appropriate songs that meet children's musical needs.

Assume for the purpose of this Etude that you are choosing songs for a group of children that has had many months of appropriate instruction. They have been immersed in all of the various meters and tonalities. The children have engaged in Rhythm Dialogue Activity, Resting Tone Activity, Macro/Micro Beat Activity, and Tonal Dialogue Activity in the various meters and tonalities in both group activities and one-on-one interaction. These long-term students have experienced play songs, art songs, and gem songs. They have had extensive musical input, whatever their level of output. All of the songs you choose for this Etude are to be from this book. Arrows → invite you to engage with the creative challenges of this Etude.

- → Review the play songs, art songs, gem songs, and songs in the higher singing range presented in this Etude.

- → Select one of the following groups of long-term students.

  Group A—Four- and five-year-old children not yet in kindergarten
  Group B—Five- and six-year-old children in kindergarten and first grade

- → Select the following types of songs for the group of children that you have chosen. (Review criteria for songs worthy of children's artistry (pp. 84-88.)

  ### Group A
  - → 1 play song
  - → 2 art songs (initial singing range)
  - → 2 gem songs (initial singing range)

  ### Group B
  - → 1 art song (initial singing range)
  - → 1 gem song (initial singing range)
  - → 3 songs in the higher singing range

→ Include in the set of songs you choose:
- 4-5 tonalities
- 3-4 meters
- At least one song that directs the musical mind to rhythm
- At least one song that directs the musical mind to tonal

> **Reminders:**
> - Songs in the initial singing range directly serve the musical mind. Those in the higher singing range serve the vocal instrument.
> - Everything we do to develop the musical mind serves vocal development.
> - Simple rhythm in song directs the musical mind to tonal. Complex rhythm in song directs the musical mind to rhythm.

Play Songs

These are the songs we choose for their joy, their words, and for their immediacy without concern for tonality, meter, or vocal range. They serve many purposes, particularly with the youngest children and with beginners, as they engage, delight, and invite participation with and without attending adults. Play songs explain themselves without any verbalization, as the words suggest how to engage with them. Play songs are particularly effective in sculpting energy.

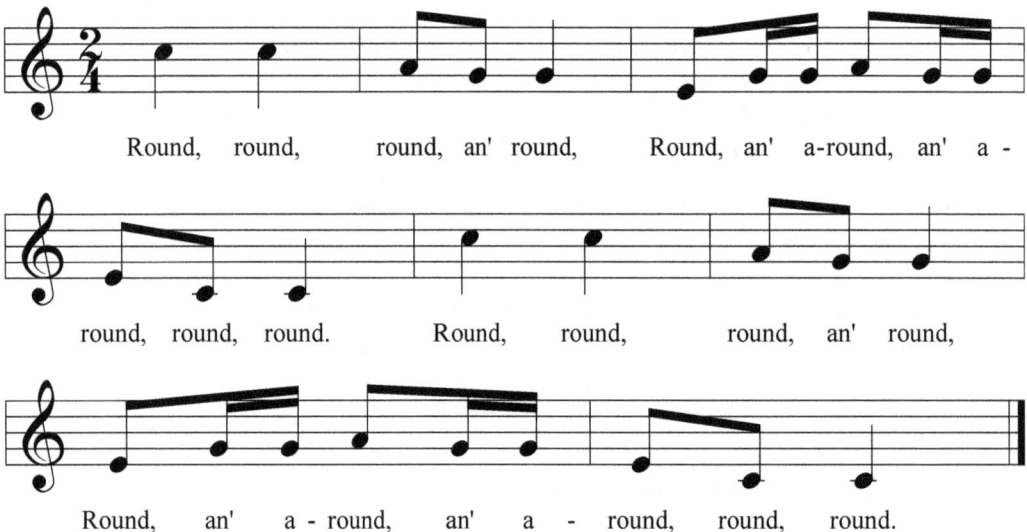

Figure 10.1   Major, Duple

2. Dance, dance, dance, an' dance,
   Dance, an' a-dance, an' a-dance, an' dance.
   Dance, dance, dance, an' dance,
   Dance, an' a-dance, an' a-dance, an' dance.

Round an' Round (Figure 10.1) offers an energetic song that brings children or parents and children together in community, with all in the circle engaging in singing and movement. Everybody circles together on the first verse and moves freely on the second verse, before returning to the first verse, with or without additional verses. This song serves well in charging energy and is particularly effective in getting everybody up and participating immediately.

Figure 10.2 Major, Duple

I Hear a Sound (Figure 10.2) is a playful song that grabs every little tyke. See how many recognizable sounds you might be able to come up with for multiple verses—fire engine, clock, cow—adapting the notated rhythm to the sound. Choose a few options and then bring the song back in a few weeks, starting with the train verse and using different sounds. This song serves well in sculpting energy, settling children in a sitting position after being up and engaged in a more active song.

I Have a Friend

Figure 10.3   Major, Triple

I Have a Friend (Figure 10.3) is a tender little song that invites a moment of one-on-one intimacy with each child as we sing each child's name in successive verses. The song might include verses for Mommy, Grandpa, or whoever is special to the children. The song serves well to calm children after high energy activity, but more than that it provides one-on-one attention to each child in a very non-threatening way.

I Went To The Zoo

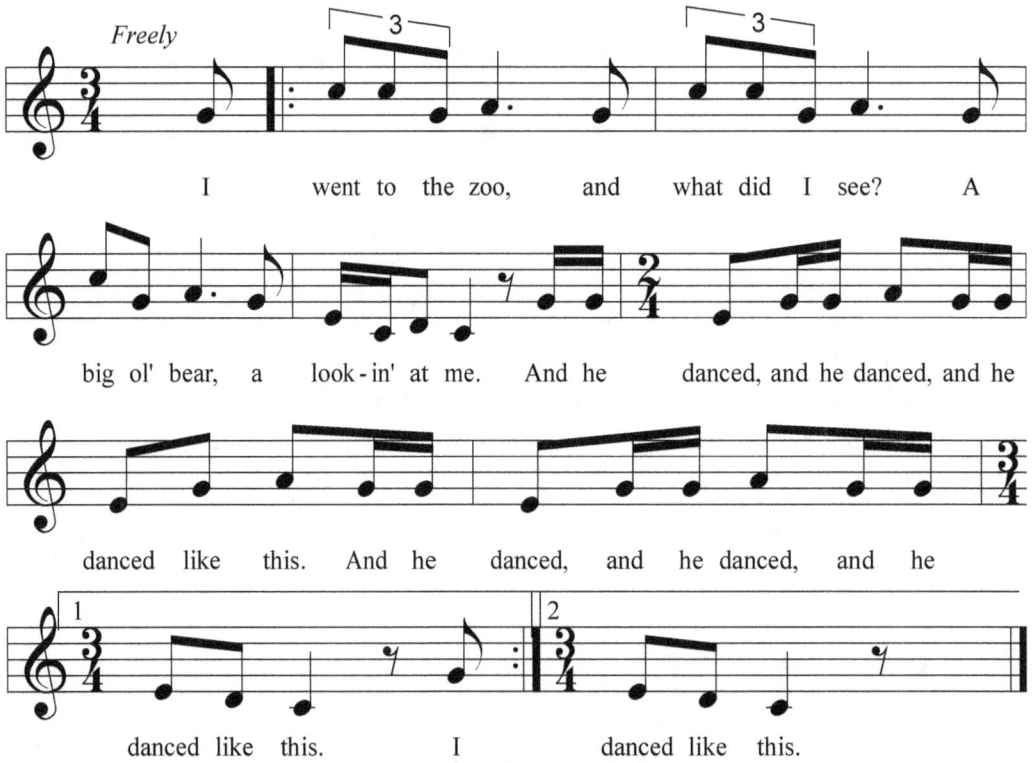

Figure 10.4   Major, Triple/Duple

232   Unveiling Artistry in Early Childhood Music

I Went to the Zoo (Figure 10.4) presents an active song that charms all. Lead the children in movement through several verses, dancing like a different animal in each verse. Bring the song back in a few weeks, starting with the bear and a different set of animals to vary the experience of the song. *I Went to the Zoo* serves well to get children up and moving after seated activity, and to encourage parents and children to be their playful selves in class.

Figure 10.5   Major, Triple

It's Time to Say Goodbye (Figure 10.5) offers an effective ending to any class, perhaps preceded by a song of great energy and followed only by a signature song. *It's Time to Say Goodbye* prepares little children for parting, as it is often difficult for little ones to leave something they love. Shaking each child's hand while they are in their safe space with an attending adult can add a personal touch, helping to ease any fear of being approached. Older children might prefer that we replace "little friends" with "my friends." The tenderness of this song touches the hearts of both children and attending adults before parting.

Additional play songs in this book that can be included in your choices are *Who Can Walk Like a Duck?* (p. 12) and *David Has a Dirty Face* (p. 12).

Art Songs

Art songs for tender ages are little kernels of art waiting to bloom in children. These songs compel the musical mind with tonality, meter, and the way rhythm, tonal, and text come together, with songs in the least common tonalities the most compelling. Each of these songs is short, with translated haiku texts, and in the singing range that best serves the musical mind. These little art songs serve children of all ages from birth, and they can be transposed up a third to serve the vocal instrument of older, more developed children, and even adult singers. Art songs are accompanied only by flowing movement or movment with the energy of the line, without props, prescribed movements, or verbalizations about the words. Little children receive the words of art songs as sound rather than for their literal meaning. This set of art songs includes several with considerably greater rhythmic challenge than those of Etude 1.

The Crescent Moon

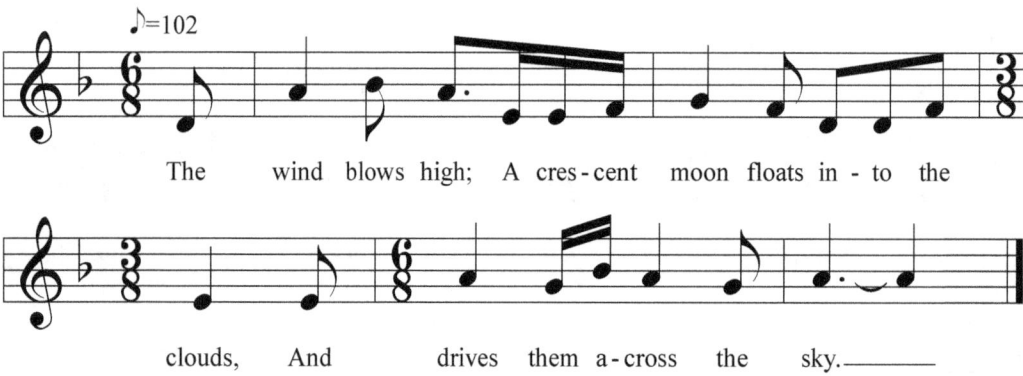

Figure 10.6   Phrygian, Triple

The Crescent Moon (Figure 10.6) is set in Phrygian tonality and Triple meter. The single 3/8 measure propels the turbulence of the wind, driving energy and the clouds across the sky. Rhythm, tonal, and text of the translated haiku each supports the other, with both rhythm and tonal supporting the musical mind; although the melodic contour, with much of the song beneath the resting tone, increases difficulty. Multiple repetitions of this song, started with tonality and meter preps and accompanied only by flowing movement or movement with the energy of the line, increases the experience of musicality with each repetition. This song can be used effectively with very young children for the musical experience of the song. It can be used with a broad range of ages for expression and articulation, and when transposed up a third, it can be used with more developed children in kindergarten and older.

Poppies

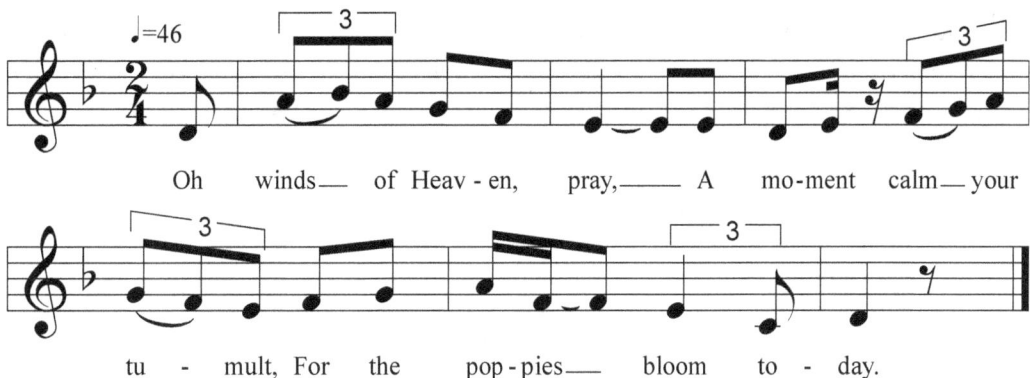

Figure 10.7 Aeolian, Combined

Poppies (Figure 10.7) offers a translated haiku text set in Aeolian tonality and Combined meter. The rhythmic challenge captures the tumult of the wind differently than *The Crescent Moon*, amidst the joyous blooming of the poppies. Tonal and rhythm preps prepare the musical mind for this song, with the beat grouping in Combined meter being 3/2, even though beat groupings throughout the song vary. Many successive repetitions, accompanied only by movement with the energy of the line, animate artistry at every level as children experience Combined meter shifting between groupings of threes and twos. This song serves well for the musical experience with all ages, whether or not the children are yet actively engaging in singing and movement. It also serves well as a warm-up for more developed singers in kindergarten and beyond when transposed up a third.

Dreams of Flowers

Figure 10.8 Lydian, Duple/Triple

Etudes / Etude 3 235

Dreams of Flowers (Figure 10.8) offers a setting of a translated haiku text in Lydian tonality, shifting between Duple and Triple meters. Tonal supports the musical mind, and rhythm, tonal, and text align. The tricky rhythm, with its shifting meters, elongations, ties, and upbeats increases the challenge and provides for a meaningful delivery of the text, as the rhythm mirrors the text. The shifting energy of the meters draws out greater musical depth. Starting with tonal and rhythm preps in Lydian tonality and Duple meter prepares the musical mind. Movement with the energy of the line of this song echoes its expression, whether with very young children or those old enough to engage in movement with the energy of the line. The song also serves well as a warm-up with older singers when transposed up a third. Multiple repetitions of this song cast a magical spell over children of all ages.

A Pair of Butterflies

Figure 10.9   Dorian, Unusual Paired

A Pair of Butterflies (Figure 10.9) offers a translated haiku text set in Dorian tonality and Unusual Paired meter. Rhythm and tonal anchors align with the natural pronunciation of text, such that this little song flows with great ease. Rhythm and tonal preps set up the musical mind for this song, with the beat grouping of 2/3 in Unusual Paired meter. (See Appendix B for beat groupings.) Movement might include flowing movement, macro and micro beat movement, and movement with the energy of the line. The song floats comfortably over all, becoming more compelling with each successive repetition. The song serves well with all ages, including as a warm-up for older singers when transposed up a third. Young children with the musical readiness for this song are as mesmerized by the song as they are butterflies.

A Lantern Dance

All night long the dance goes on, Till dew up-on the danc-ers' sleeves Pro - claim that it is dawn.

Figure 10.10   Minor, Unusual Paired

A Lantern Dance (Figure 10.10) sets the translated haiku text in Minor tonality, with Unusual Paired meter switching to and from Triple meter. The tempo of this song makes it still more difficult. Tonal supports the musical mind, despite the rhythm challenges, with rhythm, tonal, and text supporting each other. Tonal and rhythm preps set the aural stage, with the beat grouping of 2/3 for the rhythm prep in Unusual Paired meter. (See Appendix B for beat groupings.) Movement, perhaps a combination of flowing movement, macro/micro beat movement, and movement with the energy of the line, magnifies the drama of this little song. Multiple repetitions build intensity, with each successive repetition building greater excitement, whether in this key with young children or transposed up a third for a choral warm-up with older singers. This song becomes addictive. Children don't want the song to end.

There are many little art songs with haiku texts presented in this book that can be included among your choices, in addition to those in this Etude, *The Frog and the Cherry Petal* (pp. 7 & 214), *Never in a Hurry* (pp. 13 & 216), *The Modest Violet* (p. 65), *Quaint Fancy* (p. 80), Butterfly Dreams (p. 128), *Fish in the River* (p. 215), *The Little Fly* (p. 215), *Fluttering Butterflies* (p. 217), *The New Year's Here Again* (p. 217), and *The Pheasant* (p. 218).

Gem Songs

Gem songs, like art songs, compel the musical mind with tonality and meter, with the more unusual tonalities the most compelling. Gem songs become musically sophisticated play songs, with well-set texts in the various tonalities and meters. They have all the charm of play songs but with far greater musical challenge. Gem songs speak directly to the musical mind, while also delighting children with their texts. Youngsters with extended experience with the various tonalities and meters and with some experience with art songs are ready for the occasional gem song, used without props and accompanied only by movement. Every age and stage grows on gem songs that meet children's musical needs, with some more appropriate for younger children and others for older children. Gem songs provide for children at every age to bask in both the musicality and delight of the songs. This set of gem songs begins and ends with a play-party, each of which shifts in and out of unusual meters. It also includes three songs of varying types of difficulty to meet advancing musical needs. All are in the initial singing range.

I Need a Partner!

Figure 10.11 Mixolydian, Duple/Unusual Unpaired

I Need a Partner! (Figure 10.11) invites high energy in a play-party in Mixolydian tonality, with meter shifting between Duple and Unusual Unpaired meter. This little song is electric as children discover the excitement of the shifting meters at a quick tempo as well as the joy of finding a new partner with each repetition. Verbal instructions are not necessary, as the song and our trying to find a partner draws children right in. This song, unlike play songs, requires readiness both rhythmically and tonally, as the musical mind has to sustain tonality amidst such turbulent rhythm and activity. We set up the tonality and meter, using the prep for Duple meter, as the song begins in Duple. Everybody scrambles to find a partner during the first six measures of the song. Partners hold hands and dance throughout the rest of the song as we lead movement on macro beats by shifting weight on macro beats with our partner. The whole process begins anew with each verse, delighting children and attending adults, even if a child always chooses his parent for a partner. The utter delight of this song complements its musical sophistication, both of which are reflected in the joy of participants.

There Was an Owl

Figure 10.12 Lydian, Triple

There Was an Owl (Figure 10.12) offers an English rhyme set in Lydian tonality and Triple meter. The delightful words make this gem song pure fun to sing or experience. We start with tonal and rhythm preps. The melodic contour supports the musical mind, with the repeated characteristic fourth of Lydian tonality reassuring the musical mind that the owl is indeed in Lydian tonality. The rhythm, with Triple meter, upbeats, and ties presents some complexity but follows the natural pronunciation of the words. Rhythm, tonal and text support each other. Young musical minds steeped in tonalities and meters, but young enough to play with nonsense words, find multiple repetitions of this song irresistible, especially with movement of the energy of the line playing into the rhythm of the words in the final two measures.

Bang-Whang-Whang

Figure 10.13 Major, Unusual Unpaired

Bang-Whang-Whang (Figure 10.13), a setting of the words of Robert Browning in Major tonality and Unusual Unpaired meter, is considerably more difficult than *There Was An Owl*. Melodic contour supports the musical mind, and rhythm anchors, tonal anchors, and text align, but the rhythm is far more difficult and the text more sophisticated. The whole song is in Unusual Unpaired meter but with varying beat groupings as indicated by the shifts in time signatures. (See Appendix B for different beat groupings in this meter.) Tonal and rhythm preps for Major tonality and Unusual Unpaired meter sets up the musical mind for the 8/8 measure with three macro beats of uneven length, even though the beat groupings in the meter shift in the second measure and again in the third. The shift in beat groupings may challenge you, perhaps in notation if not sound, but children with the readiness for this song rhythmically will be very comfortable with it, as the rhythm reflects a natural expression of the words. The more adept we become in this meter with the various beat groupings, the more this little song just flows with exciting energy. Our movement with macro beats through multiple repetitions might start a parade.

When Woods Awake

When— woods a-wake— and trees are green And— leaves are large— and long,— 'Tis mer-ry to walk in the for-est fair— And hear the small— birds' song.

Figure 10.14 Dorian, Duple/Triple

When Woods Awake (Figure 10.14) offers an old English rhyme set in Dorian tonality, shifting between Duple and Triple meter. This song takes us into a different type of experience that serves very well with children on the older end of early childhood, challenging musical minds that need experience in the various meters and tonalities in the initial singing range. The sophistication of text and its expression take children directly into the choral art, inviting them to deliver with crisp articulation in the Duple section contrasted by the more flowing section in Triple meter.

Melodic contour and alignment of rhythm anchors, tonal anchors, and text support the musical mind, as do tonal and rhythm preps. Rhythm and melody are dictated by the text, and the shifting meters and melodic twists and turns reflect and deliver the expression of text. The shifting meters, rests, ties, and upbeats present some rhythm challenge. The shifting meters through multiple repetitions, with movement of the energy of the line, allow children to tangibly feel the impact of the meter change on the style and articulation of the text.

The melody and rhythm express the delightful text, setting the stage in the Duple section for the joy of the walk in the woods in the Triple section, and evoking merriment in the sound of the voices. Deliberate articulation of the words, carried out in movement, prepares young singers for singing with such musicality. This song serves well in the initial singing range to develop the musical mind of all ages, while transposing it up a third makes it a fine warm-up for more developed children as well as for adult singers.

Hat Party

Figure 10.15 Mixolydian, Duple/Unusual Paired/Unusual Unpaired

Hat Party (Figure 10.15) is an utterly joyous play-party for young children, yet the rhythm is highly complex. We set up Mixolydian tonality and Duple meter, as the song begins in Duple, but the meter shifts throughout between Duple, Unusual Paired, Unusual Unpaired, and Triple meters. This song surely requires readiness, both for the rhythmic complexity of shifting meters and for navigating tonality amidst the changing meters. Each verse of the song plays with words and their natural rhythms, making each verse catchy, as the rhythm is consistent with the pronunciation of the playful wordiness. The repetitive melodic line supports tonality in the musical mind, with the characteristic lowered seventh of Mixolydian securing tonality while helping drive the energy of the song. We can set up tonal and meter preps, but the meter shifts so quickly that setting up Duple meter hardly prepares the musical mind for such turbulence. We might just set up the tonality and then spontaneously break into this song as we might a play song, but only with children who have the musical readiness for this song.

Multiple types of recognizable hats can be offered with this song—firefighter, baker, construction worker. No instructions are necessary, as the song says it all, and each verse is repeated to allow time for each task. We keep the hats hidden until the song starts, then the collection of hats appears out of nowhere during the first verse, surprising the children and fueling anticipation for the "hat party." Each child picks a hat from the selection during the second verse. We all don our hats for the hat party in the third verse, with everybody proudly displaying their chosen hat on their head as we lead swaying movement on macro beats. We collect the hats on verse four, repeating the verse as needed to collect all of the hats and hide the collection. The song continues as it began, with no hats in verse five. Storing the collection of hats in a wagon behind a closed door makes it easy for the hats to magically appear and disappear. The complexity of the meter makes the song utterly joyful for children with the musical readiness for *Hat Party*, while the hats and the whole idea of a hat party charm children and attending adults alike.[1]

Other gem songs offered in this book, in addition to those in this Etude, can be included among your choices. See *Otto Would a Riding Go* (p. 14), *Under the Chair* (p. 15), *Lie-A-Bed** (p. 64), *Wake Up Jacob* (p. 79), *Willie Boy, Willie Boy* (p. 81), *Little Bubble* (p. 86), *Here How the Birds** (p. 86), and *O Sailor, Come Ashore** (p. 87). (*Songs with an asterisk might also be considered art songs.)

Songs in the Higher Singing Range

Songs in the higher singing range presented here are for children on the older end of early childhood who are sufficiently developed in the various tonalities and meters, art songs, and gem songs in the lower singing range, and in the process of developing the vocal instrument. Songs of increasing difficulty in the higher singing range offer greater musical and vocal challenge that grows with the children, inspiring artistry at every level throughout childhood.

Songs in the higher singing range that give voice to children's artistry compel the musical mind, prompt artistic expression, and enable vocal technique. They offer well-set texts in various tonalities and meters. We choose them to meet children's musical needs and to match the expressive range of the children. This set includes songs of varying levels of difficulty to meet children's musical needs at various ages and maturity levels.

Winter Moon

Figure 10.16 Aeolian, Duple

Winter Moon (Figure 10.16) offers a lovely poem of Langston Hughes. This one, set in Aeolian tonality and Duple meter, invites expressive and impressive singing. Rhythm, tonal, and text support each other in the musical mind. The rhythm and tonal translation of text captures the drama of Langston Hughes's words, eliciting expression with crisp articulation leading to the peak of the song. The built-in expression enables vocal technique as young singers deliver this song with their whole being. Children at this level can handle the challenges of the somewhat melismatic passages and sustain energy on the long notes. Vocal placement is in the optimal range for children's voices and the song draws a lovely sound out of those voices.

Children love shading vowels to make their singing even more beautiful, focusing on the "ah" sound in the words "night" and "white" and sustaining that open sound throughout the peak of the song with the two different vowel sounds in "ghost" and "white." Tonal and rhythm preps prepare the musical mind, and movement with the energy of the line while singing encourages articulation, building of the line, and enhanced vocal technique, complete with breath support at the peak of the song. Presenting this song in concert with piano accompaniment, with an introduction and interlude between repetitions, makes a lovely addition to any concert. The quality sound and expression of our young singers paint the picture that Langston Hughes painted with words.

My Maid Mary

Figure 10.17   Mixolydian, Duple

My Maid Mary (Figure 10.17), an English rhyme set in Mixolydian tonality and Duple meter, offers pure merriment that promotes children's artistry. The setting charges energy, with the long notes of the last line building tension that bursts into joy. The delightful text demands clean articulation with the many Duple meter divisions, yet evokes a carefree manner, freeing the voice to be utterly musical. Tonal and rhythm preps set up the musical mind, while macro/micro beat movement with appropriate weight distribution can drive the song to still greater musicality. Vocal placement is in the optimal range for children's voices. *My Maid Mary* elicits a lovely sound from children at this level. Successive repetitions render this song addictive, whether used as a warm-up or at the end of a class to send children merrily on their way.

Butterflies, Butterflies

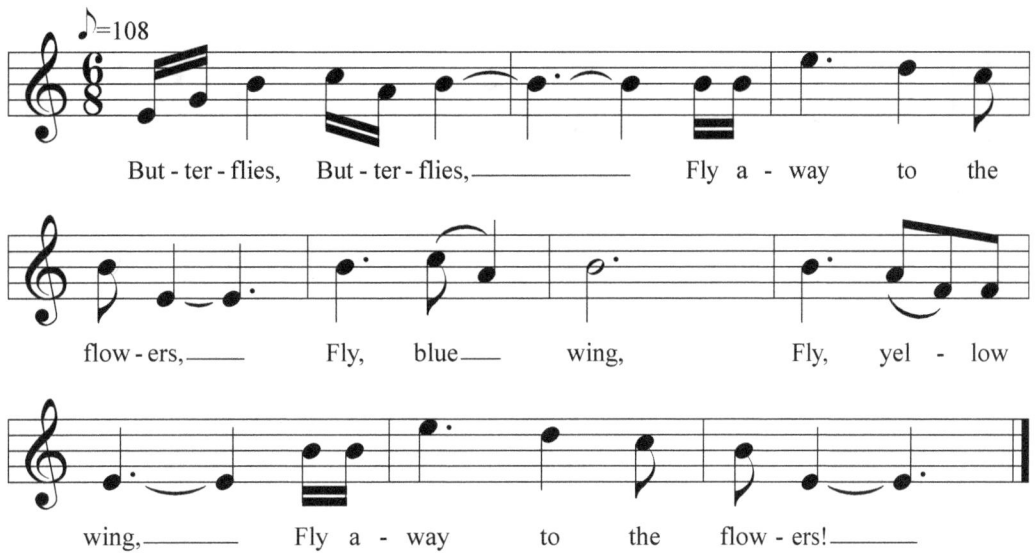

Figure 10.18   Phrygian, Triple

Butterflies, Butterflies (Figure 10.18) presents a Native American Pueblo text set in Phrygian tonality and Triple meter, taking young singers further into the wonder of the choral art and the wonder of their own artistry. The setting in Phrygian tonality compels the musical mind while evoking sheer artistry. Rhythm anchors, tonal anchors and text align, with the melodic rhythm the rhythm of the text and the melodic line the expression of the text. Neither the meter nor the tonality is established clearly until the seventh measure, requiring some established skill before reaching this song. The rhythm is challenging with its ties and upbeats, and the slow tempo is particularly challenging with the long notes, likely requiring rehearsal with macro/micro beat movement.

Voice placement in this song is optimal for vocal sound, and the ensemble sound elicited in this Phrygian song is stunning. The musical figure of the repeated word "Butterflies" builds the line to the peak of the song while stimulating energy and breath. The middle section of the song sustains the beauty of the line, with the natural expression of the song generating breath and energy once again for the repetition of the peak of the song. Our young artists can shape the sound of the second vowel of the word "away" with a bit of "ee" coloring, opening it to a more beautiful sound. This song might be used just for the experience of the song, as a warm-up, or as a song that evokes the kind of sound that can be a model for other song literature. The text, the tonality, and the melodic line of *Butterflies, Butterflies* move children deeply into their own artistry as it soars with the butterflies.

Snail

Figure 10.19 Lydian, Triple

Snail (Figure 10.19) offers the lovely words of Langston Hughes set in Lydian tonality and Triple meter. This song moves the young voice up to the high F. Children with well-bred musical minds who sing beautifully above the voice break sing the high F with ease. The length and seeming simplicity of the text is appropriate for young singers, but the text becomes more sophisticated as it goes. Song architecture supports the musical mind, scaffolding singers as the vocal range and text sophistication move children forward. The range and tessitura of this song together with other dimensions of its song architecture elicit quality sound from children's voices.

The rhythm is quite easy for children at this level. Tonal includes the characteristic fourth of Lydian in the first measure and reinforces it throughout. Stepwise passages with skips within the harmonic functions that define the tonality make the melody easy for singers, despite the high F. (See Appendix D for harmonic functions that define the tonality.) Starting the song with rhythm and tonal preps assures that the well-bred musical minds will be seated in Lydian tonality, and rehearsing with macro/micro beat movement assures momentum with the underlying Triple meter. Movement with the energy of the line can guide expression and vocal technique to the peak of the song, resolving down to the resting tone. Children enjoy coloring the word "see" with a bit of "ooh" to create a more beautiful sound. A piano accompaniment with introduction and interlude between repetitions makes this song suitable for any concert. The text marvels at the beauty of the snail while the song exposes the beauty of children, the beauty of children's voices, and the beauty of children's artistry.

The Morning Song

Etudes / Etude 3

Figure 10.20 Mixolydian, Triple

The Morning Song (Figure 10.20) will wake up singers and teachers alike. This haunting little song in Mixolydian tonality and Triple meter draws the heart and soul out of children as it builds to the peak of the song and then resolves with a repeat of the opening phrase. Multiple verses energize the building of the line and the joy of the morning. The rhythm is a bit challenging, particularly with the long notes. Building through the tie from the second line to the third builds intensity that draws both breath and energy to reach the peak of the song. The repeated text makes the song easy, though learning multiple verses always adds its own challenge. Rhythm and tonal preps prepare the musical mind and macro/micro beat movement secures meter underneath the melody.

Vocal placement in this song is optimal for children's voices. Movement with the energy of the line invites all to build with outstretched arms to the peak of the song, celebrating the new day in movement as well as voice. Children of all ages sing their hearts out in *The Morning Song*, as its song architecture elicits the joy and drama of the song from all singers. The song can serve well with a children's chorus of mixed ages and experience levels. The addition of a piano accompaniment makes this song a fine addition to any concert. An extra verse might even be added. "And we are singing to wake the morning" celebrates children's joy in singing this song. You might occasionally find this song accompanying you in the car or on a morning walk, as it is a song that everybody goes home singing.

Additional songs in the higher singing range presented in this book that can be among your choices for this Etude include *Where Are My Roses* (p. 179), *I Have a Funny Clown* (p. 181), *I'm the King!* (p. 183), *Firefly* (p. 185, *Cricket* (p. 186), *Snowflake* (p. 188),

Hop, Mother Annika! (p. 189), *Dance to Your Daddie* (p. 190), *Winter Sweetness* (p. 191), *The Leaves Fall* (p. 193), *Wild Flowers* (p. 194), *Bumblebee* (p. 196), *Ant* (p. 198), *Penguin* (p. 200), *Autumn Thought* (p. 201), and *What Does Little Birdie Say* (p. 203).

The process you have gone through in this Etude to select songs for a particular group of children will help you in selecting songs for all of your early childhood music classes. You have reviewed the musical properties of songs in relation to children's musical needs, age, and range of expression. You have included four or five different tonalities in the songs you have chosen, three or four different meters, and at least one song that directs the musical mind to rhythm and one to tonal, creating a well-balanced set of songs for any group of children. Now you can add that favorite folk song, spiritual, or seasonal song, assured that the set of songs you have chosen in this Etude serve children's artistry.

Songs that meet the musical needs of young children feed the process of developing artistry and serve as the vehicle for the expression of children's artistry. Well-chosen songs give flight to children's artistry at every level. Let us raise our young voices with songs that inspire children's artistry.

Appendices

Appendix A
Meters and Tonalities Used in This Book

Meters

Rhythm examples in each meter present macro beats, micro beats, and divisions in relation to each other.

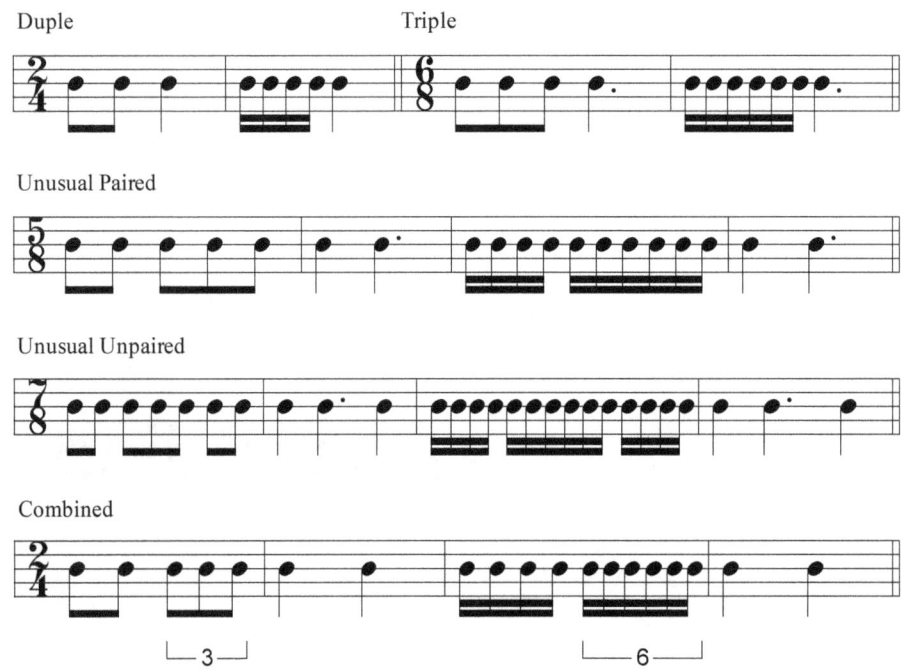

Tonalities

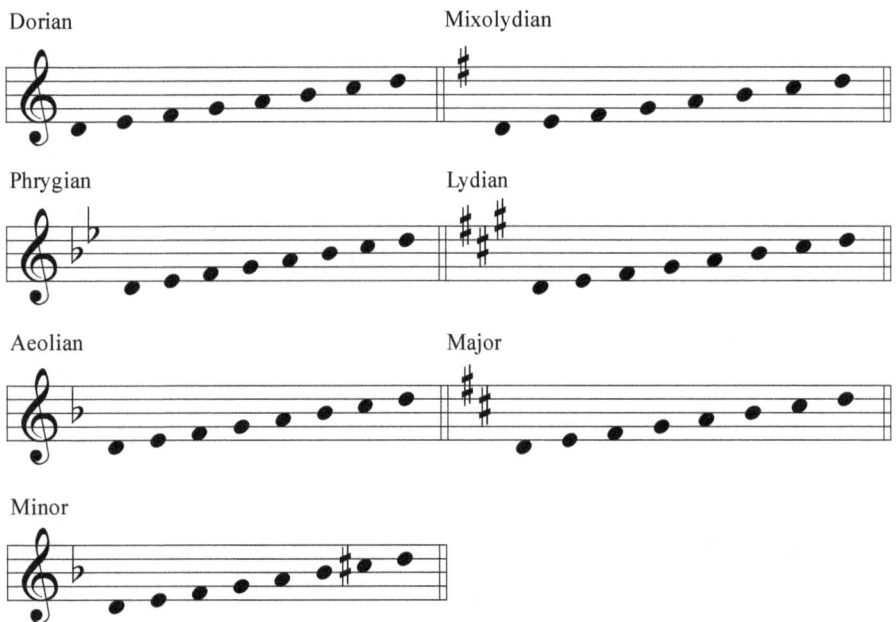

Appendix B

Weight Distribution with Various Beat Groupings
in Unusual Meters Used in this Book

⬇ Represents macro beat weight in the various beat groupings within each meter.

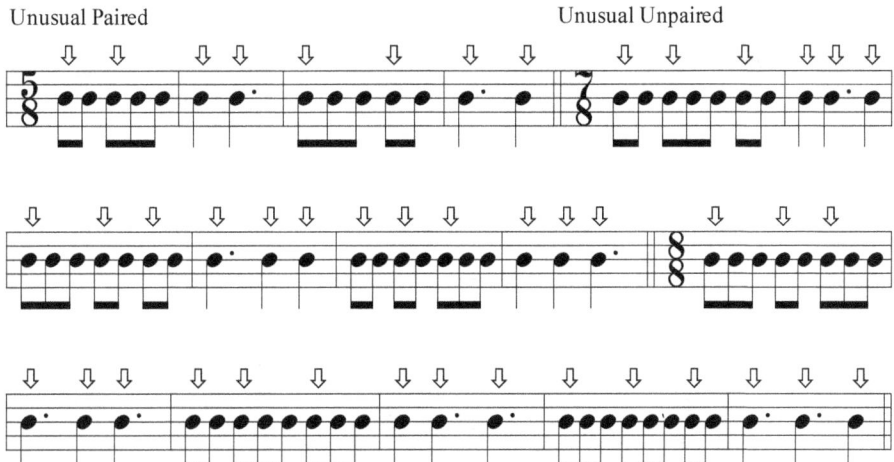

Appendix C
Characteristic Tones of Each Tonality

Characteristic tones of each tonality are presented here in relation to Major tonality. Each tonality on the left includes a major third, while those on the right each include a minor third.

⬇ Characteristic tone one-half step lower than Major
⬆ Characteristic tone one-half step higher than Major
◠ Characteristic tone of tonality, though same as Major, despite the minor third

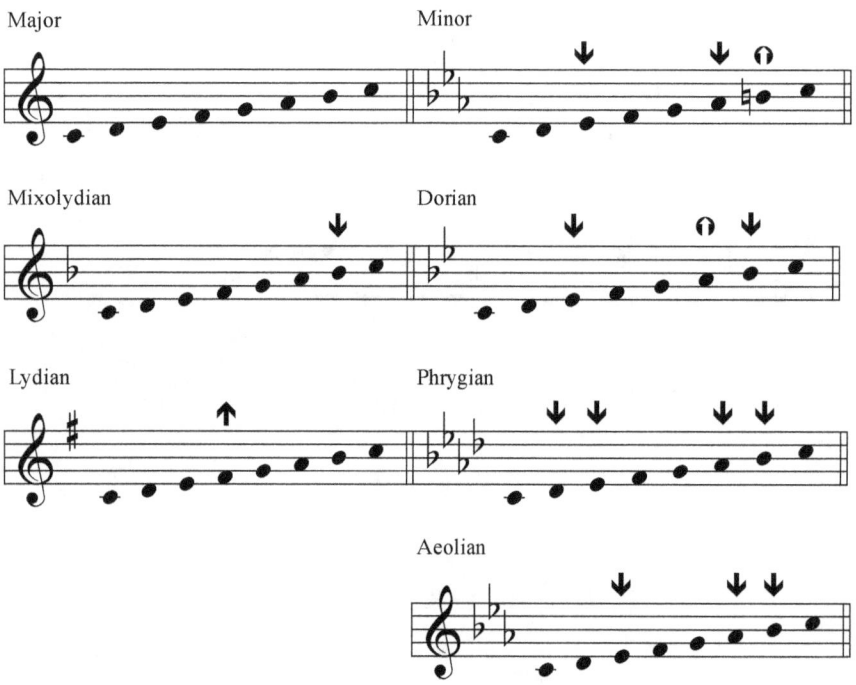

Appendix D

Harmonic Functions that Define Each Tonality

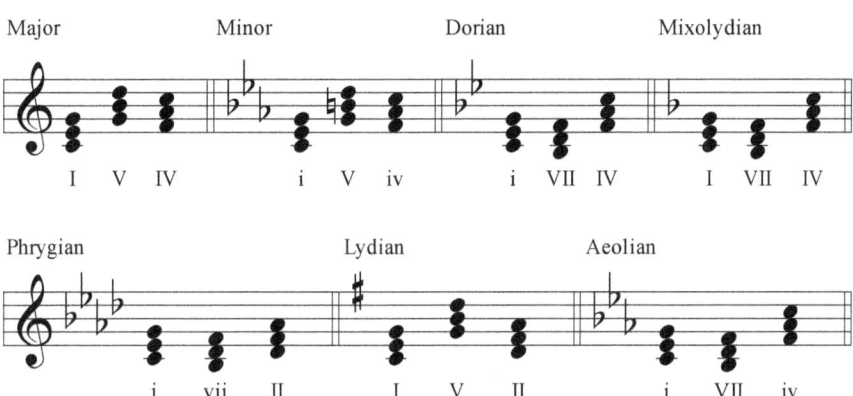

Appendix E

Pronunciation Guide and More about the
Rhythm and Tonal Syllables Used in This Book

Rhythm Syllables[1]

Pronunciation:

Vowels are pronounced the same in each meter. The consonants shift to reflect the difference between the meters but macro beats in all meters are du.

Vowel sounds:

u	=	*oo*
e	=	*ay*
a	=	*ah*
i	=	*ee*

Varying beat groupings shift the placement of twos and threes, so syllables shift with them. For example, Unusual Paired meter could be grouped as 2/3 or 3/2. The syllables for the 2/3 grouping are "du be, du ba bi" and the syllables for the 3/2 grouping are "du ba bi, du be."

More:

- Go to Appendix G for teacher acquisition of syllables.
- Go to Gordon's Learning Sequences book[2] for additional information about his rhythm syllables, their comparison to other rhythm syllable systems, and their consistency with more difficult rhythm patterns.

258   Unveiling Artistry in Early Childhood Music

Tonal Syllables

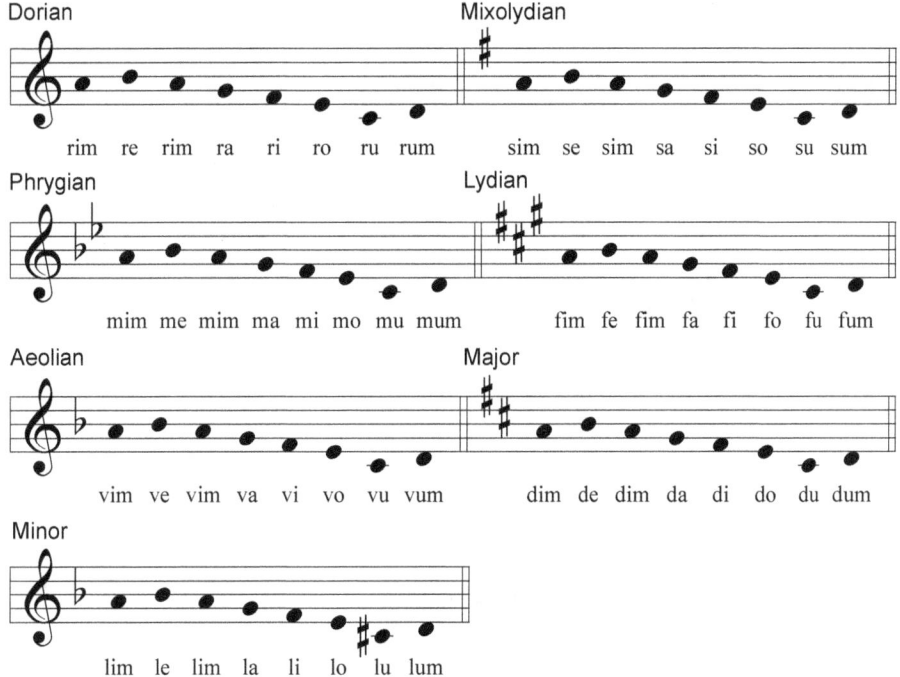

Pronunciation:

Consonants change to reflect the uniqueness of each tonality, but vowels are consistent across tonalities, reflecting the sameness in melodic function across tonalities. The "m" on both resting tone and fifth highlights tonal anchors.

Vowel Sounds

im	=	ĭm
e	=	*ay*
a	=	*ah*
i	=	*ee*
o	=	*oh*
u	=	*oo*
um	=	ŭ*m*

Chromatic syllables in each tonality are accommodated by adding "s" to the syllables for raised half steps, and "f" for lowered half steps (deleting the "m" on altered tonic and dominant), i.e., major ascending—"dum dus do dos di," descending—"di dif do dof dum."

More :

- Go to Appendix G for teacher acquisition of syllables.
- Go to https://comechildrensing.com/letters9.html for additional information about this tonal syllable system, including its rationale and attributes in comparison to solfege syllables with a "do" based major and "la" based minor.[3]

Appendix F

Teacher Reference Music Reading

Figure 6.2 (p.134)

Duple Meter

Figure 6.9 (p.147)

Mixolydian Tonality

Appendices

Figure 6.10 Examples with Key Signatures (p. 149)

Appendix G

Teacher Acquisition of Syllables

Our greatest challenge as an adult in acquiring rhythm and tonal syllables is to get our own thinking mind out of the way. Rhythm and tonal syllables that mirror the musical mind speak to both the musical mind and the thinking mind, but our thinking mind generally wants to take over, unwittingly silencing our own musical mind. Our thinking mind often tries to employ music theory, translate syllables from a more familiar rhythm or tonal syllable system, or apply tactile associations with a keyboard or other instrument to rhythm and tonal syllables, but such mental gymnastics get in the way of the musical mind's acquisition of syllables. We have to use our thinking mind to teach our musical mind, but then get the thinking mind out of the way so our musical mind can acquire syllables in sound. Guidelines are offered here for learning the recommended rhythm and tonal syllables using the materials of this book.

Etude 1, which is designed to develop competence with the various meters and tonalities in sound, can also serve the teacher learning syllables. Securing meters and tonalities in the musical mind is necessary first, however, before attempting rhythm and tonal syllables. Use this Appendix only after your musical mind feels competent and confident with the various meters and tonalities. Then go through Etude 1 with syllables, engaging in each step with rhythm or tonal syllables. Suggested movement will help to keep the thinking mind from focusing on the syllables. Rhythm and tonal preps with syllables will help the musical mind to grasp the syllables, and recordings with syllables can help you to learn syllables in sound. Don't give into the temptation of writing the syllables under the notation. Syllables have meaning only in sound. Written syllables can serve as reference for the thinking mind, but they get in the way of the musical mind.

Any new language takes time to learn, but the adult thinking mind wants immediate command of the syllables. It further assumes that its background in music theory enables going from an intellectual grasp of syllables to reading complex music with syllables. Reading music involves collaboration between the musical mind and the thinking mind, but the take-charge adult thinking mind can easily intimidate and shut down the musical mind or just give up on the syllables. Quieting the thinking mind provides the space the musical mind needs to grasp the new syllables in sound and then to apply them to more difficult tasks.

Follow the procedure below, giving your musical mind the time it needs to grow into each of the four challenges. Engaging in the various meters and tonalities with children who are ready for syllables will also propel your acquisition of syllables.

Rhythm Syllables

- **Rhythm Narratives**—Go through the rhythm section of Etude 1 (p. 208-212), now with rhythm syllables, using Appendix E as a guide to the right syllables.

- **Rhythm Patterns**—Try delivering macro and micro beat patterns and division patterns with syllables in each meter, increasing rhythm difficulty as you become more secure with the syllables.

- **Rhythm Reading**—Try reading the rhythm materials of Chapter 6 on syllables (p. 132-145) . You might create recordings to simulate the experience of having music read to you on syllables while you follow the notation. Apply this process to more difficult examples as you progress.

- **Rhythm Writing**—Try writing a four-bar chant with macro and micro beat patterns and divisions in the meter of your choice, using syllables and beaming micro beats. Write a similar chant in another meter, and then another, all with beamed micro beats, and observe the collaboration between your own musical mind and thinking mind to see how your process of writing macro and micro beat patterns and divisions in one meter may or may not transfer to another.

Tonal Syllables

- **Tonal Narratives**—Go through the tonal narratives of Etude 1 (p. 212-218), now with tonal syllables and without the more difficult art songs, using Appendix E as a guide to the right syllables. Add a couple of measures of 5-1 in syllables between multiple verses.

- **Tonal Segments**—Try delivering basic tonal segments with syllables in each tonality. Notice the similarities across tonalities.

- **Tonal Reading**—Try reading the tonal materials of Chapter 6 on syllables (p. 145-155). You might create recordings to simulate the experience of having music read to you on syllables while you follow the notation. Apply this process to more difficult examples as you progress.

- **Tonal Writing**—Try writing a simple four-bar melody in the tonality of your choice, using tonal syllables and just macro and micro beats. Locate the resting tone and fifth on lines or spaces; include all characteristic tones of the tonality in your melody; and create a melodic contour that supports the musical mind (p. 63). Then write a simple four-bar melody in another tonality with the same parameters and using the same resting tone and fifth. Try it in yet another tonality. Observe the collaboration between your own musical mind and thinking mind to see how your process of writing a simple melody in one tonality may or may not transfer to writing in another tonality when the resting tone and fifth are the same, with or without key signatures. Then write another similar melody in a higher key and see how that process does or doesn't relate to your process of writing melodies in different tonalities with the same resting tone and fifth.

Notes

Chapter 1

1 Edwin Gordon began working with little children relatively late in his career and it changed his approach to research, leading him to value children's responses more than hard data. He addresses this throughout an article/conversation in 1998 for musicstaff.com. Edwin Gordon "A Conversation with Edwin Gordon," interview by Mary Ellen Pinzino, 1998, accessed March 15, 2024. https://www.comechildrensing.com/pdf/other_articles_by_MEP/2_A_Conversation_with_Edwin_Gordon.pdf.

2 Current research in a number of disciplines relate to a variety of topics in this book. The bibliography includes earlier sources that most impacted the work presented in this book, with the hopes that those pursuing music learning will tap into the timeless wisdom of these rich resources on learning and on speech and language development to inform their teaching, their research on music learning, and their relationship with the work of Edwin Gordon. Ann Berthoff's *The Sense of Learning* and *The Making of Meaning*, for example, alongside the work of Edwin Gordon, broaden perspectives from which to view the process of music learning.

3 Edwin Gordon introduced the importance of the various tonalities and meters as well as songs and chants without words for young children. His views can be found in Gordon, *A Music Learning Theory for Newborn and Young Children*.

4 Pinzino, "Online Teacher Education Center: Moved by the Music," https://www.comechildrensing.com/teachers/blog_details.php?type=local&blog_id=351&catCode=64.

5 Pinzino, "Online Teacher Education Center: It's Not About Butterflies!," https://www.comechildrensing.com/teachers/blog_details.php?type=local&blog_id=355&catCode=64.

6 The term "tonal" is used as both an adjective and a noun, as is rhythm.

7 Pinzino, Come Children Sing Institute SONG LIBRARY, https://www.comechildrensing.com/sl.php.

8 Pinzino, "Online Teacher Education Center: Enchanting Children's Energy," https://www.comechildrensing.com/teachers/blog_details.php?type=local&blog_id=488&catCode=63.

9 See note 7 above.

10 Pinzino, "Online Teacher Education Center: The Art of Teaching Early Childhood Music," https://www.comechildrensing.com/teachers/blog_details.php?type=local&blog_id=542&catCode=63.

Chapter 2

1 Pinzino, "Online Teacher Education Center: Music for Learning or Music Learning?," https://www.comechildrensing.com/teachers/blog_details.php?type=local&blog_id=348&catCode=64.

2 Pinzino, *Letters on Music Learning*, 8.

3 The study of speech and language development can guide our understanding of music learning from infancy through advanced music reading and writing. Language acquisition is a similar process to music acquisition, and research on language learning opens new avenues for research on music learning.

4 The suggested audible breath serves the development of tonal knowing in the young musical mind. Vocal technique is addressed in Chapter 7.

5 See note 2 above.

6 It is essential that this activity use the squat as punctuation to a musical phrase rather than as an abrupt interruption.

7 The first eight bars of this example of Tonal Dialogue Activity can serve as a tonal narrative with somewhat developed children. Those just beginning Tonal Dialogue Activity are better served with a longer tonal narrative to seat the tonality before moving into Tonal Dialogue.

8 See note 4 above.

9 Pinzino, SONG LIBRARY, https://www.comechildrensing.com/sl.php.

10 We can also use a drum, recorder, another instrument, or a recording to expose children of all ages to musical material that is beyond their current level of development.

11 Pinzino, "Online Teacher Education Center: The Art of Eliciting Musical Response from Little Children," https://www.comechildrensing.com/teachers/blog_details.php?type=local&blog_id=365&catCode=64.

Chapter 3

1. Gordon, *Learning Sequences*, 161-172.
2. "Unusual Paired" and "Unusual Unpaired" meters, labeled by Gordon, include macro beats of uneven length with micro beats of even length. The more "usual" Duple and Triple meters have macro beats of equal duration as well as micro beats of equal duration. Some music teachers have more recently referred to the unusual meters as "uneven paired" and "uneven unpaired."
3. Edwin Gordon originally used the term "melodic rhythm" to refer to the rhythm of the melody in relation to macro and micro beats, later preferring the term "rhythm patterns." This book uses "rhythm patterns" when referring to individual rhythm patterns and "melodic rhythm" when referring to the greater context.
4. Edwin Gordon always separated tonal from rhythm to teach tonal. (See Gordon, *Learning Sequences*, 137-149.) Early accounts of the findings at the Come Children Sing Institute about adding rhythm to elicit tonal response are in Mary Ellen Pinzino, *Letters on Music Learning*, 30-32.
5. "Tonal segments" from this point forward refer to tonal patterns with rhythm, differentiating them from Gordon's use of tonal patterns without rhythm.
6. Pinzino, *Giving Voice to Children's Artistry: A Guide for Music Teachers and Choral Conductors*, 44.
7. Gordon poses a series of absolute stages of young children's music development. Children at the Come Children Sing Institute demonstrated a far more fluid process of development, as detailed in this book. Gordon's views on early childhood music learning can be found in Gordon, *A Music Learning Theory for Newborn and Young Children*.
8. Pinzino, "Online Teacher Education Center: Tunefulness and Rhythmicity in Young Children," https://www.comechildrensing.com/teachers/blog_details.php?type=local&blog_id=372&catCode=64.
9. Pinzino, "Online Teacher Education Center: Instructing Parents Initially," https://www.comechildrensing.com/teachers/blog_details.php?type=local&blog_id=485&catCode=63.
10. Pinzino, "Online Teacher Education Center: Parents," https://www.comechildrensing.com/teachers/blog_details.php?type=local&blog_id=492&catCode=63.
11. See Note 10.

Chapter 4

1. Pinzino, *Giving Voice*, 90.
2. Edwin Gordon considers Combined meter to be easier than the unusual meters because of the even macro beats, but children of all ages at the Come Children Sing Institute regularly acquired skill with Unusual Paired meter and Unusual Unpaired meter before they did with Combined meter. Children with some skill in the unusual meters were then readily able to function in Combined meter. (See Gordon, *Learning Sequences*, 163-165).
3. Gordon, "Sugarloaf Seminars." Rhythm and tonal preps were always presented orally. Notation here represents implementation at the Come Children Sing Institute.
4. Repeating the rhythm prep of the more difficult meters before the silent beats can be helpful.
5. See note 3.
6. Gordon, "Sugarloaf Seminars."
7. The simplicity and construction of rhythm and tonal narratives used in this book distinguish them from the more commonly used songs and chants without words. Developmental rhythm and tonal narratives in the various meters, tonalities, and levels of difficulty can be found in the Come Children Sing Institute SONG LIBRARY.

Chapter 5

1. Gordon considers "verbal association," the acquisition of syllables, to be a higher level of music learning than what he calls "aural/oral," and he does not take very young children beyond aural/oral. (See Gordon, *Learning Sequences*, 95-104).
2. Early accounts of the research that led to these findings can be found in Pinzino, *Letters on Music Learning*.
3. Gordon's rhythm syllables are based on beat function, and he teaches them to older children through rhythm patterns rather than rhythm narratives. More about his rhythm syllable system can be found in Gordon, *Learning Sequences*, 78-83.
4. Pinzino, *Letters on Music Learning*: "A New Tonal Syllable System," 57-62.
5. Gordon uses traditional solfege syllables with a "do" based major and "la" based minor, and he teaches them in the

context of tonal patterns without rhythm rather than through tonal narratives. More about his chosen tonal syllables and application can be found in Gordon, *Learning Sequences*, 56-69.

6 Introducing syllables with a puppet "from another country" that speaks "a different language" is highly effective in teaching rhythm and tonal syllables. Little children readily welcome the visitor, embracing both the syllables and the new culture. Use puppets, names, and made-up homelands that would be endearing to the families you work with and that would reflect positively on any inferred cultures.

7 Little children do not distinguish between chanting and singing. It is all singing to them. Musical examples notated with a single line of the staff are always chanted expressively without discreet pitches, with or without puppets.

8 See note 6.

9 Some of the playful ideas offered for rhythm and tonal discrimination can also be applied to harmonic discrimination, however, rhythm and tonal knowing provide the foundation for harmonic learning. A sense of tonality being developed through a variety of tonalities and then strengthened through tonal syllables leads the musical mind to an awareness of melodic function, which prepares the musical mind for harmonic function.

10 Gordon designed his rhythm syllables to be used only in the context of rhythm. They do serve well, however, with children who are familiar with the syllables in the context of rhythm, to draw attention to rhythm and meter in the context of song. Gordon's application of his rhythm syllables can be found in Gordon, *Learning Sequences*, 78-83.

Chapter 6

1 Gordon, *Learning Sequences*.
2 Early accounts of this research can be found in Pinzino, *Letters on Music Learning*.
3 Pinzino, *Letters on Music Learning*: "There's More to Music Reading than Meets the Eye or the Ear," 64-69.
4 Music reading books for each child to take home can be printed in landscape mode on 8 ½ x 11 inch paper and folded in half, with whatever you choose on the cover. You might choose to laminate, use card stock, or use book covers that allow for inserting a different sheet each week.
5 Constance Weaver's *Reading Process and Practice* sheds light on the problem solving process that is reading, opening our eyes to our own reading process in language as well as children's. Marie M. Clay's *Becoming Literate* presents an insightful analysis of emerging literacy. Both sources feed our understanding of the process of emerging literacy in language, which parallels emerging music literacy.
6 Tonal and rhythm "stories" are tonal and rhythm narratives with the parameters of song architecture that support the musical mind. The music reading materials are also designed to facilitate reading, providing for children to learn by reading. All are seen as "stories" by young children. "Today we are going to read in Dorian tonality" can be more appropriate for older children.
7 See note 4 above.
8 Pinzino, *Come Children Sing Institute Music Reading Library*.
9 The research presented in *Literacy Before Schooling*, by Emilia Ferreiro and Ana Teberosky. offers a compelling picture of very young children's attempts to make meaning in print with language, illuminating young children's music writing. This stimulating study serves music learning as much as it does language.
10 Pinzino, *Letters on Music Learning*: "Children's Notes on Music Reading," 70-106.
11 See note 10 above.
12 See note 10 above.
13 See note 10 above.
14 See note 10 above.
15 See note 10 above.
16 See note 10 above.
17 The problem solving process of music reading is addressed in greater detail in Pinzino, *Letters on Music Learning*: "There's More to Music Reading than Meets the Eye or the Ear," 64-69.
18 Pinzino, *Children's Notes*, 70-106.
19 Pinzino, *Music Reading Library*.

Chapter 7

1 Pinzino, *SONG LIBRARY*, https://www.comechildrensing.com/sl.php.
2 Pinzino, *Giving Voice*, 29-30.

3 Pinzino, *Giving Voice*, 40.
4 See Chapter 5, note 6.
5 Pinzino, *Giving Voice*, 30.
6 Pinzino, *SONG LIBRARY*, https://www.comechildrensing.com/sl.php.
7 Pinzino, Giving Voice.
8 Pinzino, *SONG LIBRARY*, https://www.comechildrensing.com/sl.php.

Etude 1

1 Pinzino, *SONG LIBRARY*, https://www.comechildrensing.com/sl.php.
2 Pinzino, *Giving Voice*, 70-81. Procedure with these musical materials can also be found in this source. Wording has been tweaked somewhat for this context.
3 See note 2 above.

Etude 3

1 Any concerns about re-using hats on different heads can be addressed by printing paper hats for each class. Little children are happy to join the hat party by holding up a line drawing of a hat.

Appendix E

1 Gordon, *Learning Sequences*, 78-83.
2 See note 1 above
3 Pinzino, *Letters on Music Learning*, 57-62.

Bibliography

Berthoff, Ann E., and James Stephens. *Forming Thinking Writing*, 2nd ed. Portsmouth, NH: Boynton/Cook Publishers, Inc.,1982.

Berthoff, Ann E. *Reclaiming the Imagination: Philosophical Perspectives for Writers and Teachers of Writing*. Portsmouth, NH: Boynton/Cook Heinemann, 1984.

Berthoff, Ann E. ed. *The Making of Meaning: Metaphors, Models, and Maxims for Writing Teachers*. Portsmouth, NH: Boynton/Cook Heinemann, 1981.

Berthoff, Ann E. *The Sense of Learning*. Portsmouth, NH: Boynton/Cook Heinemann, 1990.

Britton, James. *Language and Learning*: The Importance of Speech in Children's Development. London: Penguin Books, 1970, available Heinemann.

Bruner, Jerome. *Acts of Meaning*. Cambridge, MA: Harvard University Press, 1990.

Bruner, Jerome. *Child's Talk*. New York: Norton, 1983.

Clay, Marie M. *Becoming Literate: The Construction of Inner Control*. Portsmouth, NH: Heinemann, 1991.

Ferreiro, Emilia, and Ana Teberosky. *Literacy Before Schooling*. Trans. Karen Goodman Castro. Portsmouth, NH: Heinemann, 1989.

Gordon, Edwin. "A Conversation with Edwin Gordon." interviewed by Mary Ellen Pinzino. 1998, https://www.comechildrensing.com/pdf/other_articles_by_MEP/2_A_Conversation_with_Edwin_Gordon.pdf.

Gordon, Edwin E. *A Music Learning Theory for Newborn and Young Children*. 1997 ed., Chicago: GIA Publications, Inc., 1997.

Gordon, Edwin E. *Learning Sequences in Music: Skill, Content, and Patterns: A Music Learning Theory*. 1997 ed., Chicago: GIA Publications, Inc., 1997.

Gordon, Edwin. "Sugarloaf Seminars on Music Learning." Annual seminars at Temple University Sugarloaf Conference Center (now The Commonwealth Chateau at SugarLoaf). c. 1985-1993.

Mayher, John S. *Uncommon Sense*: Theoretical Practice in Language Education. Portsmouth, NH: Boynton/Cook Heinemann, 1990.

Pinzino, Mary Ellen. Come Children Sing Institute SONG LIBRARY accessed June 18th, 2025, Homewood, IL: Self-published (subscription), 2011. https://www.comechildrensing.com/sl.php.

Pinzino, Mary Ellen. Come Children Sing Institute *Music Reading Library*. Homewood, IL: Self-published, 1999.

Pinzino, Mary Ellen. *Giving Voice to Children's Artistry, a Guide for Music Teachers and Choral Conductors*. New York: Oxford University Press, 2022.

Pinzino, Mary Ellen. *Letters on Music Learning*, Compiled Electronic Edition. Homewood, IL: Self-published, 2007.

Pinzino, Mary Ellen. "Online Teacher Education Center," 2011, accessed June 18th, 2025: Homewood, IL: Self-published (subscription). https://www.comechildrensing.com/teachers/.

Vygotsky, Lev. *Mind in Society*: The Development of Higher Psychological Processes. Cambridge, MA: Harvard University Press, 1978.

Vygotsky, Lev. *Thought and Language*. Cambridge, MA: MIT Press, 1986.

Weaver, Constance. *Reading Process and Practice: From Socio-Psycholinguistics to Whole Language*. Portsmouth, NH: Heinemann, 1988.

Yaden, David B. Jr., and Shane Templeton, eds. *Metalinguistic Awareness and Beginning Literacy: Conceptualizing What It Means to Read and Write*. Portsmouth, NH: Heinemann, 1986.

Song Index

Ant *198*
Autumn Thought *201*
Bang-Whang-Whang *240*
Bumblebee *196*
Butterflies, Butterflies *247*
Butterfly Dreams *128*
Crescent Moon, The *234*
Cricket *186*
Dance to Your Daddie *190*
David Has a Dirty Face *12*
Dreams of Flowers *235*
Firefly *185*
Fish in the River *215*
Fluttering Butterflies *217*
Frog and the Cherry Petal, The *7, 214*
Hat Party *242*
Hear How the Birds *86*
Hop, Mother Annika! *189*
I Have a Friend *232*
I Have a Funny Clown *181*
I Hear a Sound *231*
I'm the King! *183*
I Need a Partner! *238*
It's Time to Say Goodbye *233*
I Went to the Zoo *232*
Lantern Dance, A *237*
Leaves Fall, The *193*
Lie A-Bed *64*
Little Bubble *86*
Little Fly, The *215*
Modest Violet, The *65*
Morning Song *249*
My Maid Mary *246*
Never In a Hurry *13, 216*

New Year's Here Again, The *217*
O Sailor, Come Ashore *87*
Otto Would A-Riding Go *14*
Pair of Butterflies, A *236*
Penguin *200*
Pheasant, The *218*
Poppies *235*
Quaint Fancy *80*
Round 'an Round *230*
Snail *248*
Snowflake *188*
There Was An Owl *239*
Under the Chair *15*
Wake Up, Jacob *79*
What Does Little Birdie Say? *203*
When Woods Awake *241*
Where Are My Roses? *179*
Who Can Walk Like a Duck? *12*
Wild Flowers *194*
Willie Boy, Willie Boy *81*
Winter Moon *245*
Winter Sweetness *191*

Index

A
Aeolian tonality, about, 38–39
art songs. *See* song
artistry in teaching, 16, 17–22, 41–48, 67–78, 93–104

C
children's response, 6–7, 20–22
    deer-in-the-headlights stare, 6, 26, 76, 78, 112, 115
    Macro/Micro Beat Activity, 36–37
    movement, 8–9, 26, 27, 28–29, 78, 175–178
    music reading, 131–133, 139, 174
    music writing, 155, 159–160, 164
    one-on-one, 30–40, 44–48
    playing music, 9–10
    progression of development, 67–69
    progression tonally, 59, 83–84
    progression rhythmically, 55
    progression vocally, 83–84
    props, 9–10
    Resting Tone Activity, 34–35
    Rhythm Dialogue Activity, 32–33
    rhythm reading, 133–145
    rhythm syllables, 112–113, 126
    rhythm writing, 158–160
    song, 6–7, 82, 178, 179–181, 181–182, 183. 187, 197
    Tonal Dialogue Activity, 38–39
    tonal reading, 146–148, 151
    tonal syllables, 115–117
    tonal writing, 163-164
Combined meter, about, 80

D
Dorian tonality, about, 55–56, 56–57
Duple meter, about, 50

E
energy,
    children's, 18–20, 176–177
    musical, 19–20
    sculpting (*see* sculpting energy)
    teacher's, 176
energy of the line, definition, 78–82
    See also movement
ensemble development, 72–75, 82
    vocal, 82, 175–176, 177–181, 184, 185–186

G
gem songs. *See* song
Gordon, Edwin, 2, 2n1, 6n3, 59n4, 67n7, 89
    higher levels of learning, 107, 107n1, 130–132
    rhythm, 50, 50n2, 51n3, 81n2
    syllables, 108-111, 108n3, 111n5, 128n10
intonation, 6, 74–75, 179, 182, 185, 193, 199

L
language learning, 5–6, 11, 29–31, 107, 130
lesson planning. *See* planning lessons
Lydian tonality, about, 58

M
Macro/Micro Beat Activity. *See* music activities
Major tonality, about, 25, 55–56, 172–173
melodic contour. *See* song architecture
melody. *See* song architecture
meter, 6, 24–25, 36–37, 50
    difficulty, 50, 80–81, 180
    See also, sense of meter
Minor tonality, about, 55–56, 59–60, 172
Mixolydian tonality, about, 57–58
movement, 8–9, 26–29, 177–178
    energy of the line, 78–82, 177
    fancy footwork, 177, 194
    flowing, 26–27, 29, 177
    full body, 26–27
    hand-to-hand contact, with, 70–72
    macro/micro beat, 27–29, 36–37, 71, 72–74, 177
    song, with, 20, 79–82, 177–178, 185
    voice, with, 177–178
    weighted, 27–29, 177
music activities, 31–33
    Macro/Micro Beat Activity, 36–37, 71, 72–74, 113
    Resting Tone Activity, 34–36, 70–71, 115–116
    Rhythm Dialogue Activity, 32–33, 53, 70, 113
    rhythm syllables, with, 111–114, 119–122
    Tonal Dialogue Activity, 38–39, 71, 116
    tonal syllables, with, 114–118, 122–124
    See also music reading; music writing
music reading, 130–155
    process, 131–132, 133, 173
    process, rhythm, 132–146, 135–137, 141–145, 156, 172
    process, tonal, 145–155, 172

progression, 159, 173
syllables, with, 131
music writing, 132, 155–171
    process, 155, 160, 173
    process, rhythm, 156, 158–160
    process, tonal, 163–164
    progression, 159–173
musical mind
    aural framework, 24–25
    body connection, 37, 70–75, 82
    breath, 34–35, 38–39, 47, 71–72
    continuum of development, 3, 67–69, 175–176
    contrast to thinking mind, 4–9, 118
    directing focus of, 60–61, 88–92
    immersion, 5–6, 24–25, 31, 33, 39–40, 43
    language of, 8–9, 46, 107–108
    making meaning, 29–40, 67–69
    movement, with, 8–9, 26–29, 177–178
    music reading, in (*see* music reading)
    music writing, in (*see* music writing)
    progression rhythmically, 55
    progression tonally, 59, 83–84
    progression vocally, 83–84, 175
    prompting the, 88–92
    props, with, 9–11
    song, in 11, 60–66, 184
    syllables, with (*see* syllables)
    tower of blocks, 49, 60, 63–64, 83, 176, 180
    voice connection, 82, 175–176

P

parents, 75–77
Pentatonic, about, 58
Phrygian tonality, about, 57
piano accompaniment, 180, 202
planning lessons, 93–104, 219–228
    alternating tonal and rhythm, 95, 207, 220
    beginners, 95–96, 219, 220–224
    contrasting meters, 94, 207, 220
    contrasting tonalities, 94–95, 207, 220
    creativity in, 101–104
    ensemble singing, 176–177
    group to solo, 40
    long-term students, 95–96, 97, 219, 224–228
    music reading and writing, 131–132, 172–174
    rhythm content, 96, 221–224
    rhythm reading, 132–145
    rhythm syllables, 111–114, 118–122
    rotating meters, 94, 207, 220
    rotating tonalities, 94–95, 207, 220
    separating meters, 91, 65, 118
    separating tonalities, 91, 65, 118
    sets of rhythm, tonal, song (RTS), 93–95, 219
    tonal content, 96–97, 221, 224
    tonal reading, 145
    tonal syllables, 111, 114–118, 118, 122–124
play songs. *See* song
playing music, 9–10
    Macro/Micro Beat Activity, 37, 54, 72–74
    props, 9–10, 41–44, 72–73, 101–104
    Resting Tone Activity, 35–36
    Rhythm Dialogue Activiy, 33, 53
    Tonal Dialogue Activity, 39
    rhythm syllables,111–114, 119–122
    tonal syllables, 111, 114–118, 122–124
props. *See* playing music

R

Resting Tone Activity. *See* music activities
rhythm
    anchors, 50-51
    beat function, 109
    difficulty, 50–55
    macro/micro beats, 24, 27–29, 50–51
    melodic rhythm, 50–53
    precision, 50–51
    See also meter
Rhythm Dialogue Activity. *See* music activities
rhythm narratives, 4–6
rhythm prep, 88–92, 98

S

sculpting energy, 18–20, 176–177, 222, 226
sense of meter, 24–25, 27–28
    developing, 32–33, 36–37, 50–55, 78
    See also meter; rhythm
sense of tonality, 25, 34–36, 38–39, 78
    developing, 38–39, 78
    See also tonal; tonality
singing
    ensemble, 82, 176–177, 178–204
    unison, 198
    See also vocal instrument
song, 11–16, 84–88, 175, 184
    architecture (*see* song architecture)
    art songs, 6–7, 13–14, 16, 214–218, 234–237
    criteria, 16, 84–88, 178, 180, 184, 192, 204
    gem songs, 14–16, 237–244
    higher singing range, 175–176, 244–251
    play songs, 11–13, 25–27
    progression of difficulty, 175–176, 192
    unison, 198
song architecture, 65–66, 84–88
    alignment of rhythm and tonal, 61–62
    alignment of rhythm, tonal, and text, 63–64
    definition of, 65, 178
    directing focus, 60–61
    directing rhythm focus, 60–61

directing tonal focus, 60–61
interaction of rhythm and tonal, 60–63
interaction of rhythm, tonal and text, 65–66
meeting musical needs, 84–88
melodic contour, 63
melody, 60–63
musical translation of text, 16, 82, 84, 180, 199
rhythm difficulty, 62–63
song analysis, 178–204
supporting artistic expression, 178, 190–191, 194–195, 198–199, 201–202, 202–203
supporting musical mind, 65–66, 178, 190–191 193, 198–199, 201–202, 202
supporting vocal technique, 178, 199, 202, 202–203
tonal difficulty, 62–63

song texts
    Browning, Robert, 240
    folk rhymes, 14, 79, 81, 179, 189, 190, 239, 241, 246
    haiku translations, 7, 13, 65, 80, 128, 214–218, 234–237
    Hughes, Langston, 191, 201, 245, 248
    Newell, Peter, 194
    Native American, Pueblo, 247
    Pope, Alexander, 86
    Rossetti, Christina, 64, 87
    Tennyson, Alfred Lord, 202–203

syllables
    beat function, 109
    discrimination between meters, 119–122
    discrimination between tonalities, 122–124
    melodic function, 109
    meta-language, 107–108, 118, 129
    naming meters/tonalities, 125–126
    neutral, 5, 32–33, 34–35, 37, 38–39
    reading music, with, 131
    song, with, 127–129, 197
    rhythm syllables, 108–109, 197
    tonal syllables, 109–111

T

teaching, reflecting on, 4, 6, 7, 9, 16, 17–18, 20–22
    classroom laboratory, 20–22, 98–101
    music reading, 139, 153

tonal
    anchors, 55
    difficulty, 59–60, 62–63
    melodic function, 109
    resting tone, 25, 34, 38–39
    rhythm, with, 58–59
    segments, 58–59, 97, 116
    See also, tonality

Tonal Dialogue Activity. *See* music activities
tonal narratives, 4–6
tonal prep, 88–92, 98

tonality, 6–7, 25, 55–58
    characteristic tones, 55–59
    recommended sequence, 59–60
    See also sense of tonality
tonguing, 28, 37
tunefulness, 83–84, 181–184
Triple meter, about, 50, 180

U

Unusual Paired meter, about, 29, 50, 187
Unusual Unpaired meter, about, 50, 196

V

vocal instrument, 175–177, 199
    learning to use, 72, 82, 83–84, 177–178, 179–184, 184, 187, 188
vocal placement, 175–176
vocal range, 60, 175–176
vocal sound, 179–180, 185, 187, 188, 193, 199
vocal technique, 199
vocal warm-ups, 194

Permissions

The United Educators, Inc. Song texts: Figure 1.3 "The Frog and the Cherry Petal;" Figure 1.6 "Never in a Hurry;" Figure 3.32 "The Modest Violet;" Figure 4.2 "Quaint Fancy;" Figure 5.9 "Butterfly Dreams;" Figure 8.12 "The Frog and the Cherry Petal;" Figure 8.14 "Fish in the River;" Figure 8.16 "The Little Fly;" Figure 8.18 "Never in a Hurry;" Figure 8.20 "Fluttering Butterflies;" Figure 8.22 The New Year's Here Again;" Figure 8.24 "The Pheasant;" Figure 10.6 "The Crescent Moon;" Figure 10.7 "Poppies;" Figure 10.8 "Dreams of Flowers;" Figure 10.9 "A Pair of Butterflies;" Figure 10.10 "Lantern Dance." Words from LITTLE PICTURES OF JAPAN, Edited by Olive Beaupre Miller. Copyright 1925, The United Educators, Inc. Used with permission. Now in public domain.

Figure 1.7 "Otto Would a Riding Go," words of Swedish Rhyme; Figure 3.30 "Lie-a-Bed," words by Christina Rossetti; Figure 4.1 "Wake Up, Jacob," words of American rhyme; Figure 4.3 "Willie Boy, Willie Boy," words of English rhyme; Figure 4.5 "Hear How the Birds," words by Alexander Pope; Figure 4.6 "O Sailor, Come Ashore," words by Christina Rossetti; Figure 7.1 "Where Are My Roses?," words from ancient Greece; Figure 7.8 "Hop, Mother Annika!," words of Swedish Rhyme; Figure 7.9 "Dance to Your Daddie," words of English Rhyme; Figure 7.12 "Wild Flowers," words by Peter Newell; Figure 7.17 "What Does Little Birdie Say?," words by Alfred Lord Tennyson; Figure 10.12 "There Was an Owl," words of English Rhyme; Figure 10.13 "Bang-Whang-Whang," words by Robert Browning; Figure 10.14 "When Woods Awake," words from old English; Figure 10.17 "My Maid Mary," words of English rhyme; Figure 10.18 "Butterflies, Butterflies," words of Native American Pueblo; Words from the 1937 edition of MY BOOK HOUSE, edited by Olive Beaupre Miller. Copyright 1937, 1971, The United Educators, Inc. Used with permission. Now in public domain.

Estate of Langston Hughes: Song texts: Figure 7.10 "Winter Sweetness;" Figure 7.16 "Autumn Thought;" Figure 10.16 "Winter Moon;" Figure 10.19 "Snail;" Words by Langston Hughes from THE DREAM KEEPER and other poems By Langston Hughes. Copyright © 1994 by the Estate of Langston Hughes. Reprinted by permission of Harold Ober Associates, now International Literary Properties LLC, Copyright by the Langston Hughes Estate.

GIA: Rhythm syllables of Edwin Gordon from *Learning Sequences in Music: Skill, Content, and Patterns: A Music Learning Theory*, Copyright 1997 edition. Used with permission.

Mary Ellen Pinzino: Figure 1.1, Figure 1.2; Figure 1.3 "The Frog and the Cherry Petal;" Figure 1.4 "Who Can Walk Like a Duck?;" Figure 1.5 "David Has a Dirty Face;" Figure 1.6 "Never in a Hurry;" Figure 1.7 "Otto Would a Riding Go;" Figure 1.8 "Under the Chair;" Figure 2.3, Figure 2.5, Figure 2.6, Figure 2.7, Figure 2.8, Figure 2.9, Figure 3.9, Figure 3.10, Figure 3.12, Figure 3.26, Figure 3.28, Figure 3.30 "Lie-a-Bed;" Figure 3.32 "The Modest Violet;" Figure 4.1 "Wake Up, Jacob;" Figure 4.2 "Quaint Fancy;" Figure 4.3 "Willie Boy, Willie Boy;" Figure 4.4 "Little Bubble;" Figure 4.5 "Hear How the Birds;" Figure 4.6 "O Sailor, Come Ashore;" Figure 4.7, Figure 5.3, Figure 5.4, Figure 5.6, Figure 6.7, Figure 5.8, Figure 5.9 "Butterfly Dreams;" Figure 6.1, Figure 6.2, Figure 6.3, Figure 6.4, Figure 6.5, Figure 6.6, Figure 6.7, Figure 6.8, Figure 6.9, Figure 6.10, Figure 6.11, Figure 6.12; Figure 7.1 "Where Are My Roses?;" Figure 7.2 "I Have a Funny Clown;" Figure 7.3; Figure 7.4 "I'm the King;" Figure 7.5 "Firefly;" Figure 7.6 "Cricket;" Figure 7.7 "Snowflake;" Figure 7.8 "Hop, Mother Annika!;" Figure 7.9 "Dance to Your Daddie;" Figure 7.10 "Winter Sweetness;" Figure 7.11 "The Leaves Fall;" Figure 7.12 "Wild Flowers;" Figure 7.13 "Bumblebee;" Figure 7.14 "Ant;" Figure 7.15 "Penguin;" Figure 7.16 "Autumn Thought;" Figure 7.17 "What Does Little Birdie Say?;" Figure 8.1, Figure 8.2, Figure 8.3, Figure 8.4, Figure 8.5, Figure 8.6, Figure 8.7, Figure 8.8, Figure 8.9, Figure 8.10, Figure 8.11; Figure 8.12 "The Frog and the Cherry Petal;" Figure 8.13; Figure 8.14 "Fish in the River;" Figure 8.15; Figure 8.16 "The Little Fly;" Figure 8.17; Figure 8.18 "Never in a Hurry;" Figure 8.19; Figure 8.20 "Fluttering Butterflies;" Figure 8.21; Figure 8.22 "The New Year's Here Again;" Figure 8.23; Figure 8.24 "The Pheasant;" Figure 10.1 "Round an' Round;" Figure 10.2 "I Hear a Sound;" Figure 10.3 "I Have a Friend;" Figure 10.4 "I Went to the Zoo;" Figure 10.5 "It's Time to Say Goodbye;" Figure 10.6 "The Crescent Moon;" Figure 10.7 "Poppies;" Figure 10.8 "Dreams of Flowers;" Figure 10.9 "A Pair of Butterflies;" Figure 10.10 "Lantern Dance;" Figure 10.11 "I Need a Partner!;" Figure 10.12 "There Was an Owl;" Figure 10.13 "Bang-Whang-Whang;" Figure 10.14 "When Woods Awake;" Figure 10.15 "Hat Party;" Figure 10.16 "Winter Moon;" Figure 10.17 "My Maid Mary;" Figure 10.18 "Butterflies, Butterflies;" Figure 10.19 "Snail;" Figure 10.20 "The Morning Song." All from the Come Children Sing Institute SONG LIBRARY, composed by Mary Ellen Pinzino, Copyright © 1997 Mary Ellen Pinzino. Used with permission.

Figure 6.1, Figure 6.2, Figure 6.3, Figure 6.4, Figure 6.5, Figure 6.6, Figure 6.7, Figure 6.8, Figure 6.9, Figure 6.10, Figure 6.11, Figure 6.12, Figure 6.13, Figure 6.17. From the Children Children Sing Institute *Music Reading Library*, composed by Mary Ellen Pinzino, Copyright © 1999 Mary Ellen Pinzino. Used with permission

Figure 5.2, 6.14, 6.15, 6.16, 6.18, 6.19, 6.20. From *Letters on Music Learning*, Copyright © 1992, 1993, 2007, Mary Ellen Pinzino. Used with permission.

About the Author

Mary Ellen Pinzino is the Founder/Director of the Come Children Sing Institute, a center for research and development in music learning since 1984. She is the author of *Giving Voice to Children's Artistry: A Guide for Music Teachers and Choral Conductors*, which takes children's artistry beyond early childhood, and the composer of the Come Children Sing Institute SONG LIBRARY, a resource of more than 500 songs for early childhood, elementary school and children's chorus. Mary Ellen has done extensive classroom research on music learning and on song in the development of children's artistry with children from birth through thirteen, and has written copiously for music teachers and parents, including many articles for national and international publications, online music courses, and the e-book *Letters on Music Learning*. She is the creator of the Institute's Online Teacher Education Center and instructor for its many online courses and workshops for professional development. She is also the developer and teacher of Come Children, Sing Online Music Classes for very young children.

Mary Ellen has taught all ages from birth through graduate students, teaching early childhood music classes and conducting children's choruses at the Come Children Sing Institute and directing the Institute's teacher training program. She has also taught elementary school music, held both high school and college choral positions, and taught graduate school music education courses. Mary Ellen's comprehensive work with very young children, her work with children's choirs and choruses of all levels, her extensive research, and her many compositions for children have put her on the cutting edge in the field of music education.

Mary Ellen has presented nationally and internationally for music educators organizations, including the International Society for Music Education, the Music Educators National Conference, the American Orff-Schulwerk Association, the Organization of American Kodaly Educators, the American Choral Directors Association, the Gordon Institute for Music Learning, and Suzuki Institutes. Mary Ellen has presented internationally in Portugal at the University of Lisbon, Indonesia, for the East Asia Regional Council of Overseas Schools and the Jakarta International School, and for the International Music Education Conference in Vilnius, Lithuania.

Mary Ellen received bachelor's and master's degrees in music education from the University of Illinois at Urbana-Champaign and studied extensively with Edwin Gordon. She lives with her husband in Homewood, Illinois. Their two sons inspired Come Children, Sing! as babies and continued to inform her early childhood programs and children's choruses until their voices changed. Their four grandchildren have offered yet another intimate view of the process of music learning from infants to teens.

www.ingramcontent.com/pod-product-compliance
Lightning Source LLC
Chambersburg PA
CBHW081353290426
44110CB00018B/2362